SHIELDING

Corporeal Matters

is a publication series on arts-based research, in particular practices and concepts that place the body at the core. It illuminates how the body appears simultaneously as witness, document, and agent in contemporary life, and offers insights into corporeality as the often-neglected dimension that cuts through ethics, aesthetics, and politics. From multiple perspectives and fields of application and grounded in moments of research, encounter and debate generated in the context of the HZT-Inter-University Centre for Dance Berlin, the series hosts edited volumes, authored publications, workbooks and other formats.

Series Editors

Janez Janša, Sandra Noeth and Sandra Umathum

SHIELDING

Body-based Studies on Integrity and Protection

Sandra Noeth, Sandra Umathum &
Janez Janša (eds.)

Contents

Janez Janša, Sandra Noeth and Sandra Umathum

Shielding.
Introductory Notes

The work on this book began in January 2022 as part of the Research Week, which is regularly held at the HZT-Inter-University Centre for Dance Berlin and explores body-based artistic and non-artistic research practices in a wider social and political context. During Research Week, students and staff from all degree programs engage with a chosen topic together with guest experts from various fields.

The idea to dedicate the Research Week to aspects and ways of shielding was prompted by the wish to continue Sandra Noeth's research on issues of bodily integrity and un/protection.[1] By gathering different perspectives on shielding, on the one hand, we took up recent developments in realpolitik, where bodies become shields in a very literal, material sense; in warfare or political conflict, as human shields, for example. On the other hand, we were interested in the micropolitics of shielding in everyday life; in the small movements and gestures we make when we feel uncomfortable or threatened, in reaction to structural violence, for instance.

Thus, shielding became a springboard to reflection on how large-scale concepts and socio-political phenomena are translated into bodily behaviours, into codes, taboos and privileges, as well as also being embodied and ultimately instrumentalized to discipline and control bodies. The role, status and agency of the body in such processes as well as the unequal physical, but also material and ethical protection of bodies, require increased attentiveness. So how do we make space in our artistic, discursive and curatorial practices for this attentiveness? For different bodies, for the difference between bodies, for their voices, their causes or their

[1] See *Bodies, un-protected*, artistic-theoretical research project on bodies, art and protection, curated by Sandra Noeth with Künstler*innenhaus Mousonturm, 2020–22; "Bodies-Unsound: Arts-Based Research on the Integrity of Bodies and an Aesthetic Economy of Repair", in *Art in Philosophy. Philosophy in the Arts. Artistic Research and Performance Philosophy in the Making*, ed. by Arno Boehler and Susanne Valerie Granzer, Vienna: mdw-press, 2024 (forthcoming).

Janez Janša **Sandra Noeth** and **Sandra Umathum** 9

concerns? How much conflict do we invite and allow, and where do we set boundaries? Especially when, as is currently happening in Germany and many other parts of the world, the democratic value of tolerating conflicting points of view is increasingly at risk? Shielding of course, is not only about the ability to protect one's own body from danger and threat, but also the ability to protect the bodies of others.

Engaging with the shields that we put up today, individually and collectively, made us think a lot about bodily integrity both in terms of the material and physical protection of a body as well as in terms of its symbolic and ethical recognition. The idea of bodily integrity has become very precarious today. Some participants in the Research Week connected this growing precarity to a more general distrust in the power that institutions have to protect bodies, such as that offered by the state, for instance, or by other sovereign entities. International Humanitarian Law, which adopts and reproduces a particularly western understanding of the body, serves as the template here. This notion of the body is tied to the idea of the individual and conceived of as bounded and complete, a productive and ableist entity to be fixed and saved. But where is the place for, and the recognition of, bodies that do not correspond to this framework; of bodies that do not have the possibility to access the protective resources deposited there?

Throughout our research we kept asking ourselves to what extent these are also questions of aesthetics, i.e. how our ways of staging and framing bodies feed into or challenge these dynamics. Paying attention to the performative, movement-based and somatic practices of shielding reminded us that shielding is also always a matter of scale. It may be internalized, but it can still be read and traced in gestures and motions that express avoidance, the desire to evade, to shy away from or to get out of situations; be it a debate, a conflict, or even a relationship. Then again, shielding can appear as aggression or an attack, it can come in the form of violence and violation, which in turn evokes the need for protection and self-protection. This ambivalence inherent in the idea and the practice of shielding is crucial. But in what role, in what capacity does the body appear in each case? Is it an agent, a subject, a screen, a symbolic site of power and contestation? And when do strategies of shielding in turn prescribe violence?

In recent months we have again seen how the rise of conservative, right-wing and anti-migrant movements, as well as current strategies of international warfare in Europe and beyond, have activated body-related imaginaries and representations in order to de-humanize and de-subjectivize certain bodies. Words, narratives and images, for example, that compare some bodies to animals and portray them as dangerous or infectious and posing a risk. This notorious strategy of the use and instrumentalization of the body as a symbolic battleground for the implementation of ideology and exclusion has a long history of course. Once again, however, it provides grounds to argue for shielding ourselves and communities from 'the other', both on a social and political as well as on a personal level. In the process, bodies are collectivized, even abstracted, and risk to be dehumanized. In addition to the way this affects the trust we have in existing systems of protection, it includes a message; a message that opens the floodgates for mechanisms of exclusion and for the justification of potentially violent actions by giving a kind of mandate for (self-)protection.

Our research into the practices and concepts of shielding has shown how many bodies do not actually find protection within the frameworks created for them, be they social, political, legal, but also aesthetic systems, in which existing differences, discriminations and hierarchies are structurally reproduced and reinforced. This means that shielding is neither a passive position, nor is it merely a reaction to something exterior. It is something that affects us all.

Janez Janša   **Sandra Noeth**   and   **Sandra Umathum**

Nicola Perugini

Civilians as Human Screens: Bodies, Media, and the Meaning of Violence

There is no war, then, without representation, no sophisticated weaponry without psychological mystification.
— Paul Virilio, *War and Cinema*

The battlespace is a space of struggle where different forms of mediation take place. War is also the art of organising various constitutive components of the battlespace (humans, nature, weapons, optical and sensing devices, etc.) in order to regulate the use of lethal force, and its perception. To paraphrase Paul Virilio, there is no war and no space of war without mediation. Modulating distance and proximity among the different actors and components that populate the battlefield is one of the crucial acts of mediation in war. It shapes the way we see and make sense of violence.

Usually, human beings are in control of the technologies that configure these processes of mediation. But there are instances in which humans themselves become those very technologies. Like when Germany invaded Belgium in 1914 at the beginning of World War I and perfected a series of warfare practices that resulted in the coercive involvement of Belgian civilians in the hostilities, transforming them into technologies of military mediation. As the Germans conquered new territory and expanded their empire, they forced Belgian civilians to march in front of their soldiers, sometimes for entire days. The hostages were made clearly visible to the enemy and were told that they "were to have a taste of Belgian machine-gun fire"[1]. When they were "at a distance of 150 or 200 yards", the Germans would fire at the Belgian troops, which in turn "opened fire from the flanks only, to avoid hitting their people"[2]. In other instances, the Belgian troops would completely cease their fire. The use of human shields as a tool of deterrence worked.

A year after the invasion, a Belgian governmental commission published a report that used international law to assess the crimes committed in

[1] Official Commission of the Belgian Government, *Reports on the Violation of the Rights of Nations and of the Laws and Customs of War in Belgium* (Published on Behalf of the Belgian Legation), London: H.M. Stationery Office, Harrison and Sons printers, 1915, 54.
[2] Official Commission of the Belgian Government, *Reports*, 54.

the battlefield. The issue of the systematic use of civilians as a protective buffer to conquer new territory received meticulous attention in the report. The Belgians defined the practice of forcing their soldiers to fire on Belgian fellow citizens while these were constrained to "serve as a living screen" by the Germans as the "most painful moral violence"[3]. To be sure, the use of human shields did not start in Belgium during World War I. The practice was common to other conflicts.[4] However, whereas in previous conflicts the use of human shields was relatively sporadic, in Belgium it became unprecedentedly systematic. Even more significantly, Belgium was one of the first instances in which the mobilisation of living human bodies to defend a military target was defined as an act of "screening".

This idea of screening by using the human body in war is not just a metaphor or a synonym for shielding. The notion of screen opens to a better understanding of the relationship between war and media. Interrogating the human shield as a human screen is in fact crucial to understand how the human body functions simultaneously as a weapon and a media technology. It allows me to address the central question of this short archaeological essay: namely the question of how the distance of war—from the "150 or 200 yards" from which the Germans shot at their targets, to the thousands of kilometres from which contemporary drones can kill—has historically come to be mediated by the figure of the living human screen. In this way, the human screen reveals how this peculiar intervention of the human body in the battlespace has transformed the perceptual field of war, opening to multiple interpretations of the meaning of violence on the battlefield.

Indeed, what this peculiar kind of screening ultimately allowed the Germans to do was to calibrate the distance from which they could target their enemies. And while doing so, the screen of humans behind which they hid reshaped the field of perception in the battlefield. Like optical screens, while they concealed the German troops and allowed them to advance, the bodies of the Belgian citizens used as weapons of protection, also projected an image. An image that attributed a clear ethical meaning to the violence of war, like that of *The Barricade* (Fig. 1), the painting realised by the American realist artist George Bellows in 1918 to condemn the brutality of German human screening during the invasion of Belgium.

<hr>

[3] Official Commission of the Belgian Government, *Reports,* xviii.
[4] See Neve Gordon and Nicola Perugini, *Human Shields: A History of People in the Line of Fire,* Berkeley, CA: University of California Press, 2020.

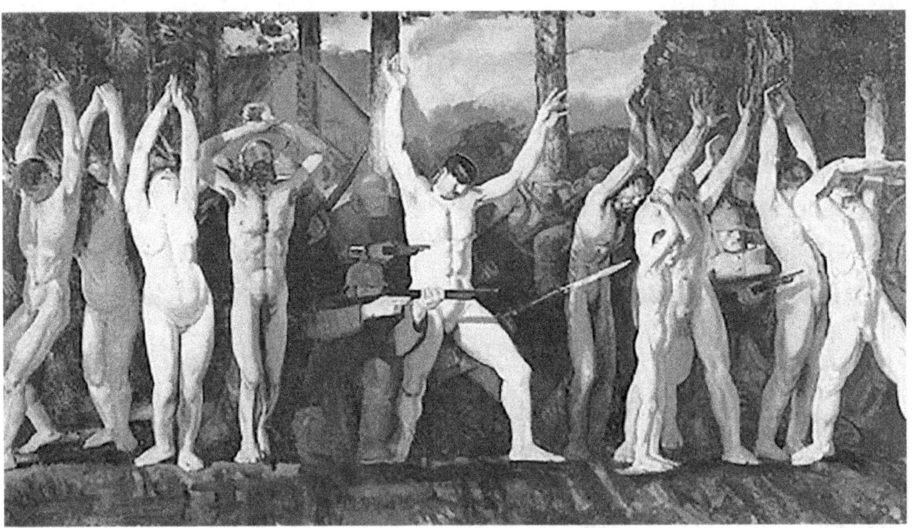

Fig. 1 — George Bellows, The Barricade, 1918. Birmingham Museum of Art.

This is not surprising if we think that screens have historically emerged as the result of this dialectical relationship between concealment and projection, invisibility and visibility, occlusion from the gaze and exposure of an image. As Rüdiger Campe has highlighted in his genealogical investigation of the notion of screen, the appearance of optical screens as technologies, which allow something to be projected and seen, can be better understood by tracing their relationship with a multiplicity of social forms of protection and concealment.[5] In the early modern world, Campe explains, the term 'screen' entertains an intimate relationship with the space of war ('screen' as a refuge for the soldier from physical danger); with the space of hunting ('screen' as a protective device allowing hunters to hunt and kill their prey safely); and with the space of socio-legal relations (legal 'screening' as a form of protection negotiated between social parties). A *Schirm*, a screen—interchangeably used in German with that of *Schild* (shield)—is a device that mediates the distance between the constitutive elements of different spaces: military, ludic, and legal. And while protecting people across these different social spaces, screens also project and allow us to see something. So, for instance, in the military realm, screens provide a refuge while allowing soldiers to re-organise their warfare tactics and strategies. In the ludic realm, while protecting hunters, the hunting screen used in the early modern era also allowed the occupant to see, observe, and target their prey (Fig. 2). Or in

[5] See Rüdiger Campe, "'Schutz und Schirm': Screening in German During Early Modern Times", in *Screen Genealogies: From Optical Device to Environmental Medium*, ed. by Craig Buckley, Rüdiger Campe and Francesco Casetti, Amsterdam: Amsterdam University Press, 2019.

the legal realm, in the case of the relationship between lords and their subjects, it is only through the screening provided by the lords to their subjects that the latter appeared—were made politically present—and acquired a legal status in social space. It is in parallel with these processes that the *Schirm* emerges also as the optical device that projects and generates a shape, an image.

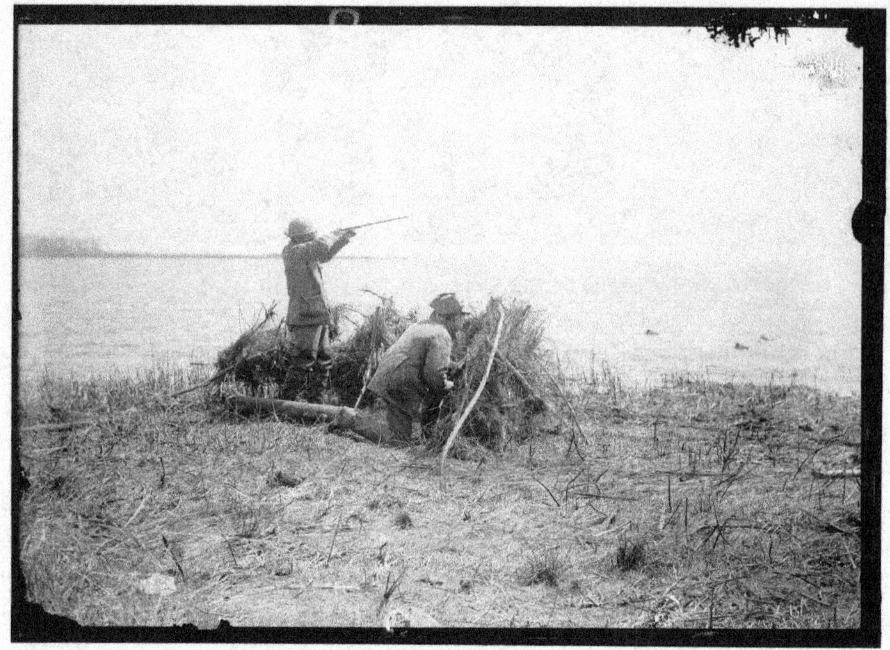

Fig. 2 — Shooting from hunters' blind by shore, 1900–1920. Library of the Congress.

Becoming Human Screens

Human screens present similarities with many other screens, but also very important peculiarities, which make them very specific political technologies that we can investigate with archaeology. Like any other kind of body or surface that becomes a screen, humans are not intrinsically screens. To put it as Francesco Casetti does, they "become screens" as the result of other processes of mediation.[6] In order to transform a wall into a screen onto which an image can be projected, a series of spatial

[6] See Francesco Casetti, "Primal Screens", in *Screen Genealogies: From Optical Device to Environmental Medium*, ed. by Craig Buckley, Rüdiger Campe and Francesco Casetti, Amsterdam: Amsterdam University Press, 2019.

and technological arrangements and mediations need to be in place. Not unlike the spatial arrangements required for cinema projections that transform walls into concrete screens, war needs to happen at a certain distance that can be modulated by the human screen, by the presence of a human body in the battlefield that ends up operating as a shield. Certain weapons and technologies of killing need to be used. Crucially, war must take place in the proximity of 'people' who can 'become' screens.

This is the fundamental specificity of human screens, which determine their political intensity. Life itself is weaponized.[7] It is life—the specific value of the life of vulnerable Belgian civilians—that allowed German soldiers to pit themselves against the machine guns of Belgian soldiers and modulate the distance from which the invading troops could fire.

This biopolitical element reveals another important peculiarity of the process we could call 'becoming human screens'. As in the case of other screens, human screens appear as a result of the intertwining of multiple historico-political forces. Human screens are assemblages of multiple historical continuities and ruptures. There would be no human screens without the military rupture which progressively led from close to distant warfare and, later, to vertical aerial bombing. Human screens would not have emerged without the development of new technologies of seeing and killing that result from this rupture. In turn—and decisively so—humans could not have become screens without the emergence of a certain kind of legal and ethical sensibility whereby certain categories of people on the battlefield come to be conceived as non-combatants to be spared and protected and whose use as war screens was prohibited. In other words, there would not be accusations of human screening without the development of a distinction between humane and inhumane forms of warfare, grounded in the idea of protecting lives that are framed as innocent.

Hence, while protecting, human screens project and reveal these historical forces which have coagulated into the figure of the human screen. An archaeology of human screens reveals that humans become screens through a twofold process of modulation: while modulating the distance in a contingent battlefield, they also modulate the flow of these historical forces—military, techno-visual, legal, ethical—which cross the body of the humans who are turned into screens. To put it in Richard Grusin's and Jay David Bolter's terms of the theory of remediation, while transforming

---

[7] See Banu Bargu, "Human Shields", in *Contemporary Political Theory* 12, n. 4 (2013); Judith Butler, "Human Shields", in *London Review of International Law* 3, n. 2 (2015); Neve Gordon and Nicola Perugini, "The Politics of Human Shielding: On the Resignification of Space and the Constitution of Civilians as Shields in Liberal Wars", in *Environment and Planning D: Society and Space* 34(1) (2016).

human bodies into mediation technologies in the midst of armed conflict, human screens 'comment on', reproduce, or refashion these existing military, techno-visual, legal, and ethical forces.[8] Through this act of remediation, a new layer appears. Certain human lives, which are deemed to be spared from the violence of war, become lives that can be sacrificed.

From Screens to Human Screens

In Ancient Greece, war was a muscular practice that often took place at very close range. "In phalanx-fighting", men armed with shields (the hoplites) operated together; they "acted as a body, not as individuals or temporary bands. Soldiers in the phalanx fought closely packed together, protecting each others' sides, forming a wall with their shields". They screened each other with the most common defensive weapon utilised across different civilisations: the shield. They moved together, proximate and across small distances, in "mass push" actions. Using a shield was an honourable practice and a symbol of heroism. "With your shield or on it", used to intimate the Spartan mother to her warrior son, since abandoning the shield in the battlespace would have constituted an unethical act of cowardice.[9]
Similarly, in the Roman Empire, the use of 'human walls' of soldiers protected by multiple forms of shields continued to constitute an important warfare technique. However, in the following centuries, war underwent important changes and the distance between soldiers and their military targets progressively increased. The introduction of both new, powerful weapons and military strategies mediated this progressive distancing of war. Arrows, catapults, and other weapons contributed to this process, until the epochal ruptures produced by the invention of gunpowder and the subsequent introduction of guns, cannons, and artillery. The art of war became more and more the art of calculating and arranging different elements in the space of the battlefield in order to find good angles for killing.
At the age of thirteen, Nicolò Tartaglia was injured in his mouth by a French soldier during the 1512 siege of the Italian town of Brescia. Two decades later, Tartaglia wrote the *Nova scientia* (The New Science), a pioneering ballistic treatise in which this Italian scientist with a strong interest for applied mathematics delineated the basic principles for making

[8] See Jay David Bolter and Richard Grusin, *Remediation. Understanding New Media*, Cambridge, MA: MIT Press, 1999, 111.
[9] J. E. Lendon, *Soldiers and Ghosts: A History of Battle in Classical Antiquity*, New Haven, CT: Yale University Press, 2005, 41.

artillery projectiles effective at a certain angle of attack, at "45 degrees over the line of the horizon" (Fig. 3). "I would like to manufacture", added Tartaglia in one of his propositions,

> an instrument for myself that I can use to level the ground and to analyze it by means of sight and [to calculate] the heights, widths, depths, and diametral and horizontal distances of perceptible objects. This instrument should also be easily usable to investigate the variety of shots of each piece of artillery and, similarly, of each mortar.[10]

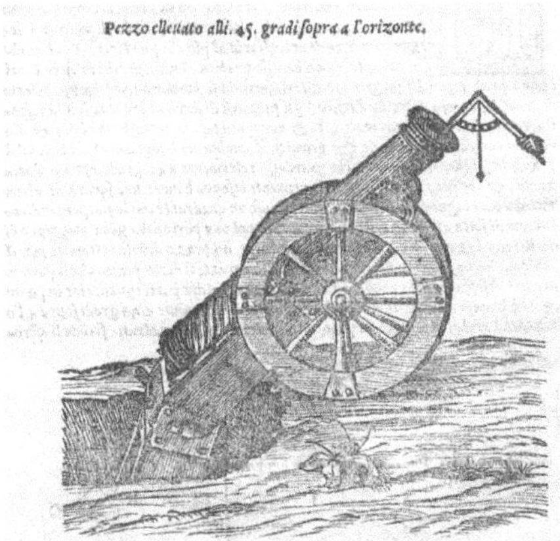

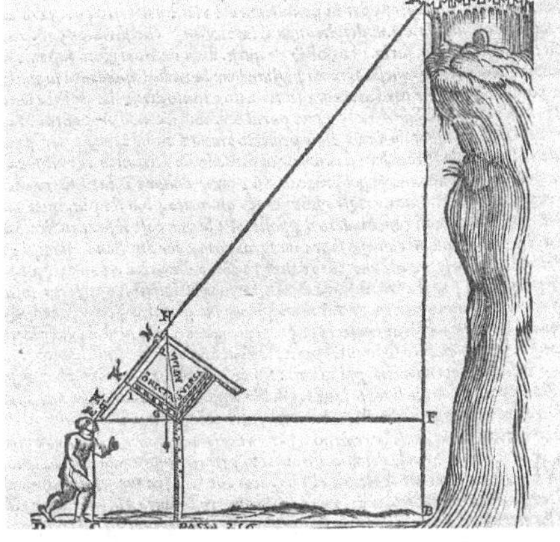

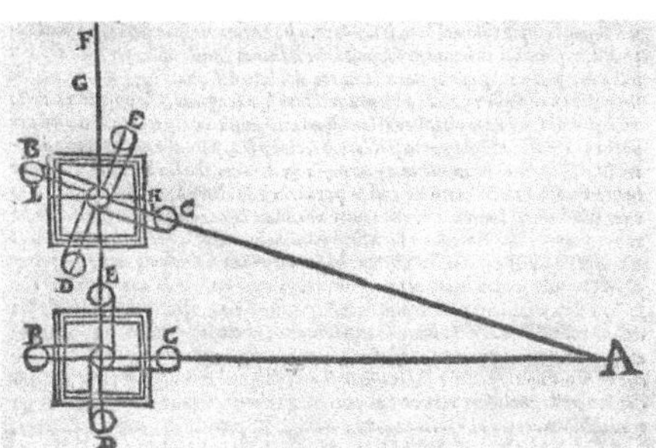

Fig. 3–5 (top-left to bottom-left) — From Matteo Valleriani, *Metallurgy, Ballistics and Epistemic Instruments: The Nova scientia of Nicolò Tartaglia – A New Edition*, Edition Open Access, 2013, 8, 24, 29.

A century after Tartaglia, Europe became a leading international force in this genre of calculations developed by the Italian mathematician and in the art of killing at a distance. In highly asymmetrical contexts like colonial wars, distance often translated as the capacity to exterminate the indigenous enemy from a relatively safe position without facing significant

[10] Cited in Matteo Valleriani, *Metallurgy, Ballistics and Epistemic Instruments: The Nova scientia of Nicolò Tartaglia – A New Edition*, Edition Open Access, 2013, 23–24.

losses, and without being seen. "At the end of the 1890s", writes Sven Lindqvist, "the revolution of the rifle was complete. All European infantry-men could now fire lying down without being spotted, in all weathers, fifteen shots in as many seconds at targets up to a distance of a thousand yards."[11] Killing at a distance meant to be able to see and kill without being seen, a practice that has, since then, become a key paradigm of contemporary warfare.[12]

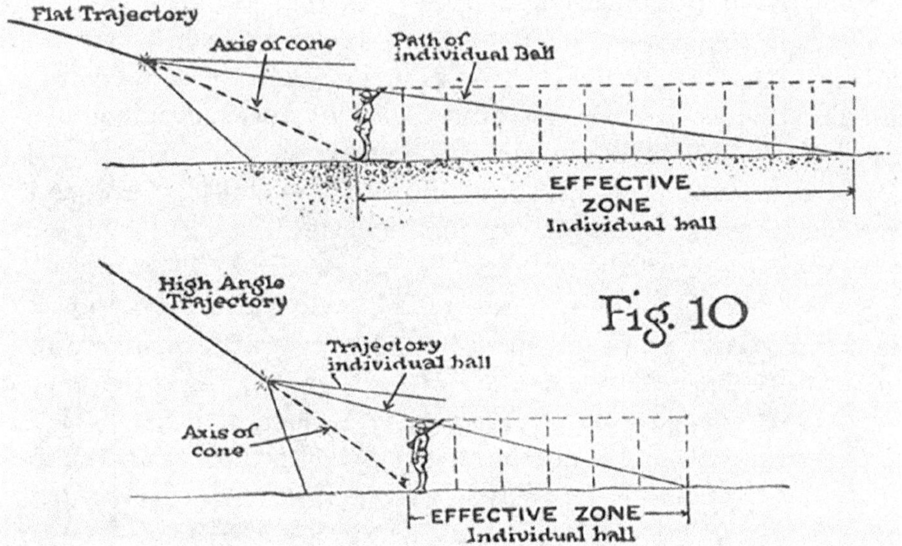

Fig. 6 — From Capt. C. Beard, "Fire and Effect of Modern Artillery", in *Professional Memoirs, Corps of Engineers, United States Army, and Engineer Department at Large*, Vol. 11, No. 58 (JULY–AUGUST, 1919), 447–494, 463.

From the Greek shield to the revolution of the rifle, what we can notice is a decrease in the 'muscularity' of war and an increase in distance that produced a whole new set of calculations and modulations. The human body has acquired new postures, new ways of fighting, and crucially, it has come to occupy new positions on the battlefield. This transformation was a fundamental passage in the creation of situations of asymmetric war epitomized by colonial and imperial aggressions but also in the emergence of a multiplicity of in-between spaces in which human screens would progressively appear, remediating the distance of war in new ways.

[11] Sven Lindqvist, *Exterminate All the Brutes*, New York: The New Press, 1996, 52.
[12] See Svea Bräunert and Meredith Malone, *To See Without Being Seen: Contemporary Art and Drone Warfare*, St. Louis: Mildred Lane Kemper Art Museum, 2016; Gregoire Chamayou, *A Theory of the Drone*, New York: The New Press, 2015.

The introduction of air power at the beginning of the nineteenth century radically increased the capacity to kill at a distance. With air bombing, distance became vertical. The aerial view was "enlisted into the practices of war" making the relationship between the art of seeing and the art of killing unprecedentedly complicit.[13] From above, aerial distance translated into a position of rational, scientific, and military control of space. As a result, aerial bombing exacerbated existing war asymmetries, transforming in particular the colonial and imperial battlefields—in which the inferior human status attributed to the life of the colonized populations allowed the deployment of brutal means of warfare—into huge laboratories of military and visual experimentation.

Every action generates a reaction. The reaction to the rational dream of making the battlefield completely visible from the air in order to increase the capacity to kill the enemy was to hide. In colonial and imperial contexts, this struggle between visibility and invisibility at a distance develops along racial lines.

During the 1935–1936 colonial invasion, Italian fascist bombing of the International Committee of the Red Cross medical facilities became a systematic practice. The issue was brought to the attention of the League of Nations, which gathered the different versions of the facts. The Italian government argued that its military aeroplanes had been precise and surgical in their choice of targets, and that it was the treacherous Ethiopian resistance that was to blame for inhumanely screening behind Red Cross tents and personnel. The fascist press echoed the government's stance and produced a series of images accusing the Ethiopians of screening behind and abusing the Red Cross emblem (Fig. 7). The Ethiopian government, however, denounced the bombing at the League of Nations

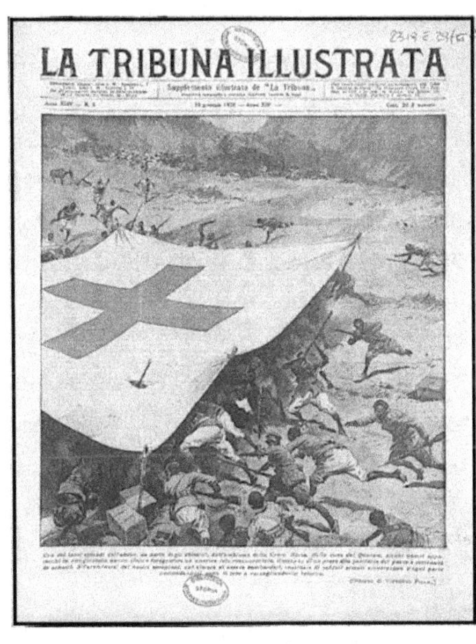

Fig. 7 — La Tribuna Illustrata, January 1936.

[13] See Peter Adey, Mark Whitehead and Alison Williams, "Introduction: Visual Culture and Verticality", in *From Above: War, Violence, and Verticality*, ed. by Peter Adey, Mark Whitehead and Alison Williams, Oxford: Oxford University Press, 2013.

and replied that the Italian actions violated the basic laws of war and were a confirmation of the intrinsic inhumanity of the fascist military.[14] In other words, human screening mediated the understanding of colonial war at vertical distance by modulating the war of perception and representation in the international political arena.

In 1950, when the United States joined the United Nations and intervened militarily against North Korea after it invaded South Korea with the support of the Soviet Union, the Korean Red Army faced a similar accusation to the one railed by the Italians against the Ethiopian resistance. In an official statement, the US representatives at the United Nations maintained that:

> The aggressor in Korea has tried all manner of tricks to divert the attention of the world from his crime. [...] Peaceful villages are used to cover the tanks of the invading army. Civilian dress is used to disguise soldiers of aggression. [The Korean Red Army is] using civilians as a *human screen* for ground forces.[15]

The Korean Red Army was among the first military formations influenced by Mao Zedong's theory of a people's war. According to Mao, people's war required the support of the entire population, including civilians. Like "fishes in the water", the anti-imperial combatants involved in these wars merged with the civilian populations that joined the war effort.[16]

A couple of decades later, the Vietnam War was a turning point in the development of the hide and seek tension that has decisively contributed to the proliferation of the idea of human screening. Faced with the Vietcong tactics of going 'invisible', the US military developed a series of techniques aimed at seeing, sensing, and better targeting the guerrilla forces blending in with the civil population. The dream was to make the enemy 'transparent'.[17] Thus, a new "fascination with the minutiae of hamlet activity emerged"[18], and Geographic Information Systems allowed the US army to produce computer-generated maps of the Vietnamese administrative units which were used as counterinsurgency tools in order to surveil and detect the intermingling of civilians and combatants.

[14] See Nicola Perugini and Neve Gordon, "Between Sovereignty and Race: The Bombardment of Hospitals in the Italo-Ethiopian War and the Colonial Imprint of International Law", in *State Crime Journal* 8, n. 1 (2019).

[15] Cited in Marjorie M. Whiteman, *Digest of International Law,* Vol. 10, Washington: Department of Defense, 1968, 140 (my emphasis).

[16] See Mao Zedong, *On Guerrilla Warfare*, Champaign, IL: University of Illinois Press, 2000.

[17] See Oliver Belcher, "Data Anxieties: Objectivity and Difference in Early Vietnam War Computing", in *Algorithmic life: Calculative Devices in the Age of Big Data*, ed. by Louise Amoore and Volha Piotukh, London: Routledge, 2015, 129.

[18] See Belcher, "Data Anxieties", 128.

The US military also developed the first bombs equipped with television tracking systems, the so-called 'smart bombs'. In addition, the use of helicopters became widespread, since they allowed for agile movement and for increasing the capacity to 'un-screen', since for the Vietcong, shooting a helicopter meant losing "the advantage of cover and concealment and generally bring a devastating return of machine gun fire and rockets"[19]. Finally, leaflets aimed at civilians were dropped on the hamlets framing the Vietcong guerrilla as a perfidious force that "hide in the midst of the people and refuse to meet the government's forces on the battlefield"[20].

These developments remediated the distances from which the war was fought. And while altering the way the war was fought and the enemy was visualized, they also helped US officials to frame the perception of the battlefield in legal and ethical terms, as a space in which a precise white air force was facing a 'treacherous Oriental Communist' human screening enemy. This argument was repeated by US officials at the beginning of the 1970s, when their military's "precision bombing" caused the death of hundreds of thousands of Vietnamese and the US came under international scrutiny and criticism. Indeed, the tension between on the one hand supposedly ethical smart bombing that can see everything at distance, and on the other hand unethical human screening—a tension about the ethics and politics of visibility—dominated the international legal debates in the years following the war in Vietnam.

Waiting for the Human Screen

The military and legal experts of global powers continued to discuss the question of civilian involvement in war and the development of precision techniques in the decades following the Vietnam War, until the First Gulf War in Iraq and then the humanitarian wars in the Balkans erupted in the last decade of the last millennium. In Iraq, the kind of war at vertical distance through the use of television bombs that had appeared in Vietnam was amplified, also for media consumption. "Warfare and war reporting became one", as Harun Farocki puts it in his film *War at a Distance* (2003). The bombs dropped from the air also became the technology through which distant targeting operations could be made closer to the spectators of war at home. The overlap between the "function of the

[19] John J. Tolson (Lieutenant General), *Airmobility, 1961–1971*, Washington DC: Department of the Army, 1973, 149.
[20] Guenter Lewy, *America in Vietnam*, Oxford: Oxford University Press, 1980, 69.

weapon and function of the eye"[21] was complete; to such an extent that images did not even need to convey any explicit propaganda message. Images became "operational images" devoid of people, Farocki explains in *War at a Distance*. One bomb, one target; that was the 'clean' message of 'surgical' warfare. In operational images, human beings disappear from the pictures. Bridges are empty (Fig. 8). The deadly targeting process is presented as smooth, devoid of human life. The images of war at a distance are operational in the sense that they are—as Farocki puts it in his film—"made to check the missile's functioning".

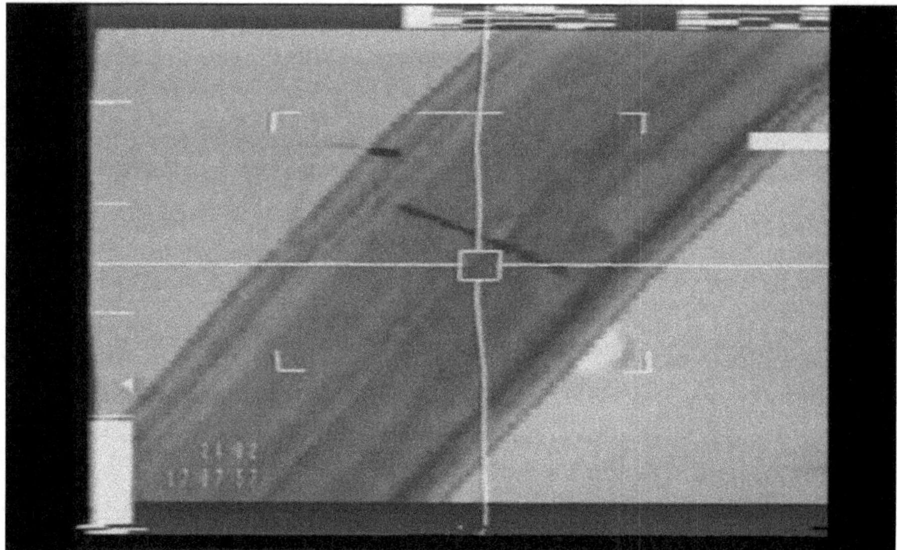

Fig. 8 — Harun Farocki, *War at a Distance*, 2003, film still.

In former Yugoslavia this cleanness and smoothness was challenged by the appearance of human screens. The paradigm of precise warfare according to which Western strikes had become 'surgical' and produced only unintended 'collateral' human deaths was defied at its roots. Like when Serbian civilians dressed as targets walked on a bridge in 1999 at the height of the NATO campaign to defend Kosovo, and as Peter Sloterdijk puts it, they served "as an apposite commentary on the reality of air warfare in the 20th century"[22]. These human screens put their bodies in-between—in the vertical axis of bombing, between the eyes of NATO pilots and a bridge that had become a potential target—the human

[21] Paul Virilio, *War and Cinema: The Logistics of Perception*, London: Verso, 2009, 26.
[22] Peter Sloterdijk, *Terror from the Air*, Los Angeles and Cambridge: MIT Press, 2009, 53.

screens projected an image that tells us that war at vertical distance cannot but terrorise and target entire civilian populations (Fig. 9). By deliberately becoming human screens who protected a civilian infrastructure, the Serbian civilians were making a comment against the normalisation of the idea of 'precision targeting'. And they were also commenting on Farocki's operational images, re-inserting the people, the human component, into the images of war.

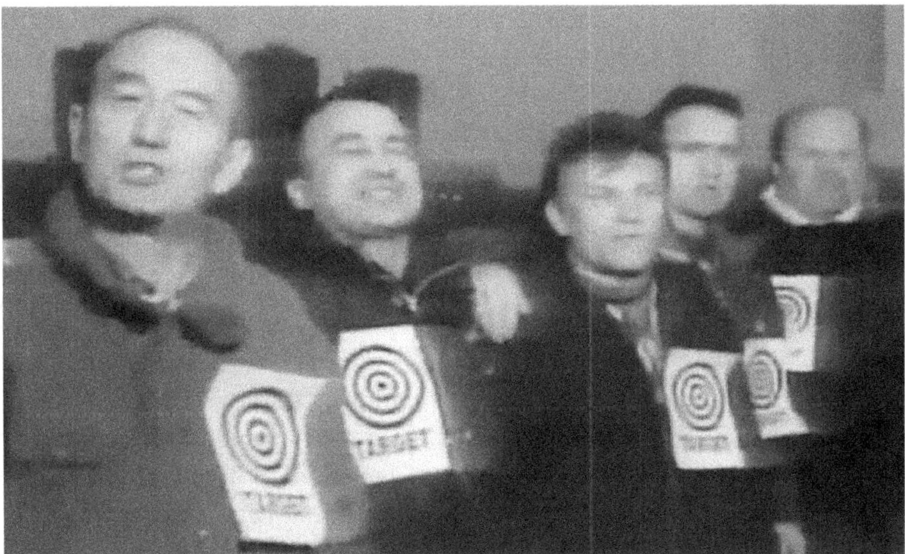

Fig. 9 — Human shields on bridges in Serbia at anti-NATO protests, 1999, film still. https://www.youtube.com/watch?v=isJvgdLidm8, accessed 17 February 2024.

In this historical struggle for the attribution and reattribution of legal and ethical meaning to war at vertical distance, the development of drone warfare should be conceived of as the most recent counter-measure adopted by international powers when they dominate global skies in order to neutralize the kind of critique embodied by the Serbian human screens.[23] Following the war in Kosovo, at the beginning of our millennium, millions of people tried to oppose the invasion of Iraq and the so-called 'War on Terror'. The protesters who took the streets of many Western capitals did not become human screens, but sent a similar message to that of the Serbian human screens: there is no 'surgical' war, all wars ultimately target civilians.

[23] On the tension between "precise" distance warfare and the meaning of violence, see Talal Asad, *On Suicide Bombing*, New York: Columbia University Press, 2007, 35.

In response to this radical critique of war, drone warfare has tried to radicalize the discourse of vertical humanity. Let us now examine how.

Drones are weapons *par excellence* in the 'War on Terror', a war against African and Asian enemies who are framed through a racialised discourse of humanity similar to that of the colonial wars of old. The 'War on Terror', the discourse goes, is fought in theatres of conflicts where inhumane terrorists deliberately intermingle with and screen behind non-combatants in order to induce the 'Forces of Good', who are driven by a higher sense of humanity, to commit war crimes and kill innocent civilians. The proponents of drone warfare often embrace this racialised world view and argue that drones, with their sight from the sky, increase the precision of warfare unprecedentedly and make the distinction between inhumane and humane warfare even more evident.

Drones, indeed, operate a radical remediation of war. They remodulate the distance of war, compressing the distance of vertical warfare—the distance between the predatory eye and the target—and transform the temporality of killing. They "compress the kill chain". Drones roam in the skies and surveil the lives of the military targets for days, offering, from the thousands of miles from which they are operated, a close visualisation of the movements of these targets and their daily social relations, as if the drone operators "were there" with their targets. What ultimately drone targeting operations try to produce is a "death of distance", as Derek Gregory puts it. The targets are surveilled and filmed at extremely "close distance", in their homes, close to their relatives, interacting with the civilian populations among which they live and operate.[24]

In such a way of war, we are told, there is almost no margin of error. The abidance by the legal and ethical standards of humanity required by contemporary precision warfare is almost total. In order to prove this point, sometimes the militaries that rely heavily on drone warfare edit drone footage and share it with the media.[25] An example of this are the images from the video distributed in 2017 by the US Department of Defense in relation to its operations against the Islamic State in the Iraqi city of Mosul (Fig. 10). Here, the figure of the human screen plays a central role and is mobilized to corroborate the discourse of vertical humanity that drone warfare tries to radicalize. The aerial surveillance footage shows what are presumed to be ISIS operatives establishing firing positions among civilians in West Mosul. Women and children can be seen within the gunsight while they walk in the compound. It is unclear if they were forced to act as screens

[24] See Derek Gregory, "Lines of Descent", in *From Above: War, Violence, and Verticality*, ed. by Peter Adey, Mark Whitehead and Alison Williams, Oxford: Oxford University Press, 2013.
[25] See Gordon and Perugini, *Human Shields*.

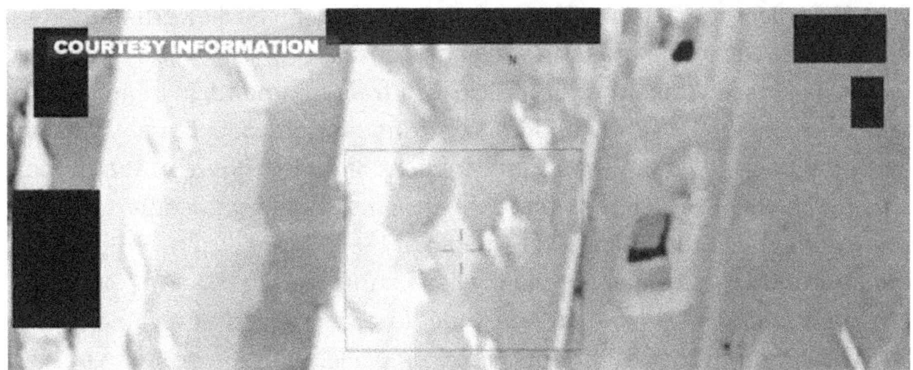

Fig. 10 — Drone video shows ISIS moving civilians into home as human shields, in *ABC News* (21 April 2017), https://abcnews.go.com/Politics/drone-video-shows-isis-moving-civilians-home-human/story?id=46945876, accessed 17 February 2024.

for the firing positions. But according to the spokesperson of the US Central Command, who was interviewed to comment on the video, there is no doubt. The civilians we see on the screen are human screens illegally deployed by an inhumane enemy, we are told. To corroborate the legal and ethical superiority of the US Central Command he added, "[t]he Coalition, through full motion video and real-time surveillance, observed the civilians and therefore did not respond with an airstrike against the position"[26].
There is, however, a different way to read this sort of military-media configuration. Indeed, as in any basic screening configuration, in which certain elements are arranged and assembled in order to render a certain surface a screen, in this military-media configuration, different technologies of surveillance and elements of the battlefield are arranged in order to wait for the appearance of the human screen. The fighters, women and children, as well as the compound in which they live, have probably been observed for extended periods of time, waiting for that specific moment; that specific configuration then framed as human screening by the US Central Command video. Ultimately, while being circulated with a justificatory legal and ethical meaning—"the coalition did not respond since we are more humane than our barbarian enemies"— these images also reveal a mechanism of embodiment, as Lauren Wilcox puts it, through which certain bodies are "produced" by the US-led coalition as "ungrievable".[27] They expose how, through the prism of a racialized enemy observed from

[26] "Drone video shows ISIS moving civilians into home as human shields", in *ABC News* (21 April 2017), https://abcnews.go.com/Politics/drone-video-shows-isismoving-civilians-home-human/story?id=46945876, accessed 17 February 2024.
[27] Lauren Wilcox, *Bodies of Violence: Theorizing Embodied Subjects in International Relations*, Oxford: Oxford University Press, 2015, 132.

the close distance of the drone's eye, certain human bodies are framed as human screens in the era of the 'War on Terror'.

Curiously, footage like that of the US Central Command, in which an attack is called off, is rarely shared by drone warfare coalitions. What we are more used to, is the systematic invocation of the figure of the human shield to justify the killing of innocent civilians, blaming the enemy for the crime, not unlike the Italians in Ethiopia or the US in Vietnam. Indeed, the configuration through which the civilians subjected to the 'War on Terror' are 'produced' as human screens should be conceived of as a necropolitical configuration. Being recognized as civilian human screens means becoming killable as human screens. It produces a radical alteration of the meaning of lethal violence on the battlefield. This passage from a 2010 drone strike communication transcript obtained by the Los Angeles Times in relation to a series of vehicles carrying civilians in Afghanistan can clarify this provisional conclusion of our archaeology. Not unlike in the US Central Command video, some civilian vehicles were observed from a drone base in Nevada for hours by a drone camera sensor operator, a pilot, a 'mission intelligence operator' and other actors of this media-military configuration.

> 1:21 (Sensor): I think they're gonna make it
> 1:21 (MC:) I hope *they get out and dry off*, and show us all their weapons
> 1:21 (Pilot): Yeah, exactly man. So what's the, we passed him *potential children and potential shields*, and I think those are both pretty accurate now, what's the ROE on that?
> 1:21 (Sensor): Ground commander assessing proportionality, distinction
> 1:21 (Pilot): Is that part of CDE, is that part of ground command? I'm not worried from our stand point so much, but that's a (expletive deleted) for them
> 1:21 (Sensor): I think if that's the case and that's what their confident with then they're gonna have to wait until they start firing, 'cause then it essentially puts any possible civilian casualties on the enemy but if we've got friendlies taking effective fire from that position, then we've gotta do what we gotta do.[28]

Military targets and civilians are intermingling. Their proximity can be seen at a close distance from a drone. Children and other civilians are framed

---

[28] Transcript available at https://gist.github.com/wiseman/52979c4451c21a0f7419, accessed 17 February 2024 (my emphases).

as "potential shields". Potential. They are not shields yet. They are not intrinsically human screens. They need to be 'produced' as screens. They will become screens only when one of the armed men opens fire on US friendlies, the drone communication transcript tells us. And while becoming human screens, they will become subjects who can be killed from a drone without legal or ethical responsibility; "it essentially puts any possible civilian casualties on the enemy", says the sensor. Indeed, human screening configurations in the era of the 'War on Terror' are military assemblages in which the forces that arrange the different elements that transform living human beings into screens are the same that pulverize these subjects-screens with impunity. In this contemporary necropolitical configuration, the body 'becomes' an illegal human screen through the work of media technologies operated by the military drone complex of the US 'War on Terror'—with the aim of destroying the body itself.

Coda

As I am finalising this essay, the Israeli military has assaulted the Gaza Strip for the fifth time since 2008. Following Hamas and other Palestinian factions' massacre in Israeli kibbutzim, towns and a desert festival, on the seventh of October 2023, several Israeli high-ranking officials proclaimed their intent to destroy "in whole or in part" the Palestinian population in Gaza, framing them as "human animals", promising to turn "Gaza into Dresden" and to "erase" and "flatten" the Strip.[29] Israel's President Herzog stated publicly that there are "no innocent civilians" in Gaza.[30] Since then, the Israeli military has been engaging in genocidal forms of violent retribution, killing more than 16,000 Palestinians, of whom over 6,000 are children. 1.8 million Palestinians have been displaced. The Israeli military has issued evacuation orders against almost the entire population in Gaza, framing those who decided to stay in their homes and not to be displaced for the second or third time in their lives as human shields. In other words, in the colonial context of Palestine, the figure of the human screen has been vertiginously transformed into a legal-ethical weapon of ethnic cleansing and mass violence.

[29] Raz Segal, "A Textbook Case of Genocide", in *Jewish Currents* (13 October 2023),
https://jewishcurrents.org/a-textbook-case-of-genocide, accessed 17 February 2024.
[30] The Wire Staff, "'No Innocent Civilians in Gaza', Israel President Says as Northern Gaza Struggles to Flee Israeli Bombs", in *The Wire* (14 October 2023),
https://thewire.in/world/northern-gaza-israel-palestine-conflict, accessed 17 February 2024.

References

Peter Adey, Mark Whitehead and Alison Williams, "Introduction: Visual Culture and Verticality", in *From Above: War, Violence, and Verticality*, ed. by Peter Adey, Mark Whitehead and Alison Williams, Oxford: Oxford University Press, 2013, 1–17.

Talal Asad, *On Suicide Bombing*, New York: Columbia University Press, 2007.

Banu Bargu, "Human Shields", in *Contemporary Political Theory* 12, n. 4 (2013), 277–295.

Capt. C. Beard, "Fire and Effect of Modern Artillery", in *Professional Memoirs, Corps of Engineers, United States Army, and Engineer Department at Large*, Vol. 11, No. 58 (JULY–AUGUST, 1919), 447–494.

Oliver Belcher, "Data Anxieties: Objectivity and Difference in Early Vietnam War Computing", in *Algorithmic Life: Calculative Devices in the Age of Big Data*, ed. by Louise Amoore and Volha Piotukh, London: Routledge, 2015, 127–142.

Jay David Bolter and Richard Grusin, *Remediation. Understanding New Media.* Cambridge, MA: MIT Press, 1999.

Svea Bräunert and Meredith Malone, *To See Without Being Seen: Contemporary Art and Drone Warfare*, St. Louis: Mildred Lane Kemper Art Museum, 2016.

Judith Butler, "Human Shields", in *London Review of International Law* 3, n. 2 (2015), 223–243.

Rüdiger Campe, "'Schutz und Schirm': Screening in German During Early Modern Times", in *Screen Genealogies: From Optical Device to Environmental Medium*, ed. by Craig Buckley, Rüdiger Campe and Francesco Casetti, Amsterdam: Amsterdam University Press, 2019, 51–72.

Francesco Casetti, "Primal Screens", in *Screen Genealogies: From Optical Device to Environmental Medium*, ed. by Francesco Casetti, Craig Buckley and Rüdiger Campe, Amsterdam: Amsterdam University Press, 2019, 27–50.

Gregoire Chamayou, *A Theory of the Drone*, New York: The New Press, 2015.

"Drone video shows ISIS moving civilians into home as human shields", in *ABC News* (21 April 2017), https://abcnews.go.com/Politics/drone-video-shows-isismoving-civilians-home-human/story?id=46945876

Neve Gordon and Nicola Perugini, *Human Shields: A History of People in the Line of Fire*, Berkeley, CA: University of California Press, 2020.

——— "Between Sovereignty and Race: The Bombardment of Hospitals in the Italo-Ethiopian War and the Colonial Imprint of International Law", in *State Crime Journal* 8, n. 1 (2019), 104–125.

——— "The Politics of Human Shielding: On the Resignification of Space and the Constitution of Civilians as Shields in Liberal Wars", in *Environment and Planning D: Society and Space* 34(1) (2016), 168–187.

Derek Gregory, "Lines of Descent", in *From Above: War, Violence, and Verticality*, ed. by Peter Adey, Mark Whitehead and Alison Williams, Oxford: Oxford University Press, 2013, 41–70.

J. E. Lendon, *Soldiers and Ghosts: A History of Battle in Classical Antiquity*, New Haven, CT: Yale University Press, 2005.

Guenter Lewy, *America in Vietnam*, Oxford: Oxford University Press, 1980.

Sven Lindqvist, *Exterminate All the Brutes*, New York: The New Press, 1996.

Official Commission of the Belgian Government, *Reports on the Violation of the Rights of Nations and of the Laws and Customs of War in Belgium. (Published on Behalf of the Belgian Legation)*, London: H.M. Stationery Office, Harrison and Sons printers, 1915.

"'No Innocent Civilians in Gaza', Israel President Says as Northern Gaza Struggles to Flee Israeli Bombs", in *The Wire* (14 October 2023), https://thewire.in/world/northern-gaza-israel-palestine-conflict

Raz Segal, "A Textbook Case of Genocide", in *Jewish Currents* (13 October 2023), https://jewishcurrents.org/a-textbook-case-of-genocide

Peter Sloterdijk, *Terror from the Air*, Los Angeles and Cambridge: MIT Press, 2009.

John J. Tolson (Lieutenant General), *Airmobility, 1961–1971,* Washington DC: Department of the Army, 1973.

Matteo Valleriani, *Metallurgy, Ballistics and Epistemic Instruments: The Nova Scientia of Nicolò Tartaglia – A New Edition*, Edition Open Access, 2013.

Paul Virilio, *War and Cinema: The Logistics of Perception*, London: Verso, 2009.

Marjorie M. Whiteman, *Digest of International Law*, Vol. 10, Washington: Department of Defense, 1968.

Lauren B. Wilcox, *Bodies of Violence: Theorizing Embodied Subjects in International Relations*, Oxford: Oxford University Press, 2015.

Mao Zedong, *On Guerrilla Warfare*, Chicago, IL: University of Illinois Press, 2000.

Rana Issa

A Woman's Wrath

One day in my early twenties, as I was stuck in one of Beirut's usual traffic jams, I peed my pants. I found myself emptying the entire contents of my bladder on the seat that now needed to be professionally cleaned. The traffic jam aggravated my bladder on that day, but this secret event was also the beginning of a new phobia that possessed me for over ten years. Since that day, I have been afraid that the accident would repeat itself. And it did.

I consulted a urologist about my condition only once. He filled my bladder with two litres of water. I was able to hold in the water without any leakages. After examining me, the doctor explained that he filled my bladder with a lot more water than a normal bladder can handle, and that what made my bladder hold so much liquid was that I felt ashamed of peeing in his presence. It seemed that I was afraid to reveal to another my awful condition, and so my bladder automatically pulled itself together and decided to not divulge its secret. The doctor speculated that my potty training as a child was incomplete, and that I had never adequately learned to heed the social conventions of urination. He said that he had seen many in my condition, habitual pissers with bladders that have no regard for rules or conventions. Still, he was optimistic that retraining me to pee in a socially acceptable manner would not be difficult, and that the probabilities for success are rather high.

I found it insufferable to try out the routine that he prescribed for more than one day. What did it even mean to train myself to accept the authority of social conventions? What were these conventions that I could trust in the wake of the end of the Lebanese civil war? Which convention of Lebanese society could I even rely upon? When the war ended, I was in my mid-teens. Like many of my generation, I did not find any reason to submit to any law or accepted rule of our violent society. Drugs were our emblem for rejecting authority, and formed the basis of our friendships. They were the silent signifier of our rejection of social frameworks that were forced upon us from the various powers, be they familial or public. We used to chat about our psychological deviance as if depression and obsession were heroic qualities we aspired to. I did not share my bladder issues with my friends, nor did they share with me their own issues with shame. I did not follow the doctor's orders, but I began the journey to search for the cause of my out-of-control bladder.

My life's instabilities as a Lebanese, Palestinian, Sunni girl living in the southern suburb of Beirut, Dahiye, at the time of the Palestinian massacre in Lebanon could be one of the reasons. I began visiting various psychologists. I did not find them so interested in the fact that here was a grown woman who pisses herself. Every time I opened the subject, it would be hushed up, and I would go home with a feeling that they did not know what to say, as if the subject was a bigger taboo than I thought, even for them. Only this one old analyst in Norway on the brink of retirement engaged with me on it, saying compassionately, this must surely be demeaning for you. *Ydmykende* she said in Norwegian. I had heard the word before, but I did not understand it properly. I looked it up in the dictionary; the word expressed a mix of humility and humiliation. In a language still new to my tongue, my consciousness found its way to a word for something I was feeling but that I had no language to express.

I then moved from one word that expressed what I felt about my condition to relating it to a complex political situation upon reading Georges Bataille's *The Story of the Eye*. All the sex and piss in the novel was a godsend for me. The text helped me decipher why I peed myself. Bataille interprets pissing as a sexual gesture that rejects the bourgeois basis of the family in the inter-war period, and casts it as a form of revolutionary violence that expresses its rebellion through a violation of bourgeois chastity and its hypocritical virginity. Bataille's characters delight in golden showers and satisfy a sexual appetite that is freed from laws governing the body, through giving free rein to pissing on the bourgeois uptightness of mothers that know nothing about their children's lives. Bataille's characters are like mammals that urinate to mark their territory and reclaim space.

Pissing on others as a form of humiliation is well-known in the handbook of political violence. This is what was witnessed in Abu Ghraib and this is what Syrian torturers do to their detainees. They piss on them like dogs piss to mark a place, to turn the body into a place. By urinating on you, the torturer occupies the space that you used to identify (before being tortured) as your body. He is a dog, and you are a place. And both of you are the property of the tyrant and are under his command and at his whim. Yassin al-Haj Saleh writes in his book about the concept of the atrocious: "humiliating torture aims to manufacture a memory, or impart a lesson that will never be forgotten"[1]. You are the tyrant's property, and only dementia may help you forget.

These days, I spend my time searching in my memories and experiences to reconstruct narratives that can bolster my psychological foundations. When the economy in Lebanon collapsed in 2019, my grandmother Izdihar came back to my mind's eye with such force. My grandmother resembled Roald Dahl's grandmothers in her vitriol at life. In the stories I tell my two children about Izdihar, I always make her an evil, dangerous witch who does not like children much. My young son hides his head under the covers as I tell him how much the witch Izdihar loved the taste of children's flesh. Truth be told, she was not a greedy woman, and she substituted biting into our arms with eating sugar. Izdihar was born during the Great Arab Revolt. She lived through the Palestinian *nakba*, which would remain a part of her until the day she died in a dilapidated hospital in the Palestinian refugee camp of Burj al-Barajneh, where rats gnaw at the flesh of Lebanon's forgotten. As I write, I stare at her ring that sits on my finger. I 'inherited' that ring from her when I found it tossed between piles of old papers in my father's house. I remembered how it grew tighter on her finger with every passing year. I tell my children that this ring has magical powers and can slay the biggest giant. I have in fact tried out its powers in my daily battles between Oslo and Beirut. All I have to do is rub it and make a wish for my heart to be filled with courage, and my tongue to breathe out fire that reduces the wicked to a pile of ash. This ring shields me in my daily travails. The power of this ring lies in my grandmother's bitterness at life. This bitterness was bequeathed to me, and it would always remain with me. It is also what has shaped my literary interests for most of my life.

I always felt my grandmother was the shameful legacy that I had to conceal from the eyes of the world. A long time would have to pass before I could accept that to lay myself bare was necessary for the writing of history. Writing her tale might not provide an adequate shield to the

[1] Yassin al-Haj Saleh, *The Atrocious and Its Representation: Deliberations on Syria's Destroyed Form and Its Laborious Formation*, Beirut: Dar al-Jadid, 2021, 49 (author's translation).

processes of brutalization storming through my life and the lives of the people I belong to, but it does offer a salve to the soul looking to exist beyond modes of survival.

I heard from my mother that Izdihar used to wet her death bed. This made my mother quite anxious, particularly after my grandmother was moved to Gaza Hospital in Burj al-Barajneh refugee camp on the outskirts of Beirut. My mother did not trust the nurses there. The hospital, like the city whose name was 'displaced' onto it, lacks everything that makes it healthy or that can bring about healing. My grandmother started wetting herself towards the end of her short life. She died at the age of 61 after hearing news that her eldest son, who had escaped to Baghdad after the massacres perpetrated against the Palestinians by the Lebanese Shia militia Haraket Amal along with the Syrian intelligence services, had disappeared. His tale is a horrific one; my mother might write about it one day in a new novel. His disappearance made his mother literally lose her balance completely, so she fell and broke her hip and died a few weeks later. I recall that my mother took us to visit her in Gaza once. The hospital, like all the places in the camp, had the smell of several layers of mould piled up with that of being forgotten. If you die in Gaza, it means that wretchedness has triumphed over you and your life, and that your dignity will remain trampled even after your death. For example, there is no guarantee that your grave, if you get a grave in the first place, will not become a garbage dump more vile than the heap of humiliation dumped on you while you were alive.

The smell of shit takes me back to my grandmother and to my memories of my mother's family in the camp. Everything there smelled repulsive. Even the people there reek of those gases. My mother explains that water comes to the camp mixed with sewage, and none of the inhabitants manage to escape that smell when they bathe. They are literally full of shit, not metaphorically nor is this a smartass way of cursing them. The stink of political discrimination manifests itself too as an odour that blocks the imagination and occupies souls, to turn foul language and foulness into a daily reality that aims at destroying the ability of Palestinians to insist on their right to a decent life. Their lives are full of shit wherever they live. Following the Sheikh Jarrah demonstrations in Jerusalem in May 2021, news started coming out about the Israeli army flooding the neighbourhood in Jerusalem with shit. The Israeli occupiers hose the area daily with skunk water, spraying the streets and the walls with what the Palestinians call the *kharrara*, or the shitter. The goal of course is to force Palestinians to leave by nauseating them. The gases stick to the walls and streets, and so people become imprisoned inside their homes out of disgust.

My grandmother's life was destroyed when her husband was assassinated. The way he was killed, with the political and national connotations it carried, bestowed upon him a glamour that comes with the halo of martyrdom. He died for the cause and left his wife with five children, the youngest of whom could not yet walk. My grandfather was a hero, a patriot, a man of principle, a martyr. Mahmud Chreih mentions him in his book *Paradise Lost,* which gives validity to the tales my mother tells about my grandfather's generosity and his popularity in the camp. As for her, his widow, Izdihar, she was a whore. That is how she was known in Juret al-Tarashiha (Tarshiha alley) and all over Burj al-Barajneh Camp. When her husband died, my grandmother was in her late twenties. Beautiful, slender, white, soft to the touch. Her murdered husband had spoiled her too much before his death and she seemed to think that after his death she would manage to maintain something of this pampered life. Her son would catch her behind the door kissing a man that supplied her with fabric. Another son would hear kids at school whispering rumours about his mother. My maternal aunt tells legends about my grandma's erotic appetite and her early marriage. She said that my grandfather married her at the age of 15 to shield her honour from gossip. After the hero died, it seemed to the relatives that Um Nizar, as my *teta* was also known, was aimlessly wandering, searching for another body to fuse with. They were not mistaken.

I prefer the tales of scandal that used to follow her to my own memories of *teta* (grandmother). I could have remembered her as a servant, even if I never saw her scrub the toilets of the well-to-do. Housework is a profession I know well. After my mother's class status was upgraded from poverty to relatively better economic conditions, she began employing women who would mop up the dirt from the corners of the house. We lived with those women whom we hardly got to know the way they got to know us. They never had enough time to answer our questions about their lives outside our house, except in snippets about fatherless children and poverty that forced them to work in the households of others, which all sounded alike. Did Izdihar work as a servant? I don't know for sure, but I recall her telling my mother that the wife of Sami al-Khatib would call for her to help cook a dinner party or that General Khatib was craving baked *kibbeh* or *moghrabieh* made by her. Her food was honey, like the piss of angels.

And this General Khatib, who was later known as the High Commissioner of Beirut during the era of the direct Ba'athist occupation of Lebanon, previously held a high position in the branch of the Lebanese intelligence service known as *al-Maktab al-Thani*, or the Deuxième Bureau, during the reign of President Fouad Shehab in the fifties. In the biography that was published by *al-Akhbar* newspaper after his death months before the outbreak of the revolution in 2019, journalist Nicholas Nassif mentions that after the coup against Shehab that was attempted by the Pan-Syrian Nationalist Party, the officer at the time, Lieutenant Sami el-Khatib was the one responsible for interrogating the leaders of that party. He was a brute of a torturer, as the article mentions. After the arrest of my grandfather Mohammad, for being one of the party's Palestinian leaders, Izdihar went to Khatib looking for her husband. She learned from him that her husband had been killed by mistake before he reached the interrogation centre. A blow to the head by the butt of a soldier's rifle killed him. Sami apologized to her, saying that he had only asked for him to be summoned for interrogation and had never ordered his killing. To console and make it up to her he asked his wife to employ her in his house as a cook, for Izdihar was a master chef, as everyone who ate her food knew. Her name itself helped as well. *Izdihar* means 'flowering' and thus prosperity. Surely her name would bring him good fortune and the prosperity it implies would reflect back on to him too. He was a police chief confronting a revolutionary coup and he was like the political dickhead in Jean Genet's play, *The Balcony*. And like Genet's dickhead, Sami al-Khatib was seeking glory and *izdihar* in order to tighten his grip over people. And he did in fact flourish in his profession, achieving *izdihar,* for the dickhead was made a minister twice. Doubtless, grandma Izdihar's *mulukhiyya* helped Sami stoke the appetites and capture the imaginations of his guests at dinner parties, and extending to him some of the prestige my *teta* had inherited from her high-class upbringing in Tarshiha, in the north of Palestine. I recall how my grandmother's face would light up each time she told my mother that she had been called to cook at the minister's house. Not once did she think to poison the food and avenge her husband. I prefer to imagine Izdihar as Irma the whore in Genet's play rather than a simple maid. In whoring there is some of that coyness that I liked about her more than her enslavement all those years at the house of her husband's killer.

The husband died when she was at the peak of her beauty, only 27 years old and a mother of five. She possessed no skills except cooking, sewing, adornment and motherhood. Her children do not think that she did well at motherhood. In her youth she liked men and sought out their attention.

The entire camp bore witness to your grandmother's elegance, says my mother on the phone. She was always dressed in sexy outfits and high heels and sported the latest hairdos. She spent time and money on love, which caused hardship for her children. They might not find anything to eat the day she left the house to visit a lover. When one of the children complained about her negligence, she would explode in a fury that echoed all over Juret al-Tarashiha.

A slave to her children, that's how society wanted her. As a widow, she was imprisoned by her mother-in-law in the house while her husband's brother gave her a pittance for her upkeep according to Muslim family law. The situation stifled her, so she used to escape to work in secret for the Khatibs to somewhat relieve her terrible penury. Her brother-in-law barely gave her any money, and the people of the camp were poor, which also made them frugal with mercy for the weakest among them. After her relatives discovered where she worked, malicious gossip began to spread in the camp. She defied them by openly bragging about her connection to powerful people who could shelter her and her children from harm. She did not care that the neighbours and the family questioned her integrity and accused her of being a spy for the Deuxième Bureau.

In Marxist literature one will not find concepts that are capable of describing an employer-employee relationship as brutal. The burden it placed on our family is not unique, for it is the kind of labour relation that is central to the savage political economy of our region. This kind of menial labour relation grinds down the soul and is widespread in economies that are clientelistic, colonial and enslaving. These labour relations promote inequality and create violent binaries that rend people apart. Palestinian workers inside the Occupied Territories are called traitors if they work in an Israeli settlement, or participate in building the apartheid wall. What shame is this, born of a hand whose owner has no other choice in the confrontation with need, where the only recourse she or he can take to feed hungry mouths at the end of the day is this betrayal? Izdihar's love for her children might have been what forced her to swallow her pride and suck in the pain of losing what was rightfully hers and compromise to secure basic necessities for her children.

Izdihar was beautiful and desirable. She was deft at employing her beauty in the same way she succeeded in making Sami al-Khatib's conscience prey upon him and give her work. Her lovers were amiable and lavish. They would buy her perfumes, fabric, and fresh fruit. As Audre Lorde writes, the erotic protects women from the feeling of incapacitation and other states of being that are not native to us, like resignation, self-effacement, and depression. Eroticism neutralizes humiliation and dissipates its impact. Without doubt, Izdihar the young widow was dreaming of a new love, but I do not know if her strict upbringing in Tarshiha permitted her to open her thighs for anyone to rub her *daghdaghan*, that tickly thing as the clitoris is called in Hebrew. Let's lay the stress on the last syllable and let the long *aaaa* wash away all the boring Arabic words for the most delightful of body parts. Izdihar may have let them kiss her and pinch her breasts, and if someone managed to taste her honey, I would be so very happy for her. Her erotic appetite was tremendous and she had her own language to speak about the body and its gestures. She used to call it *ash'oush*, the tiny bird's nest. She would tickle us between her fingers in the bath and cry out with glee, "may God protect your *ash'oush*". If one of us let go of a *foss* or smelly fart, she would also greet it with glee, "may God protect your *foss*". She owned her body like she owned nothing else. She risked her reputation because she desired.

Often, when we visited her in the camp, she would try to cover up her shameful poverty by telling us about the glorious past life she had had in Palestine. Endlessly repeated tales that spun a bygone glory; wealth, lands, influence, prestige contrasted with the moment of exodus—barefoot: they forgot their slippers at home and they had nothing with them except the clothes on their backs. The rancid smells in the camp dominate the tales of the high stature of the Qiblawi clan in Tarshiha before they were dispossessed of their homes and displaced from their land following the *nakba*. My great-grandmother was strong, rode horses, knew how to shoot a rifle; Izdihar's father was the town mayor and we own hundreds of *dunum*s of property there. Tales overflow with jasmine and orange blossom, as if the narratives were exerting themselves to overcome the smell of shit that hangs on the walls here, and is mixed with the tap water.

When I finally visited Tarshiha a few years ago, my memory dominated my senses. The smell of the camp blocked my nose from smelling the refreshing air of the town. As for the olive trees scattered over the hills facing the house of my mother's maternal cousin, they reminded me of the haphazard web of electric cables above the alleyways of the camp. These cables short-circuit every year and can reduce human bodies to charred coal during the wintertime, when they snap under the weight of the heavy rains and thus rain down gratuitous death on the people of the camp. The homes of our relatives there are spacious, and their financial situation is nothing like that of their family in Lebanon. They are strangers to us, these relatives. The political and historical connection is more obvious than the family tie. The uncanny resemblance between this stranger-cousin and my own maternal aunt shakes the foundations of my limited understanding of family as I knew it, the one with a house in the camp. It was in Tarshiha, that the *nakba* finally took hold of my consciousness decades after the fact. My concept of home was unhinged. After my visit to Tarshiha I began to understand home as revolving around the axis of the *nakba* as its historical rupture. Only now could I unpack how this rupture had become part of my senses and seeped into my pores, deforming the flesh under my skin.

The destroyed Qiblawi household now uncannily stirred up feelings of familiarity and alienation. This family that remained in Tarshiha managed to disrupt the very limited narratives I had about my Palestinian-ness and forced me to face up to the other possibilities that could have been available to my family members—Izdihar's offspring—had the *nakba* not taken place, or had they been able to remain in Tarshiha where their mother was born and raised. I ask Izdihar's cousin about why (and how) her immediate family remained in Palestine whereas mine left for Lebanon to become refugees. Her response is disarmingly straightforward. Her family walked eastward whereas mine walked north. As simple as a few kilometres difference, and new borders were drawn between the two countries. The historian Adel Manna writes about the pamphlets that the Israelis air-dropped, in which they threatened the townspeople with a massacre if they did not evacuate their village at once. They all abandoned the village. Some became refugees and others became what we call '48 Palestinians, the ones who managed to remain in Palestine after the *nakba* and were given Israeli citizenship.

Izdihar was thirteen at the time of the *nakba*. Her parents did not teach her to read or write, instead they taught her cooking, sewing and other things they believed to be useful to make her a better marriage prospect. They deliberately intended her to be *ummiya*, illiterate, to prepare her to play the role of *umuma*, motherhood, a role she would inherit from her mother, her mother's mother, and the mother of all the mothers that came before them. *Ummiya* she would remain, for she would remain created in the image of her mother, and to speak her mother's tongue. This is the concrete tongue that has no recourse to ink or pens or any of the tools to rupture the umbilical cord binding it to the maternal. She was taught only housework in preparation for her future as an *amah,* a house-slave to her husband. *Sois belle et tais-toi.* Be pretty and shut up. This is not a specifically Arab, Tarshihi legacy, it is also common in many other cultures. To ensure your silence, because your voice might give your husband a headache, your family kept you illiterate, and vowed to your cousin before they married you off to him that you would be obedient. In ancient Greek, both *amah* and *umm*—slave and mother, along with children, house and the entire estate owned by a man come under the concept of *oikos*, which is the etymological cognate in English for economy. The economic health of the family depended on these pre-assigned gender roles of slave and master within the family. In this economy, illiteracy (ensures that the woman is restricted to being *amah*, enslaved to her husband, or *umm*, mother to the children) provided stability and prosperity (*izdihar*) to the family and lifted its social standing. As for marrying her off to her cousin, my *jeddo* or granddad, this ensured that the property would not be taken over by a stranger, for whatever Izdihar inherited along with her other siblings would remain the property of the Qiblawis to add to their wealth and prestige. Today, Tarshiha is annexed to the neighbouring settlement Maalot, existing only through the hyphen that conjoins them, Maalot-Tarshiha.

Sandra Noeth

Colder

1.

Today is different.

Sitting at my desk in Berlin in early 2024, I am struggling to concentrate. There is a constant stream of news about artists cancelling their gigs in Germany, about event organisers withdrawing invitations to pro-Palestinian and Israel-critical voices and calling off events. Readings that are dropped in response to protests, intentionally or not. Open letters against an anti-Semitism clause in Berlin's local funding system, which was about to be quickly introduced politically and just as quickly abandoned—or rather postponed—due to legal uncertainties. Debates about the possibility of forced exmatriculation of students for their political opinions. Petitions—who speaks for whom?—which show how thin and yet effective the line is between a self-elected and an imposed 'we'. My body—our bodies—on the streets, while the messages on my social media channels and in the peer-to-peer networks never stop, and the political right has long since left the fringes. My attention is frazzled and the nervousness is deep in my body, all senses on alert.

The daily growing confrontation with discrimination, anti-Semitism and anti-Muslim racism and how to deal with it also affects the arts and us as art-makers to the core, here in Germany and far beyond.[1] It did not begin with the Hamas attack on Israel, not with the massacre of Jewish civilians, not with the subsequent invasion of Gaza by the Israeli army and the horror of the war that has gone from there on—even if the mood has become

[1] Parallel to the unsettling rise of anti-Semitic tendencies and resentments in Germany and Europe anti-Muslim racism has also increased significantly. In the current socio-political climate, a dangerous development can be observed in which one form of discrimination is played off against the other, creating a dynamic in which the exclusion and rejection of the two collectives are mutually constituted and fuelled, sometimes in a strategic way. Even though both forms of racial discrimination are clearly shaped by the European colonial context, this illustrates the danger of equating or relativising the specific facets and trajectories of anti-Semitism and Islamophobia.

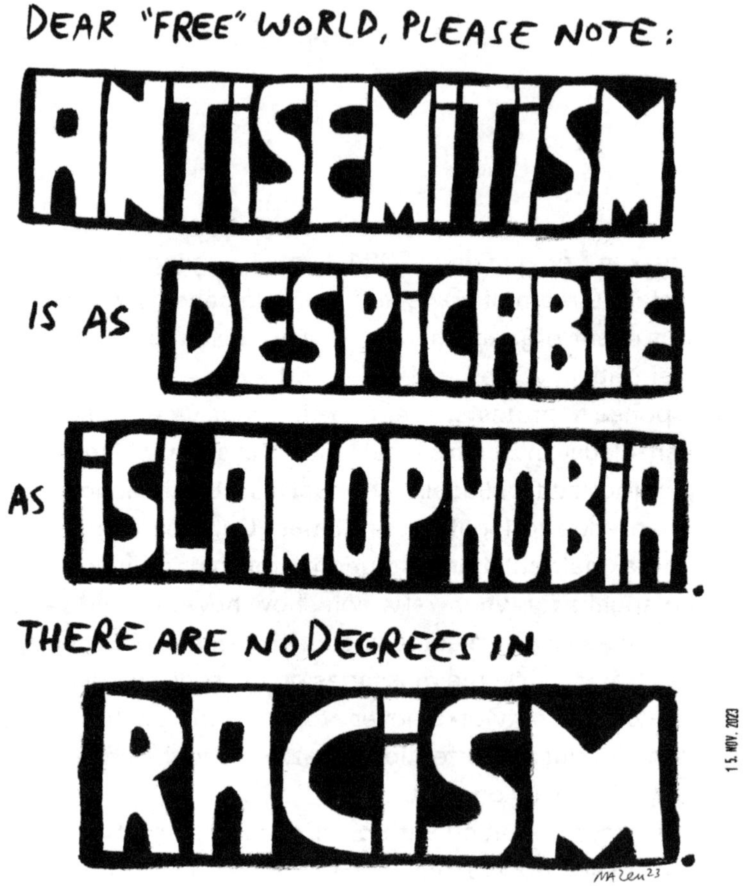

Fig. 1 — Mazen Kerbaj, Antisemitism_Islamophobia, 2023. Courtesy of Mazen Kerbaj.

more aggressive since then and the fronts have hardened. As public attention is increasingly focused on individual incidents, blow by blow, the structural dynamics that have long simmered beneath today's debates about artistic freedom and freedom of expression are being pushed further and further into the background. The drifting apart and increasing fragmentation of our societies; the recognition of our own histories and the possibility of reassessing them in today's changed circumstances; the gap between the protection mechanisms of international law and their applicability—and insufficiency—in everyday life.

Popular discourses, semi-private conversations and what remains unsaid are all about boundaries: a struggle for openness and the presence of the many on the one hand, and an attempt to seal off what are supposedly one's 'own' territories and imaginations on the other. These processes of solidarization and demarcation are also carried out through the body. A body that serves to protect what is one's own—one's own community and integrity, one's own privilege—as well as to protect against the other and the foreign. A body that at the same time transcends all distinctions between self and other and serves as a reminder that living together is first and foremost a relational matter.

2.
Promises.

Bodies are at the centre of my curatorial and theoretical practice. Bodies that encounter each other, in the arts and elsewhere, that are exposed to each other and negotiate meanings and values, the experiential and the utopian. In the face of ever louder calls to stand up and take a stance, I am reminded once again that taking up an attitude begins in the body: in glances and gestures, in postures and positions, in the projections that are directed at our bodies and that we direct at the bodies of others, in the way we move towards or away from each other. It's a corporeal matter.

I started working as a dramaturge and curator in France and Germany in the late 1990s. With freelance artists and collectives whose practice was rooted in activism and closely combined life and work. As an assistant in thematic festivals and programme series, often dealing with specific artistic and geopolitical developments in certain countries or regions; later in publicly funded institutions for dance, performance and discourse. This first professional phase fully reflected the political and artistic striving for the international and the opening up to the transdisciplinary. After the founding of the EU and the fall of the Berlin

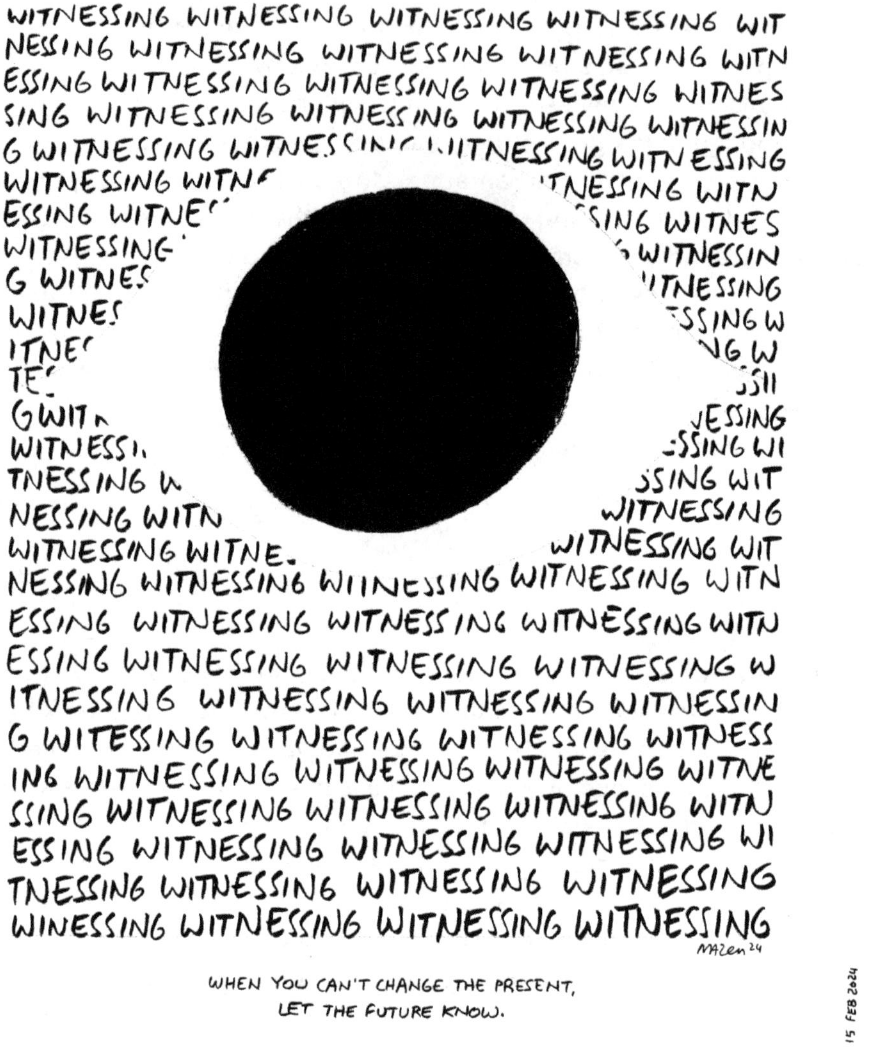

Fig. 2 — Mazen Kerbaj, Witnessing, 2024. Courtesy of Mazen Kerbaj.

Wall, numerous projects, production houses, touring and residency programmes emerged in Europe which, under the heading of cultural diplomacy, were concerned with transnational exchange and a process of integration within and beyond Europe.

A lot has happened since then, and it's not out of nostalgia that I'm revisiting this diagnosis of the times. But the value systems that were established in this environment and which still shape the cultural scene and its international invitation and production policies, are now being fundamentally questioned. How can the desire and promise to open up artistic and discursive processes and spaces to as many diverse bodies as possible and to have an integrative impact on society be realised in a socio-political climate characterised by fragmentation and intensified identity politics? How can we respond to the specific needs and experiences of individual bodies that do not, or no longer, seem compatible with dominant (funding) political, institutional, curatorial or other agendas? How can a practice of embodied critique anchored in the arts contribute to the maintenance and defence of a democratic culture?

3.
Protection.

These questions are closely related to my own curatorial and discursive practice and are embedded in important debates that critically examine the conditions that also characterise our field: discussions around institutional critique, decolonial and post-migrant perspectives, inclusion and educational justice. At its core, it is about the hegemonies that have determined the aesthetics, content and structures of body-based performing arts in Europe, and which today, in the face of increasingly narrow political and economic spaces, reinforce rather than dismantle existing inequalities and privileges.

This is also true of the idea of the international in the arts: the (self-)claim to unfold spaces for exchange, debate and non-violent confrontation, while the conditions of our coming together are increasingly regulated, or the promise to provide protective spaces for the most diverse bodies, while these are increasingly oriented towards the orders and experiences of the dominant groups. This also raises questions for curating, a practice that is fundamentally concerned with the conditions and contingencies of encounters and practical decision-making on which bodies can appear in their own right, with their own protective needs, in the aesthetic and the public realm.

These questions motivate the following observations on how bodies function as sites of identity and ideological conflict in the face of current socio-political and also military developments. Along three interrelated strategies concerning the collectivisation, distinctability and perceptibility of bodies, my aim below is to better understand how aesthetic, discursive and imaginary processes in public and political space contribute to protecting some bodies while forcing others into a calculated state of defencelessness and vulnerability.

4.
Slurrings. Collective Bodies.

Curating always has to do with translation, with strategies, framings and concepts that create a context for what is experienced and imagined; with creating openings and closures; with directing the gaze and experience towards something, or distorting it. Bodies, in the process, are assigned as belonging or excluded—symbolically or quite materially—with different outcomes. I am thinking of gestures, choreographies of movements in public spaces, or even of dances that circulate between art, activism and politics, giving trans-individual visibility to individual people and their concerns and demands across borders.[2] They show how being many can actually become politically effective—a means of self-determination and empowerment that allows marginalized communities in particular an opportunity to make their own struggle visible as a collective struggle on a systemic level, to rehearse community and to embody solidarity and resistance.[3]

But what if you have not chosen to belong to a larger group or a larger project? When national, ethnic, gender or religious frameworks and the associated expectations and clichés simply suffocate you? When becoming recognizable in discourse and politics (as a migrant, as a refugee, as

[2] The dangerous conflation of essentialist conceptions of the body with, for example, national and ethnic identities also runs deep in the history of dance, where body- and movement-based techniques developed there have been used and instrumentalized by various ideological and identity projects. See Jens Giersdorf, *The Body of the People. East German Dance since 1945*, Madison, WI: University of Wisconsin Press, 2013; Bojana Cvejić and Ana Vujanović, *Public Sphere by Performance*, Berlin: b_books, 2012; Gay Morris and Jens Giersdorf (eds.), *Choreographies of 21st Century Wars,* New York: Oxford University Press, 2016.

[3] This is all the more ambivalent as marginalized voices and perspectives are often met with ignorance and belittlement when they present their cause individually, pointing to their 'individual' responsibility for it and ignoring the structural failures of, for example, state or legal protection mechanisms. On the other hand, and against the backdrop of a global context in which bodies are increasingly the collateral damage of political conflicts, (aesthetic) collectivisation runs the risk of turning marginalized bodies into often anonymous entities to be measured and managed.

a victim or as a perpetrator) pushes bodies to become unsolicited stand-ins for the ideas, narratives and fantasies of others, especially those of dominant groups—forcing them to be transparent, to stay in place?

In the more and more heated and categorical debates about discrimination, anti-Semitism, and anti-Muslim racism in the arts, the dangers of unchosen collectivizations are once again evident. One-sided narratives that reduce complex biographies to buzzword formulas; generic images that summarize the diversity with which members of a group experience a situation in contrasting ways; rapidly circulating social media items that sometimes serve the affirmative self-understanding (and perhaps also self-affirmation) of a digital bubble more than participation in a public forum. Bodies are central to these processes: but what does it actually take to be identifiable as a 'German', as a 'Jewish' or as a 'Palestinian' body on stage, in the press or on the street, and to be able to legitimately bear witness and intervene?[4]

In the worst case, the narrowing of identity and body politics, in which individual bodies are assigned to larger collectives on the basis of body-specific markers and ideas, leads to unwelcome alliances in which individual experiences and realities are collectivized and thus simplified and schematized. Instead of fostering and sustaining polyphony, controversy and disruption, identity and supposed group membership are staged as catchy and as something self-contained and homogeneous. Set and fixed, intuitive.

The more drastic the conflict, the more individual bodies become slurred with the body of the collective, especially those bodies that do not belong to the respective dominant groups and that are always in danger of being shown as always different, other bodies. It is precisely these bodies that are systematically deprived of the possibility of being distinguishable, i. e. of being recognizable and detectable as individual bodies.

[4] There is a long and notorious history of strategies in historical and contemporary warfare and politics based on the (aesthetic and discursive) dehumanization of bodies in order to legitimize their exclusion from a particular community or system, for example by contemptuously comparing them to animals, to non-human bodies that carry diseases and don't have human rights.

THEM & US

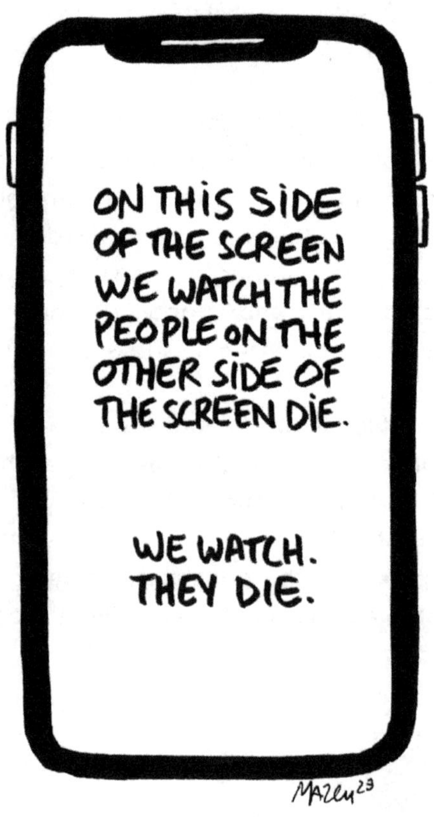

Fig. 3 — Mazen Kerbaj, Them & Us, 2023. Courtesy of Mazen Kerbaj.

5.

Being distinguishable. Body markings.

Being distinguishable is not only an aesthetic criterion, concerned with visibility and, ultimately, with agency and recognition. Being distinguishable is also a factor that relates to the legal status of a body: its ability to be evaluated as a body worthy of protection and to have access to the protective mechanisms and resources provided by law.

The protection of the body is codified, inter alia, in international constitutional and humanitarian law and the various derivations based on it: the integrity of the body—what we can do to our bodies, and the bodies of others—the protection of mental and physical health, protection from corporeal punishment, and so on.[5] However, on the levels of content, scope and application, these rights do not offer a binding definition of what it means for a specific body to be integer, safe or unharmed.

The body to which these rights and the often-abstract promises of protection they apply to is not a collective body. Rather, the body that runs through the texts and the imaginary of the law in its very foundations is first and foremost an individual body. Reflecting a dialectic, western-influenced history of ideas where the individual embodies the human condition per se, it is one that is oriented towards the subject, to a (notably male, white and bourgeois) owner, to the idea of personhood. This legal framework was designed for a body that is bounded and 'whole', i.e. not disabled, upright, functional. Its normative condition is not relational to the needs of different bodies and risks reducing the body to a commodification and object. Instead, in order to be recognized as a legal body, it must be distinguishable, and thus meet criteria that are laid down in international human rights law, which influence which bodies are worthy of protection and which are not, both in legal practice and in what is called common sense.[6]

---

[5] The right to bodily integrity is established in the Universal Declaration of Human Rights and numerous derivations. In many sources, it is stated as a freestanding, enumerated right that frames other rights, or, it exists as a delegated right inherent in some other specific rights (for instance implied in the right to the freedom from torture, cruel, inhuman, degrading treatment; rights related to privacy, health). See *Universal Declaration of Human Rights* (1948); *International Covenant on Civil and Political Rights* (1954); *Conventions on the Rights of Persons with Disabilities* (2007); Adrian Viens, *The Right to Bodily Integrity,* London, New York: Routledge, 2014; Sybille van der Walt and Christoph Menke (eds.), *Die Unversehrtheit des Körpers. Geschichte und Theorie eines elementaren Grundrechts,* Frankfurt/Main: Campus, 2007.

[6] "In other words, there would not be accusations of human screening without the development of a distinction between humane and inhumane forms of warfare, grounded in the idea of protecting lives that are framed as innocent." Cited in Nicola Perugini, "Civilians as Human Screens: Bodies, Media, and the Media of Violence", in this publication, 23.

DAILY ROUTINE

<u>Looking at:</u>

Dead babies. Dead children. Dead adults. Alive children crying for their missing parents. Alive adults crying over the bodies of their dead children. Alive adults and children saying a last goodbye to their loved ones. Bloodied survivors left to scream in overcrowded hospitals. Dust-covered survivors removed from under the rubble of their homes. Survivors in pieces. Pieces of survivors. Shrouded bodies aligned on sidewalks and waiting to be buried. Bodies turned to skeletons in the streets. People getting shot dead in front of cameras. People handcuffed and stripped down to their underwear gathered in a street and guarded by people armed and in uniforms. People blindfolded beaten and humiliated in "funny" videos posted on social media by their barefaced agressors. People fighting over a bag of flour.

<u>Hearing about:</u>

Entire families being wiped from the civil registry. Men executed against walls and in front of their families. Bodies removed from their graves and ran over by bulldozers. Bodies found with missing organs.

<u>Listening to:</u>

The lies of the people slaughtering other people. The lies of the people supporting the slaughterers. The lies of the people justifying the slaughter. The cries of the babies children women and men being slaughtered.

<u>Feeling of:</u>

Helplessnes. Hopelesness. Anger. Sadness. Outrage. Disbelief.

<u>Explaining to:</u>

People what was happening before and what is happening since the 7th of October 2023 or what is Palestine.

<u>Not being able to:</u>

Explain to my children why we cannot bring this madness to an end.

Fig. 4 — Mazen Kerbaj, Daily Routine, 2024. Courtesy of Mazen Kerbaj.

But what do 'military' and 'civilian' bodies, 'humane' and 'inhumane' bodies look like? How do 'regular' and 'unruly' bodies move? How do we identify a 'pure' or an 'impure' body, one that poses a risk or a threat to legal and governmental orders, one that needs to be sealed off from or shielded off?[7] The categories of distinction and the essentialist concept of the body inherent in international human rights law can be used to analyze the frequently articulated criticism of the universality of the Charter. It forms the basis of a system that treats certain bodies in a fundamentally unequal manner while protecting others that are framed as innocent. Bodies that are fragmented or decomposed in a material and symbolic sense—damaged, injured and dead bodies—are seen as a negative variant of a body to be protected.

These systemic inclusions and exclusions are further reinforced when bodies are addressed as collective bodies against the backdrop of strong conflicts in the public and legal, but also in the aesthetic space: The human bodies that appear crowded and strangely nameless and faceless in the reports about illegal travellers on their way to Europe. The photos of corpses laid out in rows, victims of war wrapped in cloths, bearing witness to the atrocities of war. The hooded bodies of the policemen—the hooded bodies of the protesters, which figuratively become blurred during the demonstrations. The question of how and how clearly, and to whose gaze, we mark bodies and how we make them distinguishable is about access to protective mechanisms and resources. It is also about recognizing the humanity of a body itself—also in aesthetic terms.

6.
Roaring silence. Bodies in withdrawal.

The German art and culture sector has become noisy. In the debate about anti-Semitism, racism and discrimination and their impact on the right to freedom of expression, events are coming in thick and fast. The speed with which actions and counter-actions follow one another is increasing, so are the emotions and the affects involved. At the same time, an equally loud silence is spreading. A need to pause, to digest, to adjust, to listen. A fear of the consequences of one's own expression: its compatibility with state and official guidelines, its moral judgement in one's

[7] The COVID-19 pandemic once again revealed how intersecting inequalities condition a body's access and 'right' to protection. The disparate impact that official measures had on different bodies allowed us to observe how some experienced the pandemic as a pause or rest, while others were pushed into even more precarious conditions.

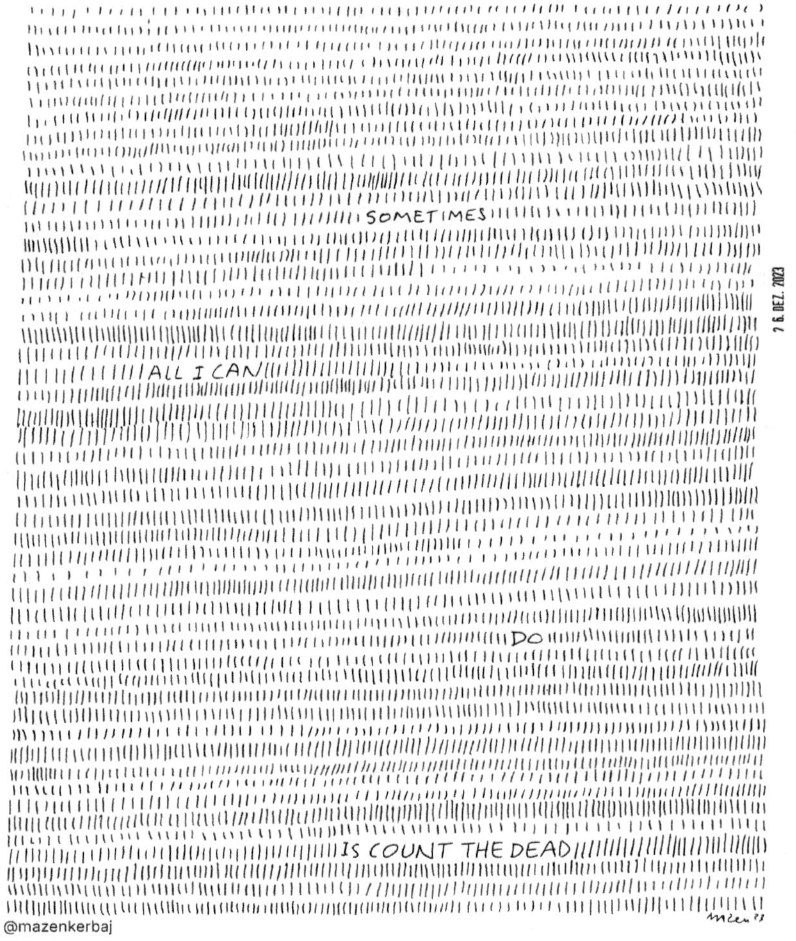

Fig. 5 — Mazen Kerbaj, Count the Dead, 2023. Courtesy of Mazen Kerbaj.

own environment or in the wider context, expected or experienced censorship, exhaustion. The fear of pushing bodies further into a state of defencelessness by speaking out. The fear of preparing properly for what comes once you break the silence. There is rage, anger and helplessness, as well.

But who can handle and control their emotions within given social protocols? Who can afford to stay quiet and remain silent, to refuse to talk, to explain, to defend and to provide evidence, to retreat into the abstract and relying on what is formulated in the in-between, in what is not said and what is kept silent—even and especially in an artistic system in which hegemonic power structures are perpetuated?[8] Where does the political and social responsibility lie with the silent majority when their active or passive restraint pushes precarious and threatened individuals further away from public discourse and action?

Patterns can be identified in the accounts of the artists who find themselves—with or without cause—at the centre of the current conflicts over anti-Semitic tendencies in art and society in Germany and who have to negotiate these on an institutional, personal and economic level. As I have been recollecting them, a repetitive repertoire of strategies and tactics of shielding has begun to emerge.

Broken off encounters and trust, that abruptly end collaborations and friendships.

Institutional wait-and-see tactics, diffuse referral strategies and opaque communication and decision-making channels are put in place until 'one sees more clearly'. Time is an issue here that conditions one's possibilities to avoid reacting immediately to potential accusations and attacks, allowing one to evaluate a situation and the means to be taken.

Hectic, driven statements that navigate complex historical and contemporary territories along broad concepts, leaving little space and attention for learning, questioning and differentiation.

Abstract formulations and an abstract presence of power act as protective shields in an ambivalent way: protecting some from being vulnerable

---

[8] While abstraction functions here as a shield for the powerful and privileged, it is also transformed into a demand that marginalized groups tend to face when it comes to validating their needs and demands at the level of politics and law. Specifically, they are encountering the necessity to abstract their claims from lived experience or affect in order to make them 'more civilized' so as not to discredit their cause.

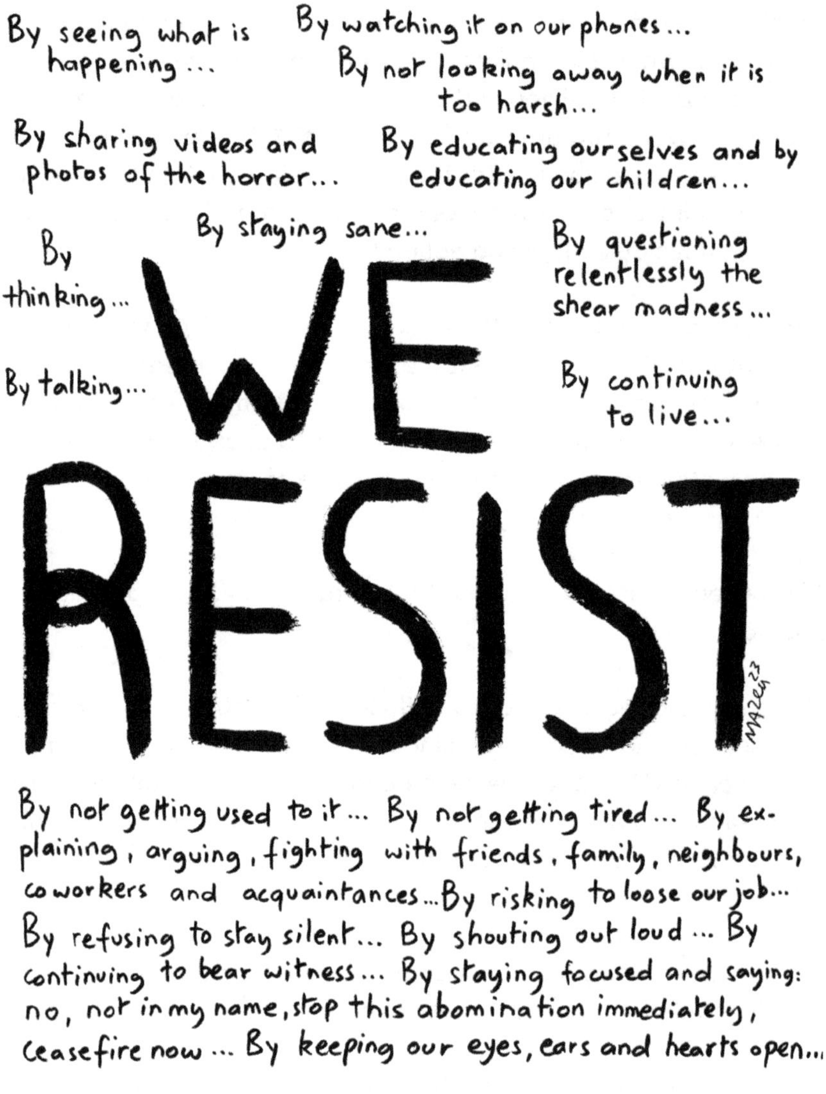

Fig. 6 — Mazen Kerbaj, We Resist, 2023. Courtesy of Mazen Kerbaj.

in an escalating situation, from losing their bearings, from being on the 'wrong' side; as protection for others from being exposed to further generalisations, rumours and accusations.

Content-related or curatorial reference systems are being realigned in the course of the current climate and confronting guests, whose presence has just been courted with doubts about their integrity that need to be refuted.

Navigating in solidarity and often also singularly, the physical, mental and sometimes simply existential pressure that these processes generate, shows how bodies are turned into places of criminalization. Their withdrawal is often barely noticeable. Their stories and their experiences come together to form a resonant body in which the voices of the individuals blur together. Humming, whistling, chattering, lamenting: they become quieter, almost unheard, in anticipation and fear of further attacks and discredit being heaped upon them. And yet there is not just a moment of paralysis and the result of being instrumentalized. Their silence thwarts all the loud words and powerful images, and it is the disquietude of their bodies and potential for disintegration that drives our actions and cannot leave us indifferent.

7.
It's gotten colder. Against aesthetic normalization.

It has gotten colder,
in the days I've been writing these thoughts. In struggling for the openings that arts can and must provide for a critical contribution to social developments, my own work is also open for critical reflection and, ultimately, failure: the moments in which it has not been possible to protect all bodies from symbolic and material damage in an art system that is always about distributing visibility, resources, access opportunities and ultimately also the ability to act, unequally. These moments hit me on a somatic and visceral level and have been inscribed in my bodily texture ever since.

It has gotten colder,
with all the hours, days and weeks in which life in war and conflict zones is defenceless and disposable. It is a dangerous moment when, in the omnipresence of images and news on our phones and screens, we run

the risk of normalizing and naturalizing the ongoing horror and accepting the absence of some bodies in the media, in our everyday lives and also in art. But how can we ever get used to abused, killed, kidnapped, and abducted, raped and starved bodies? How to ever unsee or undo their presence? How do we narrate the experience of slow, creeping violence beyond scripted patterns without reproducing it?

It has gotten colder,
and yet, in all the noise, the excessive demands and the constant reformulation of the conditions that structure our everyday navigation of the public sphere, the tasks of an art that begins in the body have become clearer. Indifference and neutrality are not an option for a body that is always already exposed to others. It is a body that experiences empathy and compassion, but also apathy and ambivalence, which cannot be easily translated into comparisons or solutions, and which must be endured and challenged: rehearsing to be together, even with those who do not belong to our group; accepting our own affiliations in the plural. 'Thinking' about it is ultimately insufficient, because practices of protection and care can only be effective if they go beyond conceptual exercises.

It has gotten colder,
and rarely have I experienced so clearly that violence is always an interruption: an interruption of normality, of friendships and relationships, of convictions and certainties. How to be equal without being equalized?

It has gotten colder,
in this time of escalation: a movement that leaves behind the normal, the familiar and the promised. Incommensurable, unexpected, sudden. A movement of rebellion and repulsion against leaving things as they are. Escalation is a movement that breaks out of the silence and gives space to what we as individuals and as a collective have for too long pushed away and kept in the unconscious. It is also a movement of toning things down; one that signals an after, dialogue and healing. That's what I'm holding on to, holding on to a transformation that makes the un-protection of bodies a collective concern.

All the drawings that accompany this text are by the artist Mazen Kerbaj. They have been with me through the writing process in a supportive and sometimes critical and challenging dialogue, and I am grateful to Mazen for making his work available for this context.

Bojana Cvejić

The Transindividual Act of Self-Burning

In this text, I will examine public acts of self-annihilation that protest against the unsustainability of life under the conditions of contemporary neoliberal capitalism by making the body the locus of violent and spectacular destruction. Following Mohamed Bouazizi's self-incineration in 2010, which served as an iconic catalyst for the popular uprising in Tunisia, the recent wave of self-burnings has spread beyond the so-called geocultural belt of self-immolations in South East Asia into the Middle East and Europe, notably France, where every fifteen days in the period 2011–13, somebody set themselves on fire.[1] While only a few instances of these burnings have been explicitly articulated as political protests against neoliberal reforms leading to dire precarization, the majority of cases appear unobtrusive, at best registered in the local (more often than national) press as suicides concluding a "personal drama"[2]. Although most of the self-burners whose acts I will examine here leave no note framing from the outset the reasons for a protest in political terms, their motives can be inferred from the public site chosen for its staging; the scene of a dramatic appeal to a government, a private company or an employer deemed responsible for their breakdown. These motives include unemployment, debt, removal of social benefits, rejection of an application for social housing, restructuring of jobs that results in excessive workloads, lay-offs or forced resignations, and administrative refusal to review one's eligibility for social welfare, to name but a few of the recurrent grievances behind the self-burnings that

[1] I am using 'self-incineration' and 'self-burning' as technical terms for a body self-destructing by fire. While they are similarly descriptive, I am relying on a rhetorical nuance in my usage: to burn oneself is more poignant—it echoes the performative threat in the words: "If you don't see me, I will burn myself"—than to 'self-incinerate', which connotes a more clinical meaning. 'Self-immolation' has become a political term for self-sacrifice, as expounded later in this text, and it includes more broadly other forms of self-mutilation that symbolize self-sacrifice.
[2] French president François Hollande, cited in Jean-Baptiste Chastand, "En s'immolant, Djamel 'a voulu faire passer un cri'", in *Le Monde* (1 June 2013), www.lemonde.fr/politique/article/2013/06/01/en-s-immolant-djamel-a-voulu-faire-passer-un-cri_3422188_823448.html, accessed 6 March 2024.

have occurred in France, the Netherlands, Luxembourg, Greece, Turkey, Algeria, Tunisia, Morocco and Mauritania since 2010. In a word, they cause a breakdown of the infrastructure of one's own life, understood here as "the living mediation of what organises life"[3]. Here, I take "breakdown of infrastructure" to mark the low point in the range of effects resulting from "governmental precarisation", which, after Isabell Lorey, denotes a complex dynamic of "interactions between an instrument of neoliberal governing and the conditions of economic exploitation"[4].

Underlining precarization as a *process* that entails a differential distribution of economic insecurity, I am concerned here with the temporal dimension of normalizing neoliberal measures that unequally affect its subjects. Precarization as an instrument of neoliberal governing implies a division between those who experience "ambivalence between subjugation and self-empowerment"[5] in navigating neoliberal restructuring of work and social welfare, and those numerous others who are in this process pauperized and dispossessed to the extent that they no longer deem their life "worthy of being lived"[6]. While it might be difficult to compare levels of precarization that precipitated these self-burners into their act, their shared state of "affliction", wherein life and death become "'interchangeable"[7], directly correlates with neoliberal reforms of work and welfare. Thus, the self-burnings I will attend to highlight the aspect of governmental precarization that causes a variety of breakdowns in which individuals become the collateral damage of an infrastructural transformation or failure and subsequent ruin. In Lauren Berlant's expansion of this term, infrastructure comprises more than roads, schools, medical insurance or families; it encompasses all "the systems that link ongoing proximity to being in a world-sustaining relation"[8]. And because infrastructural failures don't affect everyone to the same degree and at the same time, precarization is diversified and too differentially (unequally) distributed for it to act as a unifying political demand of protest for the cases I will examine.

[3] Lauren Berlant, "The commons: Infrastructures for troubling times", in *Environment and Planning D: Society and Space* 34(3) (2016), 393.
[4] Isabell Lorey, *State of Insecurity: Government of the Precarious*, London and New York, New York: Verso, 2015, 12.
[5] Lorey, *State of Insecurity*, 12.
[6] Eve Katsouraki, "A Life Not Worth Living: On the Economy of Vulnerability and Powerlessness in Political Suicide", in *Performing Antagonism*, ed. by Tony Fisher and Eve Katsouraki, Basingstoke: Palgrave Macmillan, 2017, 152.
[7] Katsouarki, 152.
[8] Berlant, "The Commons", 393.

The aim of my enquiry is to show how these scattered, isolated and seemingly individualistic acts converge in a novel category of self-burning motivated by economic insecurity, a category that I contend ought to be redeemed politically as a transindividual form of political protest. With the concept of the 'transindividual', I am drawing on Gilbert Simondon's relational ontology, which has guided Bernard Stiegler and Paolo Virno in their leftist critiques of individualism and modes of subjectivation under neoliberal capitalism.[9] Simondon reserved the neologism 'transindividual' for a more complicated relation than that of the unity between individual and society. The 'transindividual' is that which is transmitted from the interior to the collective, recreated and reassumed across time by successive individuals.[10] In a broader perspective, transindividuality refers to the capacity of 'we': what we have in common, and what we can be and can do together in social and political senses, on the condition that this relational 'we' is differentiated and reconstituted every time, in each case of transindividuation, rather than being a given identity. By unifying a relation that is interior to the individual (or the psyche) and a relation exterior to the individual (or the collective), transindividuality defines the bi-dimensional process in which the individual and the collective reciprocally co-evolve. The transindividual becomes that place, event, situation, act or collective operation in which the potentials that individuals bring in their mutual relations are put to work. For example, social forms of production and reproduction are the historical component of the potentials that are exploited or commodified in the capitalist subsumption of work or enriched and renewed in egalitarian cooperation or organized political protest, as in the solidarity movement in southern Europe and collective practices of care.[11]

In order to consider these self-burnings transindividually, I will show how the act exceeds individualist premises by redressing in the public sphere the right to a sustainable life. First, this requires that the motives of self-burning be de-individualized, demonstrating that distress and alienation are socially and politically induced by governmental precarization. Second, I will examine the power that such a self-destructive act has to 'collectivize' ('transindividuate') through confronting lives that

[9] See Bernard Stiegler, *Technics and Time I: The Fault of Epimetheus*, Stanford, CA: Stanford University Press, 1998; Paolo Virno and Jun Fujita Hirose, "Reading Gilbert Simondon", in *Radical Philosophy* 136 (2006).

[10] See Gilbert Simondon, *Individuation à la lumière des notions de forme et d'information*, Grenoble: Éditions Jérôme Million, 2005, 216 (author's translation).

[11] See Bojana Cvejić, "Solidarity as a Common Notion: The transindividual 'we' of social movements in Southern Europe since 2011", in *Performance Research* 27(5) (2023).

are not as gravely afflicted by precarization with lives that are unliveable. Moreover, this argument entails considering how one might be interpellated to respond to the violence of self-incineration with respect to the shared condition of having a body. How are we to attend to irreparable acts of self-annihilation, which stand in dire contrast to contemporary practices of vitalist self-preservation through intensive life- and self-enhancement?

These two divergent images of embodiment symbolize two facets of the biopolitical regime of power at work today, one in which the administration of life focuses on the well-being of the population and the other in which some lives are hindered or abandoned to the powers of death. This rift within the spectrum of biopower, where levels of precarization get finer with respect to the two extremes of care and disposability, is key to the revision of Foucauldian biopolitics found in Achille Mbembe's thesis on necropower, which determines whose lives matter and whose are disposable.[12] Mbembe's account of "deathworlds" is illuminating here, as it posits "[n]ew and unique forms of social existence in which vast populations are subjected to living conditions that confer upon them the status of the *living dead*"[13]. I take the acts of self-burning arising from governmental precarization to testify to necropower in Mbembe's sense as the negative underside of a contemporary regime of biopolitics. Furthermore, I will argue that they carry a transindividual potential of political protest that counters the biopolitical precept of survival at all costs.

There are several difficulties inherent to the staging of these acts that make for their political illegibility and for other obstacles to reading them as transindividual performances of protest. In the first instance, self-burnings are recognized as acts of political self-sacrifice on the condition that they protest political oppression, and are, moreover, part of an organized political struggle or movement. Thus, the political motives are inferred from self-incinerations that combat imperialist domination and foreign occupation or are orchestrated in a movement for national independence. These acts owe their status of political 'self-immolation' to inscription in the lineage that harks back to 1963 when the Buddhist monk Thích Quảng Đức performed ritual self-incineration at a Saigon intersection—an act of self-sacrifice that influenced the course

[12] See Achille Mbembe. *Necropolitics*, Durham, NC: Duke University Press, 2019, 80.
[13] Mbembe, *Necropolitics*, 92.

of the Vietnam War (1955–75). Đức's act set a historical precedent for self-burning to enter the repertoire of self-destructive practices of political resistance worldwide. Thereafter, 'self-immolation' has been used to denote sacrificial self-burning, the sense given in the word's etymology: *immolare* in Latin designates "to sprinkle [a victim] with sacrificial meal [*mola salsa*, a mixture of flour and salt], before sanctifying it by fire"[14].

While sacrifice evokes the religious background of the act, religion and individual psychopathology have often been used as "rationalising narratives"[15] to obfuscate its political significance. The latter have consistently played a prominent role in the attempts of news media or the officials interpellated by the self-burner to marginalize or explain away the political message of a public fiery protest. It also accounts for the relative paucity of the media coverage of these acts. With the exception of the literature dated after 2010, which includes Bouazizi's as the only examined case of self-burning against precarization, including Katsouraki's investigation of a "radical praxis of political protest" of suicides in Greece against the neoliberal economic capture of life,[16] most of the instances I have investigated haven't received adequate attention in print. Our knowledge of this category of self-incinerations in Europe and the Middle East is confined to scanty media reports, which present these public acts in an anecdotal fashion as personal suicides without acknowledging their social and political or, more specifically, transindividual dimension. My interest here is to interrogate the discursive silence to which the recent self-burnings in Europe and the Middle East have been subjected, and more specifically to enquire into the perplexing problems posed by these acts. How can individual life be weaponized as a transindividual form of protest if self-destruction also brings the suffering of a person to an end through an extreme public act of suffering?

[14] Anne Viola Siebert, "Immolatio", in *Brill's New Pauly*, ed. by Hubert Cancik and Helmuth Schneider (Antiquity volumes), Christine F. Salazar (English Edition), Manfred Landfester (Classical Traditional Volumes), http://dx.doi.org/10.1163/1574-9347_bnp_e523640, accessed 6 March 2024.
[15] Banu Bargu, *Starve and Immolate: The Politics of Human Weapons*, New York, NY: Columbia University Press, 2014, 22.
[16] See Karin Fierke, *Political Self-Sacrifice: Agency, Body and Emotion in International Relations*, Cambridge: Cambridge University Press, 2013; Grzegorz Ziółkowski, *A Cruel Theatre of Self-Immolations: Contemporary Suicide Protests by Fire and Their Resonances in Culture*, London: Routledge, 2020; Eve Katsouraki, "A life not worth living".

"If you don't see me, I will burn myself"

This section presents three distinctive cases of self-burning that have advanced or revealed governmental precarization as their main cause. Its title quotes Bouazizi, poignantly summarizing the calculus involved in the choice of self-destruction. Although Bouazizi's story is well known, I will rehearse it here one more time.

Bouazizi was a fruit and vegetable vendor in Sidi Bouzid (Tunisia), who had been harassed for years by the police for allegedly not having the required permit or, more likely, for not having the means to bribe the police officers. One day, the police confiscated his produce and the scales he had indebted himself in order to purchase. Outraged at losing his entire economic livelihood, Bouazizi tried to appeal to the city administrator, who declined to see him despite Bouazizi's threat ("If you don't see me, I will burn myself"). Bouazizi returned to the administration building within an hour to set himself on fire. Before he doused himself in gasoline, he was heard screaming his last words, "How do you expect me to make a living?!" Although he left no explicit statement of political intention, a large community of young Tunisians recognized themselves in his despair and chose his act as a symbol of their protest.

Bouazizi's is an act of self-burning that doesn't address itself politically to a public, yet it qualifies as a liminal act that earns the status of political protest by the effect it had in retrospect. The rhetorical question he thrust at the municipality provides a terse statement about the pain of dispossession motivating his self-incineration. A comparable, albeit more politically articulated message, stems from the case of Anas K. On 8 November 2019, a 22-year-old student and activist of the leftist student union set himself ablaze in front of the building that houses the regional student aid centre (*Centre régional des œuvres universitaires et scolaires* (CROUS)) in the French city of Lyon. The letter Anas K. left behind explicitly accused the French government and other political figures for social problems ranging from student living costs and precarious life to social inequalities and fascism in French politics. The acuteness of his words is worth citing in full:

> Today, I will do the irreparable. My target is the CROUS, a political
> site, and beyond it, the Minister of Higher Education and Research
> and the government. This year, undertaking a third L2[17], I didn't have

[17] Equivalent to year two in a three-year BA degree.

a stipend and even if I did, is 450 Euro per month enough to live on? I've been lucky to have amazing people around me, my family and my union, but should we continue to survive like we do today? And after all these studies, how long will we have to work and contribute to have a decent retirement? Will it be possible with mass unemployment? So I'd like to repeat one of my union's demands—a student wage and more generally an unconditional lifelong salary, so we don't have to waste our lives trying to earn a living. Let's move to a 32-hour working week to put an end to these uncertainties regarding unemployment, which lead hundreds of people like me each year into my situation—who die in the most complete silence. Let's fight the rise of fascism, which only divides us and of neo-liberalism, which creates inequalities. I accuse Macron, Hollande, Sarkozy and the EU of having killed me, by creating uncertainties about the future of all and I also accuse Le Pen and the pundits for having created fears that are more than secondary. My last wish is that my comrades continue to struggle, to definitively put an end to all of this. Long live socialism, long live self-management, long live social security. And sorry for the ordeal that this is. Au revoir.[18]

Anas K.'s letter indicates that his personal situation (loss of student aid) is simply a pretext for protesting against neoliberal reforms that have eclipsed social security and for advancing demands for more socially just labour conditions that would render life more sustainable for all. Despite its express political message and affiliation with the socialist struggle, his act did not achieve a large resonance with the public. Students in several cities in France rallied to counter the attempt of the government to obfuscate the political intention of the self-burning as the politicians underlined personal distress as the main motive. The French students insisted: Anas K.'s act was political!

Between Bouazizi's and Anas K.'s acts, more than fifty cases of self-destruction out of precarity have been recorded in France. For most of them however, the political import of the situation they protested has gone unrecognized. Out of seven cases featured in the internet documentary film *Le Grand Incendie*, the self-burning of Rémy Louvradoux serves as a blueprint for the acts of self-destruction caused by diminished livelihood due to neoliberal reforms to work and welfare since 2011. A technician at Orange-France Télécom since 1979, Louvradoux addressed

[18] Anas K., "Letter", trans. Austin Gross, Facebook post (14 November 2019), [page no longer available].

the management of the merger enterprise with objections to their plan for a restructure of the company (NExT), which would result in laying off 22,000 workers. Delegated by his colleagues, Louvradoux formulated their concerns in part around the notion of being treated as "surplus" ("*de trop*") in an open letter to the managers, which was followed by numerous unanswered emails over the two years leading up to 26 April 2011, when he set himself ablaze in front of his workplace, the France Telecom office in Mérignac. While the management denied knowledge of any communication, and the lawsuit against seven directors of the company charged for moral harassment and complicity in the death of Louvradoux was unsuccessful, Louvradoux's family was approached by dozens of France Telecom workers expressing their solidarity and the need to unite in order to demonstrate together their shared precarious working conditions.[19]

Two years later, the self-burning of Djamal Chaar, whose objection to the French government unemployment agency miscalculating his employment hours, which effected his unemployment benefits was twice refused, triggered a wider political echo. In a letter entitled, *The right to live, with or without employment*, several prominent public figures, philosophers, sociologists and militants including Jacques Rancière and Saïd Bouamama, asked:

> How many men and women, unemployed or working, will have to die refusing to live with indignity before the denial of their human, social, and democratic rights is finally heard?[20]

Their words pin down the political meaning of the many unreported acts whose actors remained anonymous. To gauge the performativity of these self-burnings, I will now look at the performative structure of the act.

The self-burner re-addresses their unanswered plea to the public or, in other words, they coerce the public into bearing witness to injustice, for which they blame an authority symbolically identified by its official seat: a public building or a site that serves as the context-specific stage for the act. The conditions for acquiring the status of a political performance are

[19] See Lucas Burel, "France Télécom: 'Mon père s'est immolé par le feu et les responsables ne risquent presque rien'", in *Nouvel Observateur* (5 May 2019), www.nouvelobs.com/justice/20190505.OBS12514/france-telecom-mon-pere-s-est-immole-par-le-feu-et-les-responsables-ne-risquent-presque-rien.html, accessed 6 March 2024.
[20] Raoul Marc Jennar, "Le droit de vivre, avec ou sans emploi", in *Pressenza – International Press Agency* (17 March 2013), www.pressenza.com/fr/2013/03/le-droit-de-vivre-avec-ou-sans-emploi, accessed 6 March 2024.

only partly fulfilled: the act is public and communicates with the antagonist and the broader public in the symbolic place of a state institution or private company. The interpellated antagonists (employers, public servants, co-workers, HR services) disavow their responsibility for the grievance and the accusation that the self-burner has made public. Instead, most acts are psycho-pathologized and isolated as cases of individual vulnerability, deviancy, anomaly, and in that way reduced to a glitch on the flat surface of a media report. Their disparagement rests on judging that two elements in the act misfired. First, the accusation is neutralized when the accused proves they followed the procedure correctly. Second, the actor (self-burner) is denied authority because their motives are deliberately labelled as personal distress. In a statement reported in the national news, the French president at the time, François Hollande, expressed his "strong feelings over this sign of personal distress and [of becoming] a serious situation"[21]. But as the spouse of the self-burner argued in the same article, "If it were a personal drama, as François Hollande has said, he [Djamal Chaar] would not have done it in a public space."[22] The question arises of whether the public place partly grants the act the political authority denied to its actor and the accusation. The site of the act doesn't only make it public but adds the illocutionary weight of a political accusation, with the act staged in the place that symbolizes the blamed instance. Hence, the numerous suicides caused by the same situation of dispossession and humiliation that are enacted in the private sphere—at home, for instance—risk their political significance passing unrecorded.

The spectacle of the burning body cannot escape the notice of the public eye, as the political significance of the place and the brutality of the act compel immediate and remote witnesses to ask why, what for, or even in whose name the act was committed. A person setting their body on fire wants to "leave an indelible imprint on the minds of others"[23]. The contrast between being the immediate audience of self-burning and a second-hand viewer implies a difference in degree of intensity, but not a different kind of impact. The reports and images of self-immolations that have circulated in the media act as a support for the imagination of the ordeal. What is there to witness in either the first or second degree is the rigorous determination of a subject who is unafraid to die a horrific death. The act is irreparable, as Anas K. put it in his letter and what makes

[21] Chastand, "En s'immolant, Djamel 'a voulu faire passer un cri'".
[22] Chastand, "En s'immolant, Djamel 'a voulu faire passer un cri'".
[23] Djamel Belayachi, "Arab world's revolutionary immolations and 'martyrdom' change", in *afrik news* (15 March 2011), www.afrik-news.com/article19117.html, accessed 6 March 2024.

it even more cruel, is that the self-burner addresses their plea to a public without having the possibility to receive a response. Watching or imagining self-incineration, one registers the embodiment of pain made graphic. Facing the destruction of the body as an act of self-annihilation from the perspective of an affluent society instilled with corporeal techniques of well-being is daunting and incomprehensible. It inevitably prompts the question: for there to be such a violent destruction of one's body, how much violence has this body absorbed? If such an equation holds, the self-burner condemns the violence of their situation—their life becoming unliveable—by turning that violence against themself rather than directing it at those that they publicly blame for their suffering.

Self-Burning on Behalf of Others:
'Good' Versus 'Bad' Death

When self-burning fails to politically mobilize the community of those who share the condition with the actor, the act falls under the category of a 'bad death', understood as surrendering to the disappointments of life. The phrase was coined in British anthropology in the 1980s,[24] and the notion is that individual suicide qualifies as a 'good death' when it presents a ritual in which a community is reborn: "The rebirth which occurs at death is not only a denial of individual extinction but also a reassertion of society and a renewal of life and its creative power."[25] A 'good death' entails a transfer of the vitality of life: "supreme altruistic gift of the martyr by whose death life is renewed."[26] This moral distinction reveals the conventional criteria of instrumental action that operate in the judgements made about protests by fire in liberal thought. According to prevalent liberal debates on the politics of self-incinerations, if a person doesn't burn themself 'on behalf' of others by explicitly furthering a political cause for a community, their act is not deemed political.

Judging the political character of self-burning by the criteria of instrumentality misconstrues the existential nature of corporeal performances of protest. As Banu Bargu has argued from a leftist perspective, self-destructive practices of resistance paradoxically combine instrumentality and its abolishment. Inasmuch as the self-destruction of the body

[24] See Maurice Bloch and Jonathan Parry, *Death and the Regeneration of Life*, Cambridge: Cambridge University Press, 1982, 16.
[25] Bloch and Parry: *Death and the Regeneration of Life*, 5.
[26] Fierke, *Political Self Sacrifice*, 49.

serves to publicly address a grave political concern—as is the case with self-burnings out of precarization, including, in the case of Anas K., when this self-destruction advances specific political demands—the body cannot be reduced to a mere medium of protest. "Its deployment only by way of its destruction defies the distinction between means and ends and obliterates instrumental rationality."[27]

The argument of instrumentality, which pits a 'good' death that communalizes others against a 'bad' death without a communal echo, is the product of the dichotomous conceptual framework in which self-burnings have been considered. "Martyrs" are those who self-immolate in defence of "a notion of truth" that they cannot surrender, "whereas suicide is selfish", representing "a failure of nerve, endurance, or patience and often an inability to go on despite grief, pain, dissatisfaction or deprivation"[28]. This line of argumentation has persuaded many leftist political commentaries to refrain from referring to these acts as suicides, since the term rhetorically relegates responsibility to the actor who performs the act of self-killing[29] and over-individualizes the act at the cost of its political meaning. The argument of reclaiming life's value by death in protest over life's devaluation raises the question of necropolitics: is self-burning out of precarization an instance of succumbing to necropower in Mbembe's sense, as the "subjugation of life to the power of death"[30], or is it, to use Bargu's term, a form of "necroresistance", political protest 'by death'?

The Necropolitics of Precarization

Necropolitics is bound up with governmental precarization as a regime of power that shapes life together with its attrition, whereby "slow death", in Berlant's compelling phrase,[31] characterizes the physical, but also mental attenuation of life force. Letting die in the context of administrating life can be too passive and slow a process for its full, dire meaning to be registered. Slow death might become indistinguishable from the routine stress of the underprivileged and disadvantaged. But then occasionally, this passive process of precarization amalgamates slow death in an act of self-destruction that fires the public imagination.

[27] Bargu, *Starve and Immolate*, 16.
[28] Fierke, *Political Self Sacrifice*, 5.
[29] See Bargu, *Starve and Immolate*, 18; see also Ziółkowski, *A Cruel Theatre*, 20–23.
[30] Mbembe, *Necropolitics*, 76.
[31] See Berlant, *Cruel Optimism*, 95–98.

Self-burners appear to be subjects who have lost the structure of support that sustains their life. And having exhausted other means of struggle for basic sources of livelihood, they choose to end their life in an intense form of embodied protest. Their act suggests that we expand the category of the 'living dead' to include, apart from slavery, work and death camps, also those who are left behind, dispossessed, whose lives are disposable and 'ungrievable' because they are devalued.[32] The act of self-burning marks a dramatic point in the struggle of a worker who has used up all formal channels of address. Their last resort is to make their plea public by drawing public attention to their suffering and sense of injustice. Writing for the Institute for Palestine Studies about the wave of self-burnings in the Middle East and Europe after 2010, Rashid Khalidi remarks that these are "ordinary people making eminently reasonable demands for freedom, dignity, social justice, accountability, the rule of law and democracy"[33]. When injustice is experienced as humiliation, the person's dignity is violated. The dead letter of international law (United Nations Universal Declaration of Human Rights 1948, Article 1) would mean, in practice, that dignity relates not only to a right to life but to a right to quality of life.

When the motives of self-burning are relegated to the personal, the values associated with the right to quality of life in the rationale of the act are discounted. The actor is regarded as an individual who personally suffers injustice, someone who is over-sensitive, inflexible or not robust and resilient enough to adapt to 'changes' caused by infrastructural failures. Rather than a martyr, who is applauded for audacity and generosity, the actor is regarded as a victim—someone who can no longer master their life but then becomes sovereign in refusing life under these conditions.[34] Any argument for individual sovereignty reflects the liberal habit of thought that consists in aligning agency with a strong notion of intentionality. This is characteristic of both the mainstream approaches that seek to politically ennoble the 'victim' by attributing them sovereignty in the last instance and leftist-militant views. Within the latter approach, "necroresistance" is a prominent concept coined by Bargu in praise of a negative form of biopolitical struggle, a "counterconduct to the administration of life"[35], "based not on the affirmation of life but on its wilful destruc-

[32] See Judith Butler, *Notes Toward a Performative Theory of Assembly*, Cambridge, MA: Harvard University Press, 2015.
[33] Rashid Khalidi, cited in Fierke, *Political Self-Sacrifice*, 222.
[34] See Fierke, *Political Self-Sacrifice*, 101–102; see also Nicholas Michelsen, *Politics and Suicide: The philosophy of political self-destruction*, London: Routledge, 2016, 142.
[35] Bargu, *Starve and Immolate*, 85.

tion"[36]. The claim that these self-incinerations transform the body from a "site of subjection" to a "site of insurgency"[37] applies to politically articulated self-burnings, as is, exceptionally, the case of Anas K.[38] By contrast, the self-burnings I am engaging with here are liminal and their political import (qua forms of political protest) hinges on an interpretative intervention that elucidates the transindividual dimension of the act. Thus, in what follows I suggest that the focus ought to shift from the agency of the self-burner to the affective power of the act to transindividuate.

Transindividuality in Self-Destruction

What enables us to regard self-burnings out of precarity as 'transindividual' acts of dissent? If we follow the argument about suicide as a 'bad death' then death by self-burning at first appears to counter-actualize the potential for renewing a collective because it subtracts the individual's power in a collective to co-evolve in relation to others. In Simondon's terms, self-destruction amounts to 'subjective disaster' of psychic individuation alone, which he described as "anxiety":

> In anxiety, the subject becomes their own object, the problems surge back on them alone, without being resolved in the collective. There is no world, because the subject becomes the world, filling out the times and spaces in which problems emerge.[39]

Reading Simondon with early Marx, the purported individualism of the act is a result of alienation from oneself: the individual is degraded and desubjectified as their power for social transformation is weakened to the extent that they do not see any other way out than death. But how do they enact death? "The transindividual is defined by everything that surpasses the individual while it prolongs them."[40] The conflict between the

---

[36] Bargu, *Starve and Immolate*, 27.

[37] Bargu, *Starve and Immolate*, 885.

[38] Around the two clusters of the 2011 wave of self-burnings and Anas K's political act in 2019, two more cases of political protest by fire have been registered. Piotr Szczęsny self-immolated in Warsaw, in front of the Palace of Culture, with a letter stating 19 demands of protest against the Law and Justice government in 2017. As a local leader in Varna of the Bulgarian nationwide protest against the corruption in government in 2013, Goran Plamenov self-immolated. His act was followed, arguably, by three more cases, and became a rallying point of the social justice protest that eventually led to the resignations of Varna's mayor, Plamenov's 'antagonist' and the cabinet of the Bulgarian Prime Minister Boyko Borisov.

[39] Gilbert Simondon, *Individuation à la lumière des notions de forme et d'information*, Grenoble: Éditions Jérôme Million, 2005, 250 (author's translation).

[40] Simondon, *Individuation à la lumière des notions de forme et d'information*, 274 (author's translation).

actor's witnessing the truth of injustice and the affective excess carried by this witnessing is amplified through the rage and self-consumption of the act of self-incineration. As emotions and actions, these are transindividual expressions that surpass the individual when they become public. Performing them in public doesn't restore sovereignty to the individual (as the liberal argument contends); on the contrary, the act opens up an opportunity for the public to understand the social interdependency that underlies all lives. It does so by posing a problem for the public witness in questions as to why, how, when and in relation to who and what has the individual decided to self-incinerate.

The sheer theatrics of self-burning in which an individual offers themself up, and the performances of the self in which the right to body, health, happiness and intense life is exercised, stand side by side. This juxtaposition forces a reflection upon the reasons for this irreparable act in relation to others, even if the act isn't explicitly framed as being committed on behalf of others. If the self-burner acts as a witness to social injustice, the public (even remote) bystander of the act becomes the second-degree witness to the act of self- annihilation. Bearing responsibility for things seen first and second-degree, the bystander asks: How am I implicated in this act of self-destruction? To affirm the transindividual expression of the act, one puts oneself in relation to it. This shouldn't be misconceived as feeling guilty for not having prevented a suicide. Rather, it compels one to engage in untangling one's own stake in the situation where some lives are enhanced and others are diminished. Such an operation is illustrated by the Adornian question that Butler elaborates in her *Notes Toward a Performative Theory of Assembly*:

> Implicit in the question of how to live a good life in a bad life is the idea that we might still think about what a good life might be, that we can no longer think of it exclusively in terms of the good life of the individual. If there are two such 'lives'—my life and the good life, understood as a social form of life— then the life of the one is implicated in the life of the other.[41]

'Good' life here rests on dignity guaranteed by the social rights whose denial, together with lack of political will of the government (or another antagonist) to redeem them, has led self-burners to eventually commit suicide by fire—a 'bad' death, according to the liberal argument. My point

[41] Butler, *Notes Toward a Performative Theory of Assembly*, 214.

lies elsewhere, in examining the power of the act to implicate its witnesses. The implication of one's life in the life of the other who chooses death over an unsustainable life brings forth the transindividual perspective precipitated by the ordeal of self-burning. "If you don't see me, I will burn myself"—these words encapsulate the call of the public to be more than an audience of the ordeal. In Simondon's account of the transindividual, this means: "To discover the signification of the message originating from one or several beings, is to form a collective with them, it is to individuate the individuation of the group with them."[42]

The ordeal calls for a transindividual encounter in which the individual becomes aware of what in themself is more-than-individual, that is, held in common, and, in this case, it is the question of good life and of dignity as the right to quality of life beyond survival. If the onus is on us, who attend to this act, to interpret the message by implicating ourselves, then our response might be to further the call for a transindividual politics dedicated to transforming suffering from a struggle to sustain one's life into a struggle to live within a just world.

[42] Simondon, *Individuation*, 298 (author's translation).

References

Banu Bargu, *Starve and Immolate: The Politics of Human Weapons*, New York, NY: Columbia University Press, 2014.

Djamel Belayachi, "Arab world's revolutionary immolations and 'martyrdom' change", in *afrik news* (15 March 2011), www.afrik-news.com/article19117.html

Lauren Berlant, *Cruel Optimism*, Durham, NC: Duke University Press, 2011.

——— "The commons: Infrastructures for troubling times", in *Environment and Planning D: Society and Space* 34(3) (2016), 393–419.

Maurice Bloch and Jonathan Parry, *Death and the Regeneration of Life*, Cambridge: Cambridge University Press, 1982.

Lucas Burel, "France Télécom: 'Mon père s'est immolé par le feu et les responsables ne risquent presque rien'", in *Nouvel Observateur* (5 May 2019), www.nouvelobs.com/justice/20190505.OBS12514/france-telecom-mon-pere-s-est-immole-par-le-feu-et-les-responsables-ne-risquent-presque-rien.html

Judith Butler, *Notes Toward a Performative Theory of Assembly*, Cambridge, MA: Harvard University Press, 2015.

Jean-Baptiste Chastand, "En s'immolant, Djamel 'a voulu faire passer un cri'", in *Le Monde* (1 June 2013), www.lemonde.fr/politique/article/2013/06/01/en-s-immolant-djamel-a-voulu-faire-passer-un-cri_3422188_823448.html

Bojana Cvejić, "Solidarity as a Common Notion: The transindividual 'we' of social movements in Southern Europe since 2011", in *Performance Research* 27(5) (2023), 16–25.

Karin Fierke, *Political Self-Sacrifice: Agency, Body and Emotion in International Relations*, Cambridge: Cambridge University Press, 2013.

Anas K., "Letter", trans. Austin Gross, Facebook post (14 November 2019).

Raoul Marc Jennar, "Le droit de vivre, avec ou sans emploi", in *Pressenza – International Press Agency* (17 March 2013), www.pressenza.com/fr/2013/03/le-droit-de-vivre-avec-ou-sans-emploi

Eve Katsouraki, "A Life Not Worth Living: On the Economy of Vulnerability and Powerlessness in Political Suicide", in *Performing Antagonism*, ed. by Tony Fisher and Eve Katsouraki, Basingstoke: Palgrave Macmillan, 2017, 149–70.

Isabell Lorey, *State of Insecurity: Government of the Precarious*, London and New York, NY: Verso, 2015.

Achille Mbembe, *Necropolitics*, Durham, NC: Duke University Press, 2019.

Nicholas Michelsen, *Politics and Suicide: The philosophy of political self-destruction*, London: Routledge, 2016.

Anne Viola Siebert, "Immolatio", in *Brill's New Pauly*, ed. by Hubert Cancik and Helmuth Schneider (Antiquity volumes), Christine F. Salazar (English Edition), Manfred Landfester (Classical Traditional Volumes), http://dx.doi.org/10.1163/1574-9347_bnp_e523640

Gilbert Simondon, *Individuation à la lumière des notions de forme et d'information*, Grenoble: Éditions Jérôme Million, 2005.

Bernard Stiegler, *Technics and Time I: The Fault of Epimetheus*, Stanford, CA: Stanford University Press, 1998.

Paolo Virno and Jun Fujita Hirose, "Reading Gilbert Simondon", in *Radical Philosophy* 136 (2006), 34–43.

Ana Vujanović and Bojana Cvejić, *Toward a Transindividual Self*, Oslo, Brussels, Zagreb: Oslo Academy of the Arts, SARMA and Multimedijalni Institut, 2022.

Grzegorz Ziółkowski, *A Cruel Theatre of Self-Immolations: Contemporary Suicide Protests by Fire and Their Resonances in Culture*, London: Routledge, 2020.

Tenzing Sonam

I Will Burn Myself Again and Again.

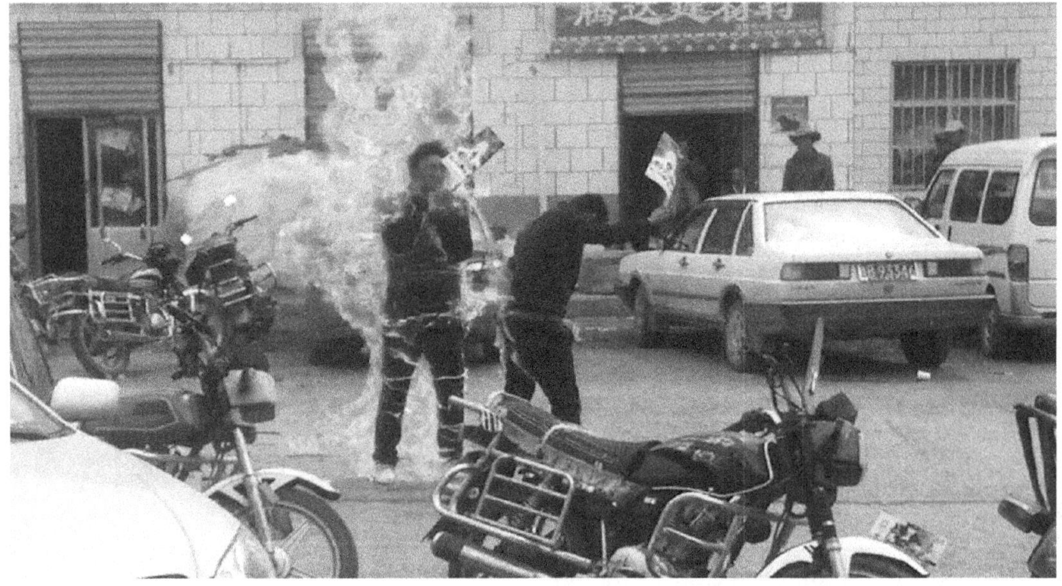

Fig. 1 — Ngawang Norphel, 24, and Tenzin Khedup, 22, self-immolated on 20 June 2012, in the town of Zatoe, Qinghai Province.

Notes on the Self-Immolations in Tibet

On 27 February 2009, a young monk named Tapey stepped onto a street in the town of Ngaba in Eastern Tibet and set himself on fire. Video footage of the event, subsequently smuggled out of the country, shows a burgundy-robed monk, arms spread wide, walking in a swaying motion, flames licking his upper body. He is holding a photo of the Dalai Lama in one hand and the Tibetan national flag in the other, both banned symbols of resistance. Policemen run after him and smother him in a cloud of fire extinguisher spray. He runs in a cloud of smoke and the video stops abruptly. Eyewitness accounts state that Tapey was then shot several times by the policemen before being taken away. His fate remained unknown for years but it later transpired that he had survived.

Tapey's was not the first self-immolation attempt by a Tibetan–Thupten Ngodup, a Tibetan exile, had set himself on fire at a political protest in New Delhi on 27 April 1998 and succumbed to his injuries–but his was the first inside Tibet and marked a landmark moment in Tibet's six-decade struggle for freedom from Chinese rule. Two years after Tapey's action, on 16 March 2011, another monk, 20-year-old Lobsang Phuntsok, set himself alight in public and died on the spot. His death ignited a chain of self-immolations that raged like wildfire across the Tibetan plateau.

To date, an estimated 157 Tibetans have burnt themselves inside Tibet, of which 136 have died. A further eight Tibetans have self-immolated in exile. Led initially by monks and nuns, they were soon joined by ordinary people—farmers, nomads, teachers, students—and were united by a common demand: the return of the Dalai Lama to his homeland, and freedom for Tibet, that they either shouted out as they were burning, or wrote or recorded in their last testaments.

This unprecedented form of protest was initially captured on citizen videos and smuggled to members of the exiled Tibetan community who then made them public on social media. The videos graphically brought home the full horror of a living human body being consumed by flames: the blurred outline of a figure engulfed in flames, the slow-motion collapse followed by the agonising contortion of twitching limbs that can only hint at the unimaginable pain being endured, and then the charred remains in grisly rigor mortis, all pretence of humanity stripped bare. Why would anyone do this? And was any cause worth the sacrifice of a life being offered in this most excruciatingly painful of ways?

To understand why Tibetans were pushed into resorting to such a self-brutalising form of protest, we have to return to the root causes of the Tibet issue. In 1913, the 13th Dalai Lama declared Tibet to be an independent country. Whatever the historical interpretation of Tibet's status prior to this proclamation—and Tibetan and Chinese historians are sharply divided on the issue—the fact remains that from this moment on, until its invasion and occupation in 1950, Tibet fulfilled most definitions of a modern nation state. It had a fully functioning government, a civil service, judicial and taxation systems, and its own army, postal service and currency. It even issued its own passport, which was recognized by major Western countries. Additionally, it had its own language, a long cultural and literary tradition, a unique way of life that had evolved in harmony with its high-altitude environment, and importantly, a civilization built around Tibetan Buddhism that had spread far beyond its borders.

China's violation of this sovereignty and its subsequent colonisation of the country set into motion a concatenation of events that led directly to the wave of self-immolations. Since its takeover, China has consistently and systematically marginalised Tibetans and reduced them to second-class citizens in their own country. Waves of Han migrants from the mainland have transformed Tibetan cities and towns into replicas of Chinese urban centres and altered their demographic makeup.

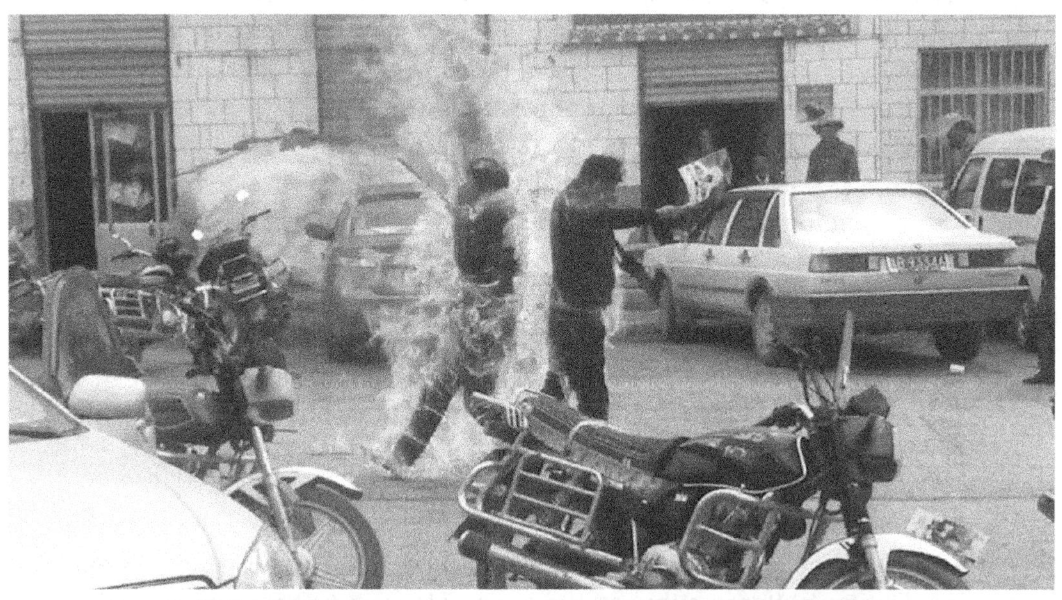
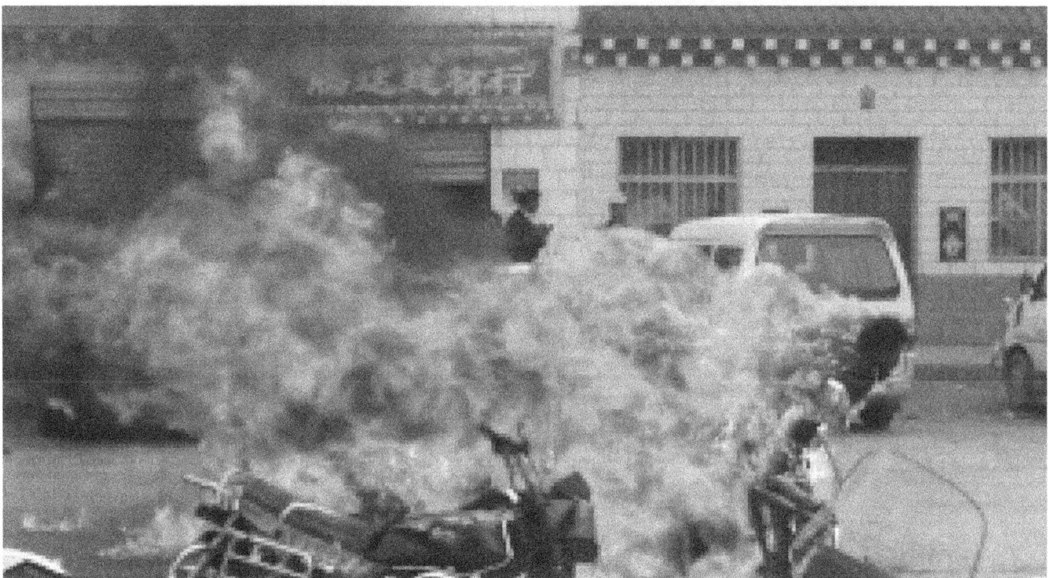

Figs. 2 and 3 — Ngawang Norphel, 24, and Tenzin Khedup, 22, self-immolated on 20 June 2012, in the town of Zatoe, Qinghai Province.

The practice of Tibetan Buddhism, the lifeblood of Tibet's culture, was singled out as a threat to Chinese rule and subjected to strict controls and regulations. Stringent rules discourage Tibetans from joining monasteries and nunneries, which are kept under tight surveillance. Monks and nuns are regularly subjected to patriotic education campaigns, which include the denunciation of the Dalai Lama, who most Tibetans consider to be their spiritual and temporal leader, and the embodiment of the Buddha of Compassion. This is one of the most humiliating and deeply hurtful acts that Tibetans are subject to. The mere possession of the Dalai Lama's photographs in Tibet is an imprisonable offence. More recently, China passed a law that authorises the Chinese government to approve the confirmation of all reincarnations of senior Buddhist lamas, including the Dalai Lama. This means that when the current Dalai Lama passes away, China will select its own Dalai Lama to replace him, a move that is guaranteed to further alienate the Tibetan people who will never accept a Chinese-approved Dalai Lama.

The study of Tibetan language has been deliberately discouraged with schools teaching in Tibetan gradually phased out. An estimated one million Tibetan children between the ages of four and 18 are now forced to attend boarding schools where the primary language of instruction is Mandarin. Tibet's substantial nomadic population, the custodians of its high grasslands for millennia, has been forced to give up herding and resettle in concrete housing blocks; the justification for this, ironically, is to protect the environment. Meanwhile, Tibet's resources are being rampantly exploited and shipped back to the mainland.

At the same time, Tibet has become a repressive police state with a huge security apparatus that includes state-of-the art electronic surveillance technology and an insidious network of informers and spies. Tibetans are subject to oppressive policies that are not enforced in other parts of China, including the requirement of special documents to travel within Tibet, a restriction that does not apply to Chinese citizens.

The pent-up discontent of the Tibetan people exploded briefly in March 2008, when large-scale demonstrations broke out in Lhasa and spread across the Tibetan plateau. This was the largest uprising against Chinese rule since 1959 and it came as a surprise to the Chinese authorities who were not prepared for the scale of resentment against their rule. Once the uprising was quelled, Tibet was made out of bounds to the international media, and only limited groups of tightly controlled foreign tourists were permitted to visit, a state of affairs that remains to this day. In the shadow of the media blackout, thousands of Tibetans were arrested, including poets, writers and musicians, for their part in the protests. New laws were put into place, further restricting even the limited rights and freedoms that had previously been granted, and contributing to the sense that the very soul of Tibet's identity was being irrevocably erased. It was in this climate of draconian repression, retaliation and heightened fear, that the wave of self-immolations began.

The spate of self-immolations and their explicit visual representation shocked exiled Tibetans like me into reappraising the political situation in Tibet. Numbed by a lifetime of estrangement from our homeland, they dramatically alerted us to the sheer magnitude of the problems our fellow countrymen were facing. Was the act of self-immolation an act of desperation born out of despair and hopelessness? Or was it an act of bravery and heroism, a refusal to surrender to one's fate, an inspirational call to action to fellow Tibetans not to give up the struggle? On this matter, the Tibetan poet and dissident writer Woeser, a trenchant critic of the Chinese regime who lives in Beijing, is very clear:

> In my interviews with international media on the topic of self-immolation, I have always tried to emphasize one area of frequent misunderstanding: self-immolation is not suicide, and it is not a gesture of despair. Rather, self-immolation is sacrifice for a greater cause, and an attempt to press for change [...]. Such an act is not to be judged by the precepts of Buddhism: it can only be judged by its political results. Each and every one of these roaring flames on the Tibetan plateau has been ignited by ethnic oppression. Each is a torch casting light on a land trapped in darkness. These flames are a continuation of the protests of 2008 and a continuation of the monks' decision that March: 'We must stand up!'[1]

As hinted at in Woeser's statement, the self-immolations sparked soul-searching and impassioned debate even within the Tibetan community about their legitimacy and ethical correctness as a non-violent weapon of protest. Was the act of burning oneself to death, even if undertaken in the interests of a larger cause, acceptable in the context of the Buddha's teachings? Was it not a form of violence against oneself and therefore counter to the fundamental tenets of Buddhism?

[1] Tsering Woeser, *Tibet on Fire: Self-Immolations Against Chinese Rule*, London: Verso Books, 2016, 26.

This was not a new dilemma. When the Vietnamese monk Thích Quảng Đức set himself alight on a Saigon-street on 11 June 1963—the first documented political self-immolation in modern times—the photograph of the incident quickly became an iconic and enduring image of struggle and resistance. But the graphic representation of a serene Buddhist monk sitting cross-legged in a blaze of fire also raised many ethical questions. Martin Luther King Jr. was one who expressed his disquietude. In response, the Vietnamese monk and Buddhist teacher, Thích Nhất Hạnh, wrote him a much-publicised letter. He explained:

> The Vietnamese monk, by burning himself, say with all his strengh [sic] and determination that he can endure the greatest of sufferings to protect his people. But why does he have to burn himself to death? The difference between burning oneself and burning oneself to death is only a difference in degree, not in nature. A man who burns himself too much must die. The importance is not to take one's life, but to burn. What he really aims at is the expression of his will and determination, not death. In the Buddhist belief, life is not confined to a period of 60 or 80 or 100 years: life is eternal. Life is not confined to this body: life is universal. To express will by burning oneself, therefore, is not to commit an act of destruction but to perform an act of construction, i.e., to suffer and to die for the sake of one's people.[2]

In this context, it makes sense that the first self-immolators in Tibet were all monks. One of the most basic Buddhist concepts they practice on a daily basis is the cultivation of compassion and altruism. This notion of self-sacrifice for the benefit of others is ingrained in Buddhist teachings, and monks and nuns, more than most people, are intimately acquainted with the concept. For at least some of the self-immolators, their decision to burn themselves would have been informed by this knowledge. There is another aspect to the Tibetan self-immolations that ties it in with the idea of self-sacrifice in the interests of a larger cause, and that is in the nature of the action itself. Lighting a lamp and burning incense are among the most common forms of making a religious offering in Tibet. This unity of fire and light as a symbolic offering of prayer and hope cannot be overlooked as yet another motivation for the self-immolators. Indeed, both the aspect of sacrifice for a larger cause and the symbolic nature of fire and

---

[2] Thích Nhất Hạnh, "In search of the Enemy of Man (addressed to (the Rev.) Martin Luther King)", in *Dialogue,* ed. by Thích Nhất Hạnh, Hồ Hữu Tường, Tam Ích, Bùi Giáng, Phạm Công Thiện, Saigon: La Boi Press, 1965, 11.

light as an offering become clear when we examine the last messages that some of the self-immolators left behind.

Lama Soepa, a high-ranking Buddhist monk, who self-immolated on 8 January 2012, recorded an audio message in which he said:

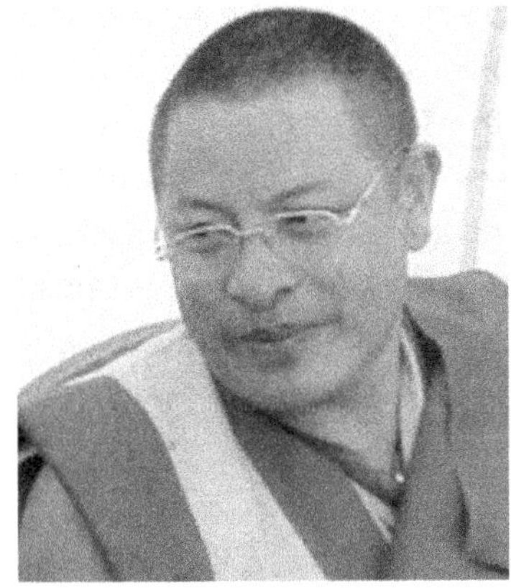

Fig. 4 — Lama Soepa, 40s, self-immolated on 8 January 2012, in the town of Darlag, Qinghai Province.

This is the twenty-first century, and this is the year in which so many Tibetan heroes have died. I am sacrificing my body both to stand in solidarity with them in flesh and blood, and to seek repentance through this highest tantric honour of offering one's body. This is not to seek personal fame or glory. I am giving away my body as an offering of light to chase away the darkness, to free all beings from suffering, and to lead them—each of whom has been our mother in the past and yet by ignorance has been led to commit immoral acts—to the Amitabha, the Buddha of infinite light.[3]

Similarly, Tsultrim Gyatso, who burnt himself on 19 December 2013, wrote in his final testament:

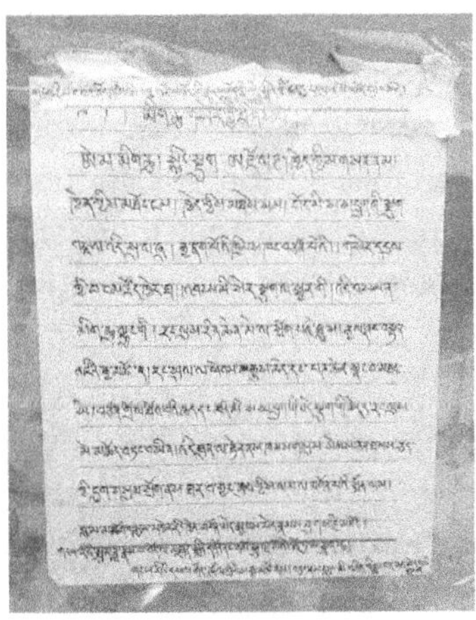

I set myself on fire for the return of His Holiness the Dalai Lama to Tibet, to free Panchen Rinpoche from prison, and for the welfare of six million Tibetans. May all sentient beings residing in the three realms be free from the three poisons and attain Buddhahood.[4]

Fig. 5 — The last testament of Tsultrim Gyatso, 43, self-immolated on 19 December 2013, in the town of Achok, Gansu Province.

[3] From an audio recording made by Lama Soepa shortly before he self-immolated, smuggled out of Tibet to the exile Tibetan government in India.
[4] From a photograph of Tsultrim Gyatso's written testament, smuggled out of Tibet to the exile Tibetan government in India.

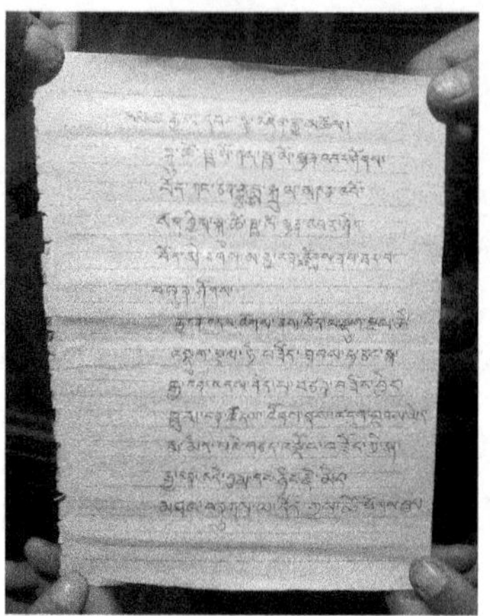

Fig. 6 – The last testament of Nangdrol, 18, self-immolated on 19 February 2012, in Dzamthang County, Sichuan Province.

18-year-old Nangdrol, who set himself alight on 19 February 2012, wrote:

Raise your head high with courage and loyalty. I, Nangdrol, call with gratitude upon my parents, siblings and relatives. The time has come for me to leave for the sake of the Tibetan people, by setting my life on fire. My requests to the Tibetans are: Be united, be Tibetan, dress Tibetan and speak Tibetan. Never forget that you are a Tibetan. Be compassionate. Respect your parents. Most of all, be united. Treat animals with compassion, do not slaughter them.[5]

Most of the letters left behind by the self-immolators stress this conviction that their action is for the larger benefit of their people and country. As Thích Nhất Hạnh emphasises, the act of self-immolation is not an act of destruction, but one of construction, in that it sends out a message of defiance and solidarity in the face of overwhelming despair.

At a time when all avenues to protest were shut down and despondency could easily lead to loss of hope, or worse, to a resigned acceptance of the situation as *fait accompli*, the self-immolators were taking the radical final step of burning themselves publicly to continue sending a message of defiance and inspiration. The message that the self-immolators sought to transmit was directed primarily at their fellow Tibetans. In their final testaments, they constantly remind Tibetans not to forget their language and traditions, and exhort them to remain united and not fight among themselves.

Since its peak in 2012, when there were 80 self-immolations, the number has steadily declined. After initially downplaying the self-immolators as mentally disturbed individuals, Chinese authorities then shifted the blame to the Dalai Lama-led exile Tibetan community and accused them of inciting unsuspecting Tibetans to commit violent acts of self-destruction. When the scale and the spread of the self-immolations became too

---

[5] From a photograph of Nangdrol's written testament, smuggled out of Tibet to the exile Tibetan government in India.

huge to explain away with these easy accusations, the state shifted its tactics. First, the flow of information about the self-immolations—particularly the graphic images and videos—was stopped by imposing harsh penalties on those caught transmitting the material, and by exercising more rigid controls on mobile phone and internet usage. Second, security personnel were armed with fire extinguishers while patrolling city streets in order to prevent death in the event of a self-immolation. Later, self-immolators sought to subvert this by drinking gasoline to ensure that they would burn from within. When the authorities could not control the extent of self-immolations, they resorted to punishing those closest to the self-immolators—their immediate family and community—by imposing harsh penalties, including imprisonment and torture, on charges of aiding and abetting. This proved effective. Those wishing to burn themselves in a political act of defiance no longer had control even over their own bodies. Killing oneself was to subject your loved ones to the consequences of the action.

The last recorded self-immolation in Tibet that the outside world is aware of took place on the 27 March 2022. As of this writing, Tibet is more tightly controlled than at any other time since its occupation. A series of policies aimed at rewriting and reimagining Tibetan culture and history to fully absorb them into the dominant Han Chinese narrative is accelerating the disappearance of Tibet's unique identity. How will Tibetans respond? One can only hope that they will continue to find new ways of fighting back, of continually reinventing their struggle, because the alternative— the extinction of an entire people and a culture—is all too real.

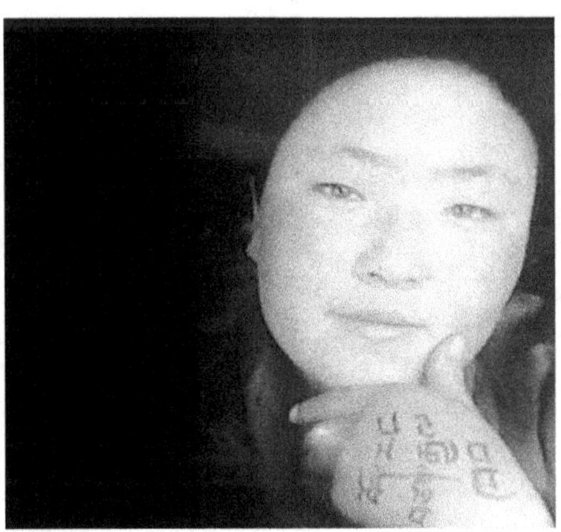

Fig. 7 — Sangye Dolma, a 17-year-old nun, self-immolated on 25 November 2012, in Barkhor Village, Gansu Province. She also left behind a note and a memory card in an envelope. In the note she wrote in Tibetan: "There is a photo of mine in the memory card. Here is the will for the photo. Sons and daughters of Tibet, the darlings of Snow lion, the brave sons of Tibet, remember you are Tibetan. My name is Sangye Dolma. Sixteen years old by the Solar calendar, seventeen years old by the Tibetan Calendar." In the photo, the words "Tibet, an independent country" are written on her hand.

I will end with a poem by the exile Tibetan poet Sungchuk Kyi, who wrote
it as a response during the height of self-immolations in Tibet.

I WILL BURN MYSELF AGAIN AND AGAIN

[...] I wish to burn, thus, without regret.
This magnificent light, like a butter lamp, is ignited by my mind.
This whole body, like an offering bowl, desires to be sacrificed without remorse.
Brothers and sisters, old and young, who will live forever in my heart,
Gods and Goddess illuminated by the conviction of my love and faith,
And the splendour of the immovable mountains and enduring rivers in my heart,
As I leave, all of you rise higher within my consciousness.
As I leave, all of you live longer through my aspirations.

From now on, aim the bullets of a hundred thousand guns only at me.
Inflict the most painful beatings and tortures only on me.
Direct all your persecution and tyranny only on me.
I offer you my precious life in return.
I assume full responsibility for this commitment.

From today, please treasure the traditions and heritage of my lineage.
Take care of the purity of my land and environment.
Respect the life force of my mother tongue.
Give freedom to all my beloved brothers and sisters.
This is my last testament, written in blood.
These are the reasons and aspirations why I burn myself again and again.
These must be fulfilled!

All the power of the gods dwelling amidst love and faith,
All the feelings of human beings living in the world,
Show your solidarity with my past.
Be witness to my present, before my eyes.
Show concern tomorrow for the welfare of my family.

I am walking thus on the path of light, to become the living proof of truth.
I am burning myself thus on the sad face of my reality.
All my brothers and sisters, young and old, living in misery and sorrow,
All people throughout the world who love freedom and peace,
And to you, tyrants of violence, oppression and torture,
What I want is a life of equality and fairness.
What I am searching for is an existence of equality and caring.
Until I accomplish this,
I will burn myself again and again.[6]

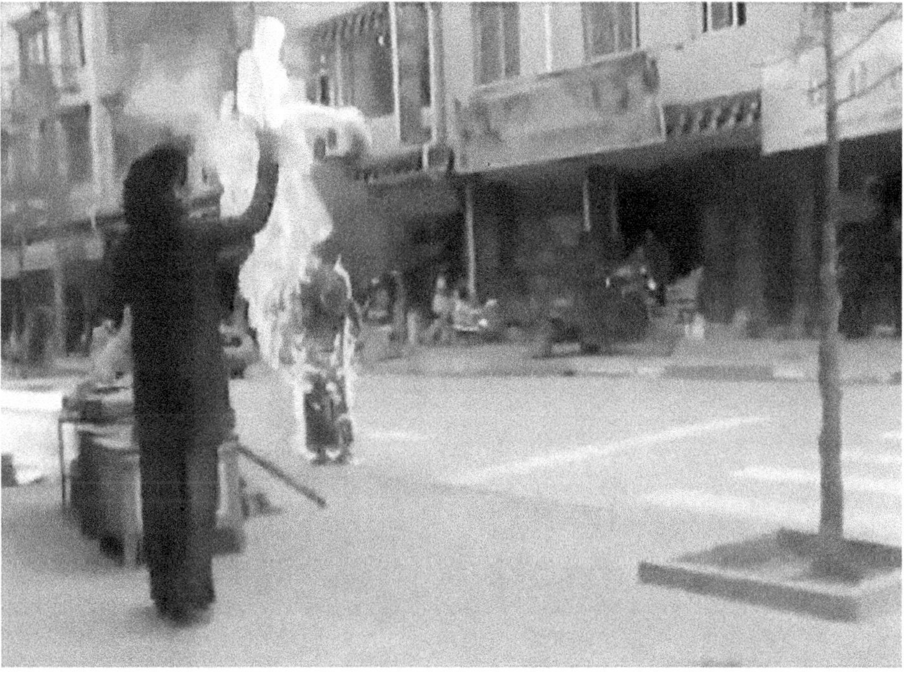

Fig. 8 — Ani Palden Choetso, 35, self-immolated on 3 November 2011, in Tawu County, Sichuan Province.

[6] Sungchuk Kyi, *I will burn myself again and again*, excerpt based on a translation by Om Gangthik (selected and altered from the Tibetan original by the author), April 2011, https://www.india-seminar.com/2013/644/644_sungchuk_kyi.htm, accessed 29 February 2024.

References

Thích Nhất Hạnh, "In search of the Enemy of Man (addressed to (the Rev.) Martin Luther King)", in *Dialogue,* ed. by Thích Nhất Hạnh, Hồ Hữu Tường, *Tam Ích*, Bùi Giáng, *Phạm Công Thiện*, Saigon: La Boi Press, 1965, 11–20.

Sungchuk Kyi, *I will burn myself again and again*, April 2011, https://www.india-seminar.com/2013/644/644_sungchuk_kyi.htm

Tsering Woeser, *Tibet on Fire: Self-Immolations Against Chinese Rule*, London: Verso Books, 2016.

Tenzing **Sonam**

Isabell Lorey

Immunized Bodies and Logistification Just-in-Time. Transformations Through the Pandemic

Amidst the Covid pandemic I was asked several times to say something about it based on my book *Figuren des Immunen*.[1] I had developed the figures of the immune more than ten years ago and for a long time I could not do much with them for the current situation. That has changed a bit, and I would like to use this paper to make a first proposal for interpretation. Central to the figures of the immune is that they are not primarily an analysis of a plague. The virus itself does not play the central role. Therefore, in the following, I will work with the figures of the immune, not so much in the context of a pandemic, but in order to work out the domination-securing dynamics through epidemic control, as well as the transformation in which we find ourselves, especially in economic and psycho-social terms.[2]

My notion of immunization is not reduced to the limited medical use that emerges in the 19th century, that is, to make immune against the causes of the disease by inoculation. When I speak of immunity and immunization, I refer to the political usage that goes back to Roman antiquity.

There are three figures, in which the politics of immunization can be condensed: Two figures of the immune that secure domination, which I have called 'juridical immunity' and 'biopolitical immunization', as well as the subversive, resistant figure of the immune: 'constituent immunization'. I will initially refer to the first two figures that secure domination; 'juridical immunity' works with the domination-securing dynamic of *Her-Ausnahme;*

[1] Isabell Lorey, *Figuren des Immunen. Elemente einer politischen Theorie*, Zürich and Berlin: diaphanes, 2011. For a summary of the main aspects, see Isabell Lorey, "Politics of Immunization and the Precarious Life", in *Dance, Politics, and Co-Immunity. Current Perspectives on Politics and Communities in the Arts*, ed. by Gerald Siegmund and Stefan Hölscher, Zürich and Berlin: diaphanes, 2013; Isabell Lorey, "Constituent Immunization Instead of Self-Immunizing Communities", in *New Alphabet: Community* (2021), https://newalphabetschool.hkw.de/constituent-immunisation-instead-of-self-immunizing-communities/, accessed 14 February 2024.
[2] See also Isabell Lorey, "Corona Effects: After Prevention, Just In Time: Digitalization and Contact Phobias", in *transversal texts. multilingual webjournal*: "Around the Crown" (2020), https://transversal.at/transversal/0420/en/en, accessed 14 February 2024.

of 'taking out as exception'. It is oriented to state and sovereignty, to limits of access, and above all, *Her-Ausnahme*, this 'taking out as exception', means immunity by privilege. The dynamic of the second figure, 'biopolitical immunization' is governmental in the Foucauldian sense: it describes the state regulation of a population through statistics and risk management, as well as by controlling the behaviour and thus the self-government of each individual. This figure depends on the circulation of commodities and people, and it uses precarization. The central dynamic of this figure is *Hereinnahme,* taking-into, incorporating.

In the current fight against the pandemic, the two figures intertwine: 'juridical immunity', which focuses on the state and privilege; and 'biopolitical immunization', which is based on governmentality, circulation, and precarization. Both politics of immunization, the juridical and the biopolitical, rely on constructions of community. Also, in the genealogy of Roman antiquity, the Latin *immunitas* is not antithetical but always complementary to *communitas*, community.

Juridical Immunity

In the fight against a plague, it is a central task of the state to regulate contagion. We already know the current means from the 19th century: Even then it was a matter of hygiene, division of space, segregation by quarantine, self-isolation, distance, risk assessment and probability calculation. Even then, infections and deaths were taken into account. The bourgeoisie constituted itself as a class of privilege, not least through epidemic control.[3]

Today, the contours of a reformation of the bourgeoisie become visible along the lines of self-discipline, re-patriarchalization, re-familialization and the cementing of relations of inequality to secure what is one's own, one's properties.[4] It is again about the privilege of being able to take oneself out: to build immunity against contacts and contagions through immobility and retreat into the home, and through secured incomes. It is about shielding the community of ownness; one's properties (family and friends), reducing contact, drawing boundaries, and controlling access. It looks as if the vaccine refusers and the so called *Querdenker* are largely

[3] See Michel Foucault, *Security, Territory, Population: Lectures at the Collège de France, 1977–78*, ed. by Michel Senellart, Basingstoke: Palgrave Macmillan, 2014.
[4] See Mike Laufenberg and Susanne Schultz, "The Pandemic State of Care: Care Familialism and Care Nationalism in the COVID-19-Crisis. The Case of Germany", in *Historical Social Research* 46, no. 4 (2021).

the complementary side of this bourgeois reformation—above all in proclaiming an individualistic, egocentric, and extremely neoliberal idea of freedom, which combines with an authoritarian populism that goes to the extreme right.[5]

The retreat into the home has gone hand in hand with a gigantic push for digitalization. In a few years, how we work, live, shop and move around has changed rapidly. Companies save a lot of money through the home office: less office space, flexible workplaces; having one's own desk becomes a luxury and a reward; co-working spaces increase, commuting and business trips decrease. In addition to those who can largely cease mobility, there are those who must remain mobile and provide mobility and circulation. They work in system-relevant, critical infrastructure, logistics, care, and nursing professions, they cannot work from home and often earn significantly less than those in the somewhere office.

On the other hand, with the home office nine-to-five over, work and leisure time can be separated even less than before.[6] Stress increases, especially for women who continue to be responsible for children and reproduction even in the home office;[7] violence in the home increases rapidly, and for many it is not a safe place. Patriarchal gender relations are reforming.

Parts of the middle class, which withdraw into the home and shield themselves, want to go to the countryside and find the amount of people in cities more and more unbearable: as well as the rising rents, they are too dangerous; everywhere there is proximity with strangers. Contact phobias are growing. Digitalization supports contact avoidance in everyday life.

In the midst of the pandemic, a broad conservative reformation of the middle class took place. Everyone was crying out for privileges and freedom. Hardly anyone spoke about the further worsening inequalities. It was

[5] See in more detail Isabell Lorey, "Corona Effects"; Sergio Bologna, „Wir dürfen der extremen Rechten nicht die Idee der Freiheit überlassen!", in *Sozial.Geschichte Online* 31 (2022), https://sozialgeschichte-online.org/2022/01/19/wir-durfen-der-extremen-rechten-nicht-die-idee-der-freiheit-uberlassen/, accessed 14 February 2024; Carolin Amlinger and Oliver Nachtwey, *Gekränkte Freiheit. Aspekte des liberalen Autoritarismus*, Berlin: Suhrkamp, 2022.

[6] On this transformation of labour under neoliberalism, see, for example, Paolo Virno, *A Grammar of the Multitude: For an Analysis of Contemporary Forms of Life*, Los Angeles: Semiotexte, 2004; Isabell Lorey, "Gefangen im Jetzt: Prekäres in der politischen Gegenwart", in *Agora 42: Das philosophische Wirtschaftsmagazin*, no. 4 (2020).

[7] During the COVID pandemic, mothers look after children more often than fathers, even if their professional workloads are equal, as the National Education Panel Study (NEPS) at the Leibniz Institute for Educational Trajectories notes in a study: "Kinderbetreuung in Corona-Zeiten: Auch bei gleicher beruflicher Belastung betreuen Mütter häufiger allein als Väter" (13 October 2020), https://www.neps-data.de/Neuigkeiten/Archiv/udt_1582_param_detail/20458, accessed 14 February 2024.

the beginning of a new *Biedermeier* period. The retreat into the working private sphere, to which only family and selected friends have access, is predestined to reinforce old gender models as well as traditional ideas of family and belonging. Community and nation, along with demarcation, play a major role again. Many people are settling into their own confined inner worlds. The desire for control in the midst of unpredictability is growing. The focus on the home and the nation not only plays right into the hands of growing authoritarian populism and its alliances but also supports a further tightening of the asylum and migration policy of the liberal left.

Understanding for everything that moves outside one's own bubble is dwindling. The longing to shut out the world and the threatening other is rampant in all social strata and all political camps. The insistence on a supposedly uncontaminated, pure body, on self-determination over one's own, this crude understanding of freedom quickly pervaded the actions of the German government. "The protection of health is a high value, but the highest value [...] is and remains freedom"[8], proclaimed Christian Lindner, German finance minister and head of the German Liberal Party. Society is not really divided; it is much more likely to move along different lines in authoritarian directions. The reactionary protests as well as those settling inside the home show that policies of immunization always rely on community closures.

Biopolitical Immunization

This figure of the immune can be developed from the Latin verb *immunio*, which primarily denotes securing and building up protection. Here, the prefix *in-* in *immunio* means a movement into something that already exists, into something worth protecting.[9] 'Biopolitical immunization' is characterized through the movement of *Hereinnahme*, of incorporating or integrating what is constructed as threatening in order to overcome its threat.[10] Liberal as well as neoliberal ways of governing can be analyzed with this figure of the immune, also dynamics of the circulation of people and commodities in order to permit the economy to prosper and grow. It inevitably involves insecurities. It is a figure that arises from

[8] This was Christian Lindner's argument against mandatory vaccination in his "speech on freedom" at the FDP's annual Epiphany meeting in January 2022.

[9] Tacitus, *Annals* (Tac. Ann. 11, 19); item, "Immunio", in *Thesaurus Linguae Latinae*, vol. VII, Leipzig: Teubner, 1979, 503.

[10] See Lorey, *Figuren des Immunen*, 260–280.

epidemic control in the 19th century, and many means of fighting the COVID pandemic actually returned, because no state and no government were prepared; they improvised and experimented.[11]

The pandemic occurred in the paradigm of neoliberalism becoming authoritarian and within its governmentality, and it exacerbated inequalities and insecurities.[12] It is part of neoliberal governmentality to be unprepared on the state side and at the same time to privatize prevention and leave it to the individual: as individualized responsibility for health and safeguarding.[13] The resulting self-government in individualizing freedom is a neoliberal practice of shielding the body to immunize against risks.

Not being able to plan for the long term is for many people not a new experience. Precarization has long become normal—not only in terms of insecurity of employment, but in terms of the insecurity of the whole life.[14] Not being able to plan destroys the fantasy of linear time—of progress, growth, of securing a standard of living.

To have been little confronted so far with unplannability is a privilege. Mainly in the middle class, in the normalization of precarization, the desire for prevention, prediction and provision persists. It is a self-disciplining control of the future in the present that the immunizing subject has been practising for decades and it is essential for neoliberal governing: everything turns around self-care. Care and nursing work with others, performed primarily by women, continue to be poorly recognized, poorly paid, or not paid at all, increasingly on call, just-in-time.

As early as the 1990s, health policy in the context of the AIDS crisis made it obvious that measures in the service of public health were primarily aimed at individualized competence and responsibility in reducing the risks of infection. During this period, a biopolitical shift in the logic of danger prevention took place: a danger that comes from outside and

---

[11] "No health system was prepared. In the future, we must have a crisis mechanism that allows us to switch over immediately", as WHO's Regional Director for Europe Hans Kluge puts it in an interview. See "Wir sind noch mitten in der ersten Welle", in *Süddeutsche Zeitung* (20 July 2020), https://www.sueddeutsche.de/gesundheit/who-corona-weltgesundheitsorganisation-hans-kluge-1.4970978?fbclid=IwAR2688upNPlzGone8tbwOSk3O_bxVj5qvxC8UVrM0o269cYbqLEH7BICJS-g&utm_campaign=who_1.4970978&utm_medium=organic&utm_source=facebook&reduced=true, accessed 24 February 2024.

[12] See Wendy Brown, *Undoing the Demos. Neoliberalism's Stealth Revolution*, New York: Zone Books, 2015.

[13] Prevention constantly fails, because of its insatiable longing for unequivocalness, security, and permanence. Some risk always remains, and new risks can arise. At the same time, prevention in the health sector is weakened by the fact that many people do not (want to) develop a preventive health-political relationship with their body through, for instance, a healthy diet, exercise, or abstention from smoking and alcohol. See also Ulrich Bröckling, "Prävention", in *Glossar der Gegenwart*, ed. by Ulrich Bröckling, Susanne Krasmann and Thomas Lemke, Frankfurt: Suhrkamp, 2004.

[14] See Isabell Lorey, *State of Insecurity: Government of the Precarious*, trans. Aileen Derieg, preface by Judith Butler London: Verso, 2015.

to which individuals are exposed becomes a risk that they themselves are responsible for through their behaviour if they do not follow official measures and medical recommendations. The neoliberal turn towards individual self-responsible risk behaviour is closely intertwined with the attribution of individual guilt when risk minimization fails. The public begins at the "openings of the body"[15], as Brigitte Weingart has said, which must be closed to avoid infection—with condoms or with masks. In neoliberalism, thinking in terms of risk is inseparable from a state invocation of self-responsibility.

'Risk factors' were invented in the 1950s in the United States as part of an emerging field of medical research: the epidemiology of chronic diseases.[16] Epidemiology is actually the study of the course of infectious diseases, but after World War II, medical research focused more on the increasing incidence of chronic cardiovascular disease. This perspective on risk factors is medically conservative because the factors do not include conditions of inequality such as housing situation or poverty, but only the behaviour of individuals. Attributing individual responsibility is simply easier to link to medical treatments and prevention requirements. Social, economic, and ecological contexts were considered too complex for uniform health policy measures. The individualizing non-contextual approach prevailed in health policy, although it has received much criticism since the 1970s in the context of left-wing social medicine.

Current epidemiology still focuses on risk minimization through statistics, probability calculations and individual diagnostics; that is, focussing on the concrete behaviour of each person, rather than on social contexts and inequalities. In epidemic control, as in neoliberal health profit, it is not a matter of everyone protecting themselves and being protected, but of calculating the costs for the social security funds in such a way that the expenses remain profitable.

Privatized, individualized prevention and risk minimization require the fears and anxieties of every single person. The provisioning behaviour in self-responsibility is demanded by the state as a reaction to increasing uncertainties, which have arisen for decades not just through deregulated labour markets, but also through the neoliberal dismantling and restructuring of the welfare state as well as the economization of the health care system. In the pandemic however, the experience of unplannability

[15] Brigitte Weingart, *Ansteckende Wörter: Repräsentationen von AIDS*, Frankfurt/Main: Suhrkamp, 2002, 119.
[16] See Carsten Timmermann, "Risikofaktoren: Der scheinbar unaufhaltsame Erfolg eines Ansatzes aus der amerikanischen Epidemiologie in der deutschen Nachkriegsmedizin", in *Das präventive Selbst: Eine Kulturgeschichte moderner Gesundheitspolitik*, ed. by Martin Lengwiler and Jeanette Madarász, Bielefeld: transcript, 2010.

becomes dominant. Individuals who have been immunizing themselves for some time were extremely irritated that prevention did not work at all in the pandemic—that all attempts to shape the future through planning and discipline in the now imploded.

In the midst of the mutating epidemic, the impossibility of autonomy and shielding was revealed. If the public begins at the openings of the body, then bodies cannot be understood as isolated, closed individuals. Vulnerability and precariousness are inevitable.[17] Bodies emerge at all only in the affection with social and ecological environments. However, contamination control works *against* affection and rearranges space to enforce distance. It alters behaviour and gives rise to new bodies that feel increasingly uncomfortable about insufficient distance from others. Epidemic control produces enormous sensitivity and high stress due to insecurity and uncontrollability. Infectious aerosols can 'float' in the air in any room, in any part of society, in any place. Despite vaccination, there remains a risk of infection. There are no absolute certainties, no reliable shielding. Boundaries between inside and outside, between mobile potential virus carriers and virus-free immobile protected persons are an illusion. They lead to loneliness, closed communities and collective immunizations, and make authoritarianism increasingly acceptable.

Logistification

Not being prepared on the government side means governing in the here and now, which necessarily becomes experimental. Governments must constantly readjust and balance risks. In the pandemic, this experimental governing shows its compatibility with just-in-time production and logistics.[18] Here, the dynamics of circulation, which are important for 'biopolitical immunization', are actualized. Despite increasing re-nationalization, the boundaries for the global political economy of logistics must remain open. The *Hereinnahme* (taking into) of economic circulation must not be blocked.

Lack of prevention corresponds to the logic of logistics, which has become detached from the promise of progress and future of liberal-democratic postwar orders. Neither the state nor the economy is interested in being prepared: too many costs, too much standstill of circulation, too

[17] See also Judith Butler, *Precarious Life. The Powers of Mourning and Violence*, London: Verso, 2004.
[18] See Rob Wallace, Alex Liebman, Luis Fernando Chaves and Rodrick Wallace, "COVID-19 and Circuits of Capital", in *transversal. multilingual webjournal*: "Around the Crown" (2020), https://transversal.at/transversal/0420/wallace-etal/en, accessed 14 February 2024.

much storage. The risk of just-in-time control of the epidemic is accepted. Policy is 'driving on sight' in an experimental way. Experimental governing intertwines not only with logistical circulation but also with psychosocial time experiences of the intensification of the now.

The virus itself is part of global supply flows that produce, transport and distribute goods on demand rather than storing them.[19] Production and distribution are moving ever closer in time to the wishes of consumers. Ordered and delivered as quickly as possible: just-in-time. Service in the now. Demand is difficult to calculate, jobs on demand are on the rise. The extreme growth in online orders since the outbreak of the pandemic is just another boom in this logistical economy, which has become hegemonic for some time now.[20]

Logistics is not a tightly organized production machinery, but a management of "contingency, experimentation, negotiation, and unstable commitments"[21]. Logistics is the management of the unpredictable, based on extreme exploitation, disenfranchisement, temporary migration on demand. At the same time, logistics serves many peoples' current understanding of freedom: having a need, ordering, and having what you want delivered immediately. People and goods are logistified—they are part of the management of the global mobility of things, capital, and data. Logistics corresponds to biopolitical-immunizing capture, which ensures shielding in the home.

In the financial markets, which were flourishing despite rising incidences, so-called stay-at-home stocks, delivery services, moreover vaccine manufacturers, and the technology industry were profiting.[22] The most important thing for the markets was that the economy did not shut down. No lockdowns and the maintenance of the so-called critical infrastructure. Service sectors with a physical presence and contact, such as restaurants, tourism or the event sector, were particularly threatened by bankruptcies. Just-in-time jobs were also on the rise here; day, week or month

---

[19] See Wallace et al., "COVID-19"; see also Alessandro Broglia and Christian Kapel, "Changing Dietary Habits in a Changing World: Emerging Drivers for the Transmission of Foodborne Parasitic Zoonoses", in *Veterinary Parasitology* 182, no. 1 (November 2011).

[20] Since the 1960s, the meaning of "logistics ... has been expanded to refer to the management of the entire supply chain, encompassing design and ordering, production, transportation and warehousing, sales, redesign and reordering". Edna Bonacich and Jake B. Wilson, *Getting the Goods: Ports, Labor, and the Logistics Revolution*, Ithaca, NY: Cornell University Press, 2008, 3.

[21] Anna Tsing, "Supply Chains and the Human Condition", in *Rethinking Marxism* 21, no. 2 (April 2009), 151; see also Sandro Mezzadra and Brett Neilson, *Border as Method, or, the Multiplication of Labor*, Durham, NC: Duke University Press, 2013, 118–22.

[22] See "So viel Börsengänge wie seit 20 Jahren nicht", in *Süddeutsche Zeitung* (7 October 2020), https://www.sueddeutsche.de/wirtschaft/anleger-so-viele-boersengaenge-wie-seit-1980-nicht-1.5057294, accessed 14 February 2024.

jobs: depending on demand and the number of orders. The worst jobs are held by migrants. Poverty is on the rise.

As part of 'biopolitical immunization', life must remain precarious. The residual risk is a prerequisite for the establishment of ever-new security mechanisms. Precarizing logistification is already inscribed in self-government and the desire of the time-scarce privileged distance workers, in the new way of life of the preventive self, which can no longer plan the future and settles in its own at home. This is perhaps the most obvious intertwining of the figures of 'jurdical immunity' and 'biopolitical immunization'.

Constituent Immunization

Even if there were always good reasons for isolation and contact avoidance in the height of the pandemic, this very practice cannot be allowed to become life-defining in the long run. Much more understanding of global connections and interdependencies is needed to allow radically different ways of living and working to become dominant, in which the interdependencies of proximity, exchange and ecologies are central.

It has long been clear that a virus such as COVID does not come from outside, cannot be externalized, but spreads with socialities and makes us focus on the now. This is good news, because we can only shape the now—not the future. It is only a fantasized crutch to bend the unpredictability of life into a progressive line to a future and make it supposedly controllable. It is necessary to lose the old orientation in order to radically end this time of progress and growth. Learning to deal with unpredictability and precarization should be used to get 'in front of the wave' of capitalist transformation and to finally think ecology, health and care together without preventive thinking, surveillance and control.

Against the neoliberal form of democracy, which relies on precarization and the self-responsibility of the individual, in which solidarity—if at all—becomes a private matter or an honorary office, new and radical approaches to democracy are needed: democratic practices, that counter and go beyond the logic of immunization that perpetuates domination and its concomitant constructions of community; go beyond the figure of the individual focused on possession and self care and all the juridical principles that are based on it: individualized freedom, independence, property—all aspects of the old norm of hegemonic white masculinity that are constituted by warding off the fundamental dependencies on others and environments.

The figure of the immune that tries to conceptualize this is the subversive and resistant figure of 'constituent immunization'. It concerns an understanding of immunization that is a far cry from its everyday meanings. The dynamics of a subversive figure of the immune can also be developed out of the verb *immunio*. Instead of a movement of incorporation into an already constituted political body, *immunio* can also be used to highlight the movement of 'constituting', in the sense of creating anew.[23] In this way, 'constituting' is very close to the practice of instituting, a creative, instituent act. It is a process of beginning and duration. The beginning anew, in this kind of ongoing process, corresponds to a recurring break, destituting existing social conditions and, at the same time, creating a breach that enables new views and new possibilities for action.[24] 'Constituent immunization' starts from inequalities and stresses a renewed ordering in which safeguarding the political body is no longer the stake, but rather the constituting of those formerly constructed as a threat, as minor and not worth protecting. Such a resistant form of the immune ruptures the dynamics of immunization in which political and economic domination functionalizes fear and precarization. The 'con-' in constituent, the 'with', is not geared towards a community, but to the common that is to be found in compositions and cooperation.[25]

In the pandemic it became obvious once again that there is a need for an exodus of the many from the reactionary re-formations of nation, family and patriarchal dominance, an exodus from logistified desires, an exodus from contact phobias, and there is a need for an exodus from the neoliberal form of democracy.[26] There were and are new radical approaches to democracy in the democracy and occupy movements of the 2010s. It is now necessary to connect these experiences to the climate movements of today.

---

[23] See also Antonio Negri, *Insurgencies: Constituent Power and Modern State*, Minnesota and London: University of Minnesota Press, 1999.

[24] See Gerald Raunig, "Instituent Practices: Fleeing, Instituting, Transforming", in *transversal. multilingual webjournal*: "do you remember institutional critique" (2006), https://transversal.at/transversal/0106/raunig/en, accessed 14 February, 2024; Gerald Raunig, "Instituent Practices, No. 2: Institutional Critique, Constituent Power, and the Persistence of Instituting", in *transversal. multilingual webjournal*: "extradisciplinaire" (2007), https://transversal.at/transversal/0507, accessed 14 February.

[25] See Lorey, *Figuren des Immunen*, 281–292.

[26] For the notion of "exodus", see Lorey, *Figuren des Immunen*. For a new conception of democracy, see Isabell Lorey, *Democracy in the Political Present: A Queer-feminist Theory*, London: Verso, 2022.

References

Carolin Amlinger and Oliver Nachtwey, *Gekränkte Freiheit. Aspekte des liberalen Autoritarismus,* Berlin: Suhrkamp, 2022.

Sergio Bologna, "Wir dürfen der extremen Rechten nicht die Idee der Freiheit überlassen!", in *Sozial. Geschichte Online* 31 (2022), https://sozialgeschichte-online.org/2022/01/19/wir-durfen-der-extremen-rechten-nicht-die-idee-der-freiheit-uberlassen/

Edna Bonacich and Jake B. Wilson, *Getting the Goods: Ports, Labor, and the Logistics Revolution,* Ithaca, NY: Cornell University Press, 2008.

Ulrich Bröckling, "Prävention", in *Glossar der Gegenwart,* ed. by Ulrich Bröckling, Susanne Krasmann and Thomas Lemke, Frankfurt: Suhrkamp, 2004, 213–14.

Alessandro Broglia and Christian Kapel, "Changing Dietary Habits in a Changing World: Emerging Drivers for the Transmission of Foodborne Parasitic Zoonoses", in *Veterinary Parasitology* 182, no. 1 (November 2011), 2–13.

Wendy Brown, *Undoing the Demos. Neoliberalism's Stealth Revolution,* New York: Zone Books, 2015.

Judith Butler, *Precarious Life. The Powers of Mourning and Violence,* London: Verso, 2004.

Michel Foucault, *Security, Territory, Population: Lectures at the Collège de France, 1977–78,* ed. by Michel Senellart, Basingstoke: Palgrave Macmillan, 2014.

"Immunio", in *Thesaurus Linguae Latinae,* vol. VII, Leipzig: Teubner, 1979, 503.

Hans Kluge, "Wir sind noch mitten in der ersten Welle", in *Süddeutsche Zeitung* (20 July 2020), https://www.sueddeutsche.de/gesundheit/who-corona-weltgesundheitsorganisation-hans-kluge-1.4970978?fbclid=IwAR2688upNPlzGone8tbwOSk3O_bxVj5qvxC8UVrM0o269cYbqLEH7BICJS-g&utm_campaign=who_1.4970978&utm_medium=organic&utm_source=facebook&reduced=true

Mike Laufenberg and Susanne Schultz, "The Pandemic State of Care: Care Familialism and Care Nationalism in the COVID-19-Crisis. The Case of Germany", in *Historical Social Research* 46, no. 4 (2021), 72–99.

Isabell Lorey, *Democracy in the Political Present: A Queer-feminist Theory,* London: Verso, 2022.

——— "Constituent Immunization Instead of Self-Immunizing Communities", in *New Alphabet: Community* (2021), https://newalphabetschool.hkw.de/constituent-immunisation-instead-of-self-immunizing-communities/

——— "Corona Effects: After Prevention, Just In Time: Digitalization and Contact Phobias", in *transversal. multilingual webjournal:* "Around the Crown" (2020), https://transversal.at/transversal/0420/en/en

——— "Gefangen im Jetzt: Prekäres in der politischen Gegenwart", in *Agora 42: Das philosophische Wirtschaftsmagazin,* no. 4 (2020), 13–16.

——— *State of Insecurity: Government of the Precarious,* trans. Aileen Derieg, preface by Judith Butler, London: Verso, 2015.

——— "Politics of Immunization and the Precarious Life", in *Dance, Politics, and Co-Immunity. Current Perspectives on Politics and Communities in the Arts*, ed. by Gerald Siegmund and Stefan Hölscher, Zürich and Berlin: diaphanes, 2013, 265–276.

——— *Figuren des Immunen. Elemente einer politischen Theorie*, Zürich and Berlin: diaphanes, 2011.

Sandro Mezzadra and Brett Neilson, *Border as Method, or, the Multiplication of Labor*, Durham, NC: Duke University Press, 2013.

National Education Panel Study (NEPS): "Kinderbetreuung in Corona-Zeiten: Auch bei gleicher beruflicher Belastung betreuen Mütter häufiger allein als Väter" (13 October 2020), https://www.neps-data.de/Neuigkeiten/Archiv/udt_1582_param_detail/20458

Antonio Negri, *Insurgencies: Constituent Power and Modern State*, Minnesota and London: University of Minnesota Press, 1999.

Gerald Raunig, "Instituent Practices, No. 2: Institutional Critique, Constituent Power, and the Persistance of Instituting", in *transversal. multilingual webjournal*: "extradisciplinaire" (2007), https://transversal.at/transversal/0507

——— "Instituent Practices: Fleeing, Instituting, Transforming", in *transversal. multilingual webjournal*: "do you remember institutional critique" (2006), https://transversal.at/transversal/0106/raunig/en

"So viel Börsengänge wie seit 20 Jahren nicht", in *Süddeutsche Zeitung* (7 October 2020), https://www.sueddeutsche.de/wirtschaft/anleger-so-viele-boersengaenge-wie-seit-1980-nicht-1.5057294

Tacitus, *Annals* (Tac. Ann. 11, 19).

Carsten Timmermann, "Risikofaktoren: Der scheinbar unaufhaltsame Erfolg eines Ansatzes aus der amerikanischen Epidemiologie in der deutschen Nachkriegsmedizin", in *Das präventive Selbst: Eine Kulturgeschichte moderner Gesundheitspolitik*, ed. by Martin Lengwiler and Jeanette Madarász, Bielefeld: transcript, 2010, 251–782.

Anna Tsing, "Supply Chains and the Human Condition", in *Rethinking Marxism* 21, no. 2 (April 2009), 148–176.

Paolo Virno, *A Grammar of the Multitude: For an Analysis of Contemporary Forms of Life*, Los Angeles: Semiotext(e), 2004.

Rob Wallace, Alex Liebman, Luis Fernando Chaves and Rodrick Wallace, "COVID-19 and Circuits of Capital", in *transversal. multilingual webjournal*: "Around the Crown" (2020), https://transversal.at/transversal/0420/wallace-etal/en

Brigitte Weingart, *Ansteckende Wörter: Repräsentationen von AIDS*, Frankfurt/Main: Suhrkamp, 2002.

Janez Janša, Janez Janša and Janez Janša
in conversation

Name as a Shield

Janez Janša

Janez, can a name act as a shield? Shortly after the Russian army invaded Ukraine, a German couple with Russian-sounding names applied to change their names, claiming that they had suffered discrimination since the start of the war. The administrative court in the German city of Koblenz rejected the application on the grounds that "merely abstract aspects, such as a change in social values and attitudes, are not sufficient for the assumption of good cause. Rather, there must be a concrete link between the significant inconvenience and the respective surname"[1]. For the court, the fact that they were born in Germany, were of non-Russian origin and therefore not refugees (for whom the name could cause difficulties in integration) and that the surname is also found in Poland, was enough to reject the appeal.

> **Janez Janša**
>
> Without going into the details of the case, it is not difficult to imagine a certain shift in the perception of a name based on what court named "a change in social values and attitudes". Overnight, the name began to sound more Russian than it did before the aggression against Ukraine. The name began to function as a name, as something that (seems to) identify you, more than a rigid label, more than an identifier. I suppose that's where the 'psychological burden' might lie: Why should I be seen differently just because of my name and the political events that overshadow it? In its

[1] Verdict of the Administratice Court of Koblenz (2023), 1–13, 10 (interviewer's translation), https://files.vogel.de/infodienste/smfiledata/1/9/4/7/6/8/235038.pdf, accessed 18 March 2024. See page 8: "The change of name under public law does not serve to protect the bearer of the name from all kinds of inconveniences and difficulties that the use of a particular name may entail [...] It cannot be inferred from the plaintiffs' submissions in the official and court proceedings that the surname represents a psychological burden for them and their daughter that can be regarded as an important reason for a name change."

decision, the Administrative Court followed the principle of the continuity of the name, putting the public interest in identification before a personal need for protection.[2] In principle, a person's name is not at the free disposal of the bearer. Therefore, a surname or first name may only be changed if there is an important reason for doing so. What would be an important reason, what would be an evidence of a 'psychological burden' that would convince the court and outweigh the principle of keeping a name? What would *free* the couple from the name given to them? The state is primarily interested in regulating its citizens and naming regimes are established to serve this regulation by identifying each individual. But with the introduction of digital, biometric, unambiguously precise means of identification—unrepeatable PIN numbers, social security and tax numbers—to what extent does the state still need to rely on the identification of citizens by name? Especially in an age of massive migration and name legislations that are not standardised within the EU legal system, let alone beyond. But, to answer your question, a name *can* act as a shield. There are numerous examples of pseudonyms that individuals have adopted in order to escape oppression, persecution, cancellation…

Janez Janša
… in Germany, the case of Willy Brandt is particularly interesting, not only because it helped him protect himself from the Nazis.

Janez Janša
Yes, the former West German chancellor (1969–74), after whom the Berlin airport, squares, streets and institutions in the new Germany are named, was born Herbert Frahm. Resisting the Nazi regime, he had to escape persecution by going into exile, choosing Norway first. There he changed his name to Willy Brandt (after using at least two other names—Gunnar Gaasland and Felix Franke). After the war, he returned to West Germany as a Norwegian citizen and decided to keep Willy Brandt as his official name. In his case, the pseudonym was so successful that it not only protected him from the Nazis,

[2] "Otherwise it would be too easy to undermine the identification function of the name, which is essential for name continuity. This applies in particular to adults, for whom the retention of the previous name is of particular importance, unlike for minors, since adults have regularly appeared under their surname for longer and more frequently in professional life, in legal transactions and to the authorities […]. [Unconscious] prejudices that lead to inconveniences that—as here—are below the threshold of a mental impairment to be taken into account are to a certain extent inherent in a society and therefore cannot be dealt with by the public right to change names." Verdict of the Administratice Court of Koblenz, 10–11.

it also erased his birth name and inscribed him in German political history. The course of history told him there was no going back to Herbert Frahm, the name which with he left Germany, that he had no other choice than to keep his newly born Norwegian name—in order to keep the symbolic capital achieved with the name Willy Brandt.

Janez Janša

So if one of the most prominent leaders of social democratic politics in Germany (the leader of the SPD from 1967 to 1987), has a survival story based on changing his name—turning a pseudonym into an official name— why can't modern legislation be based on such an example?

Janez Janša

An exception will hardly become a norm. In this respect, it is interesting to take a closer look at the cases of collective pseudonyms. Marco Deseriis introduced the concept of 'improper names' in his book of the same title, in which he examines various resistance collectives that operated by sharing the same name: from the Luddites of the 19th century, to Allen Smithee, Monty Cantsin and Luther Blissett of the 20th century, to Anonymous of the 21st century:

> Unlike a proper name, whose primary function is to fix a referent as part of the operation of a system of signs, an improper name is explicitly constructed to obscure both the identity and the number of its referents. On the one hand, the improper name embeds the shielding effect of any pseudonym, that is, the nominal function of the pseudonym to protect an individual by replacing her legal name as a marker of her identity. On the other hand, an unlawful name functions as an open multiplicity that can hardly be disambiguated and assigned a discrete referent.[3]

The classic film portrait of the multiple names that obscure the identification of an individual is the scene from Kubrick's film *Spartacus* (1960), in which the Roman general Marcus Licinius Crassus attempts to identify the rebel slave Spartacus among a group of imprisoned slaves. Just as Spartacus (played by Kirk Douglas) is about to stand up and reveal himself, one by one the slaves stand

[3] Marco Deseriis, *Improper Names. Collective Pseudonyms from the Luddities to Anonymous*, Minneapolis, London: University of Minnesota Press, 2015, 3–4.

up and shout: "I am Spartacus!" The slaves shielded Spartacus by taking his name. Spartacus was not identified, but Crassus sentenced them all to death by crucifixion. Deseriis is particularly interested in multiple names that reinforce the quality of the individual as a social being, a quality that resists the legal reduction of a living being to just an individual.

Janez Janša

In the territory of the former Yugoslavia, during the Second World War, members of the resistance were called 'illegals' ('ilegalci') and used partisan names, pseudonyms, and even collective names among themselves.[4] Today, the same word is used to discredit migrants trying to enter the EU.

Janez Janša

There is always something uncanny about a name change because of the perception that a name is so tied to an identity. We are primarily policed (by society and its repressive organs) by our names, that's why most regimes are not indifferent to a name change. Let me point to the two cases that have caused some public outrage over the *granting* of name changes. In 2017, two prisoners who had been sentenced to the highest possible punishment in their respective countries, Norway and Austria, applied for a name change. Norwegian mass murderer Anders Behring Breivik,[5] sentenced to 21 years in prison with the possibility of extension, was allowed to change his name to Fjotlof Hansen. Austrian Josef Fritzl,[6] sentenced to life imprisonment, was allowed to change his name to Joseph Mayrhoff. The public was outraged by the court's decisions to allow the name changes: "How can such a criminal get a new name?"

Janez Janša

In several legal systems, one of the reasons for not allowing a name change would be precisely the fact that the applicant has a criminal record.

---

[4] In one of the most popular partisan films, *Valter brani Sarajevo* (*Valter defends Sarajevo*, 1972), part of the plot is based on finding out who 'Valter' is: not only is the Gestapo looking for him, but also the members of the resistance movement. The answer is given in the final scene of the film, in which the retiring Nazi supreme commander of Sarajevo invites his ambitious successor to show him 'Valter'. Arriving at a vantage point from which the entire city of Sarajevo can be seen, he says: "Look at the city. That is Valter."

[5] On 22 July 2011, Anders Behring Breivik killed 8 people in front of the parliament building in Oslo and later in the day another 69 on the island of Utoya.

[6] Josef Fritzl locked his 18 year old daughter in the cellar of his house for twenty-four years (1984–2008), kept her as a slave, raped her and fathered seven children with her. He also locked three of his other children in the cellar.

Janez Janša

In some countries, having the same name as a known criminal would be a good reason to allow a name change.[7] Knowing the length of Breivik's and Fritzl's sentences, the question of traceability and identification becomes redundant. As the bodies are locked up and their social interactions reduced to a bare minimum, there is very little scope for their new names to become a crucial identification marker. From that point of view, the authorities had no problem allowing them to change their names.

Janez Janša

Yet the lawyers for both clients were careful not to disguise the reasons for their name changes. By changing their names, Breivik and Fritzl wanted to move into the realm of anonymity of names that would not associate them with their past. At the same time, their former names were imprinted on them and became generic names for people who committed similar crimes. Breivik and Fritzl wanted to cut with the past via a name change—but is changing your name enough to become someone else? Or rather, to become no-names within the same body—which we can assume is the goal of Breivik/Hansen and Fritzl/Mayrhoff? When you become a name, when you become recognised socially as your name in the first place, when your name does more for you than you can do for yourself, then it is hard to count on a (new) name as a shield.[8]

Janez Janša

Indeed. The status of 'protected witnesses' provides a good answer to the question of a new name as a reliable shield. Protected witnesses are usually given not just a new name, but a whole set of characteristics that cut all ties with their previous life in a way that makes them untraceable for revenge and that does not compromise new social interactions that they will—or might have—to face. A new name alone is not enough for a protected witness to be sufficiently shielded. They are protected by a scripted identity, a new biography in which the biggest threat is the shadow of the former life.

---

[7] See Tadej Kovačič, "Juridical Regulation of a Name Change", in *Performance Research*, 22:5 (2017), 72–79.

[8] Despite the name change, media reports on current events involving them have largely ignored their new legal names.

Janez Janša

It seems that we cannot escape (the shadow of) a name. The name is given, it is imposed on us, it is something we have not asked for—just like life. The name is sometimes at work before we are born, and it certainly continues to work on us after we are dead.

Janez Janša

Not only this: with our names, we don't only perform ourselves but also others; those we may or may not have heard of. We perform collective identities, we contribute to the continuation of constructed ethnic, national and other identities and narratives by carrying the names given to us.[9] A name always already carries common sense and context beyond our individual biographies. The question is how—not whether—we can control the performance of our names. Ariella Aïsha Azoulay tells her family story, which provides another insight into the mutability of naming regimes:

> When I was about twelve years old, my older sister suggested that we change our last name to a Hebrew one. This was a common practice, mandatory among people in official positions and voluntary among those who wanted to dissociate themselves from their lineage and assimilate into Israeliness. In Israel a Hebrew name means an Israeli one—one distinct from those that carry the mark of what Israel defines as 'its' diaspora. This regime of name changing affected *ashkenazim* and *mizrahim* alike; as the state imposed itself as the center of 'Jewish life,' it endowed its fabricated Jewish subject, 'the Israeli,' with an epigraphic history and future. I was unable to discern this conflation between Hebrew and Israeli. However, through my sister's request, I could no longer shield myself from the truth that my teacher uttered every day when she read our family name aloud: there was something wrong about our name and about us. We were like 'them,' those North Africans from whom we were supposed to distinguish ourselves. With a child's intuition, I understood that I had to support my sister's plan. Yet my parents rejected her suggestion, asserting: 'One

[9] "I had insisted on their [my childrens'] names being chosen, not according to the fashion of the moment, but in memory of people I have been fond of. Their names made the children into revenants. [Ihre Namen machen die Kinder zu Revenants.] And after all, I reflected, was not having children our own path to immortality?" Sigmund Freud cited in Mladen Dolar, *What's in a Name?* Ljubljana: Aksioma, 2014, 36.

doesn't change one's name.' This was a lesson for me, one that turned our difference into a source of power and liberation. Who our family is surpassed what is inscribed in our name; our name is not reminiscent of bygone times. At that point I still didn't understand what an identity meant, but I did understand that I was heir to an ancestral refusal of colonial nomenclature, evidenced by my parents' determination to keep our name intact.[10]

Janez Janša

Every change in the political order is radically manifested in the naming regime. The Italian fascists under Mussolini systematically Italianised names of Slavic origin in the occupied parts of present-day Slovenia and Croatia. My parents' surnames were changed from Hrvatin to Crevatin and from Rabak to Rabbaccio. A few years after my grandparents died in the 1990s, my father asked the Croatian authorities to change his parents' names, as they were still registered with their Italianised names. Even though they had lived in socialist Yugoslavia for 45 years! There, by the way, my father's name Vito, clearly of Romanic origin, got its Slavic version by adding *-mir* to the end of the name: he lived part of his life with the name Vitomir, given to him by the state.[11]

Janez Janša

How can we protect our names from being changed against our will?

Janez Janša

If you were to protect your name, what would that mean for others? In North Korea, for example, the name of the leader is reserved for him alone. People were forbidden to have the same name as the regime's founder, Kim Il-sung, and his successor, Kim Jong-il. After the current leader, Kim Jong-un, came to power, the state forced people named Jong-un and Sol-ju, the name of his wife, to change their names, and since 2023 the same has been demanded of people who have the same name as the leader's daughter, Ju-ae.

[10] Ariella Aïsha Azoulay, "Unlearning Our Settler Colonial Tongues. On language and belonging.", in *Boston Review* (30 November 2021), https://www.bostonreview.net/articles/unlearning-our-settler-colonial-tongues, accessed 18 March 2024.
[11] Many names in the former Yugoslavia were given extensions *-mir* (male) or *-mira* (female), *-mir* meaning 'peace', and *-slav* or *-slava*, referring both to 'Slavic' and 'glory'.

Janez Janša

An easier solution for the absolutist is the mostly abandoned practice of adding numbers to the name that would be repeated. There is only one Richard III and only one John Paul II. Like the names of the streets in Manhattan, which can hardly be changed. But can you, as an ordinary citizen, protect your name in liberal democratic legal systems?

Janez Janša

Protect from what or in which sense? From being adopted by others? From being multiplied and losing their uniqueness? Or from forcefully being stolen? "Though the name embodies so much of a person, it cannot be considered as a thing or good on which one holds property rights"[12], writes Audrey Guinchard in her comparative analysis of French and English law on proper names. Put simply, we cannot legally protect our names and pretend that the name given to us is unique. There is no legal basis for your name to be unique. Your name is repeatable and it should come as no surprise to bump into someone with the same name as you. But, as Guinchard points out, "the debate about the nature of the name is not on whether the name is property or not, but on what the relationship should be between a person and his name."[13] However, we may regard them as unique—unique at least to us—they are given to us to imprint upon us a certain regime that a name-giver wanted us to belong to or was obliged to follow. There is always an extension of something a name refers to and there is always an announcement of something a name bearer can contribute. There is something in a name that doesn't want to die. The name is the place where memory and potentiality negotiate in the clearest way. There is not much a bearer can do about a name that has been given to them, but there is a lot they can do to make it not unbearable.

---

[12] Audrey Guinchard, "Is the name property? Comparing the English and the French Evolution", in *Journal of Civil Law Studies* (2008), 1–21, 1. Many celebrities protect their name as a trademark, including Greta Thunberg. See her Instagram post from 29 January 2020: "Impostors, trademarks, commercial interests, royalties and foundation... First: Unfortunately there are still people who are trying to impersonate me or falsely claim that they 'represent' me in order to communicate with high profile people, politicians, media, artists etc. Please be aware that this is happening and be extremely suspicious if you are contacted by 'me' or someone saying they 'represent' me. I apologize to anyone who has been contacted - and even misled - by this kind of behavior. Second: My name and the #FridaysForFuture movement are constantly being used for commercial purposes without any consent whatsoever. It happens for instance in marketing, selling of products and people collecting money in my and the movement's name. That is why I've applied to register my name, Fridays For Future, Skolstrejk för klimatet etc [sic] as trademarks." Greta Thunberg (29 January 2020), https://www.instagram.com/p/B76KMRjJPRn/, accessed 18 March 2024.
[13] Guinchard, "Is the name property?", 21.

Janez Janša®

Janez Janša® is a registered trademark owned by Janez Janša, Janez Janša and Janez Janša.

Frédéric Pouillaude

On Aesthetic Shielding: Walls, Windows and Screens

I will focus on three elementary kinds of shields in the daily environment: walls, windows, and screens. Through these figures I would like to interrogate the connection between art or aesthetic experience and the need for self-protection; for being safe. Art and aesthetic experience need safe places to be developed; they require a basic situation of security to exist. At the same time, if they have to be something important, something not completely inoffensive or anaesthetized, they must take some risks and even be exposed not only to risks but also to real violence. This conceptual and existential tension between art's need for safe places (white cubes, black boxes, in other words: the separation between art and life) on the one hand, and the artistic, political and ethical requirement of an exposure to violence (the violence of the world, the violence of life, in other words: a blurring of art and actual existence) on the other hand—this conceptual tension is probably as ancient as art is.

Mediations:
Walls, Windows, Screens

I have a very basic and simplistic position in media theory: everything which looks like media—a mediation—is a wall, period. And all these walls, obviously, are shields.

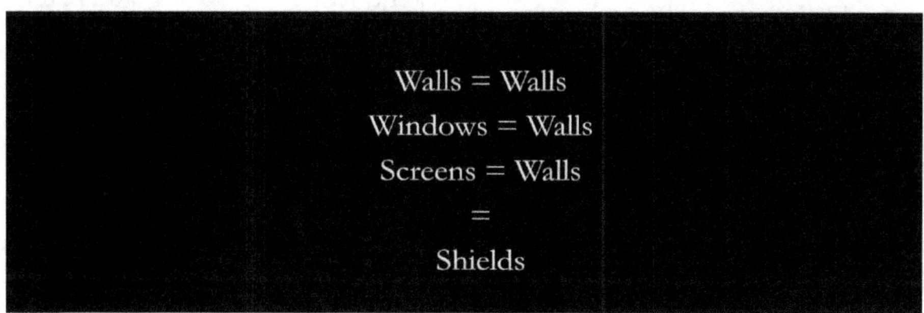

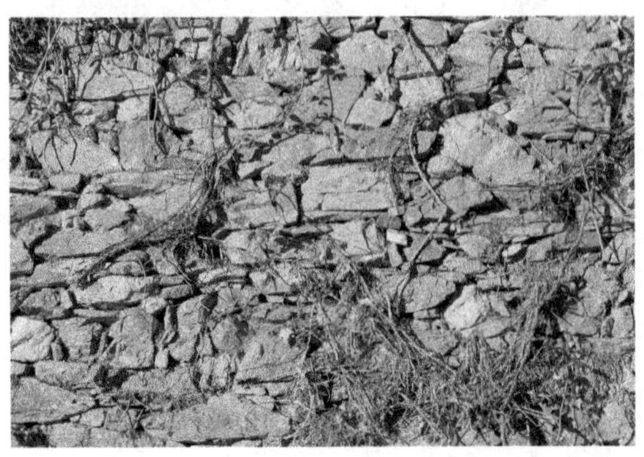

A wall is a static, non-mobile shield. Its two faces create an interior and an exterior, an inside and an outside. Being a solid structure, its basic function is to protect the inside from the outside, to keep the integrity of the things and beings that are inside against the potential aggressivity and harmfulness of outside elements. Whether it belongs to a house, an estate or a country, it blocks movements and creates an outside considered as a threat. In this way, a wall is a large non-mobile shield.

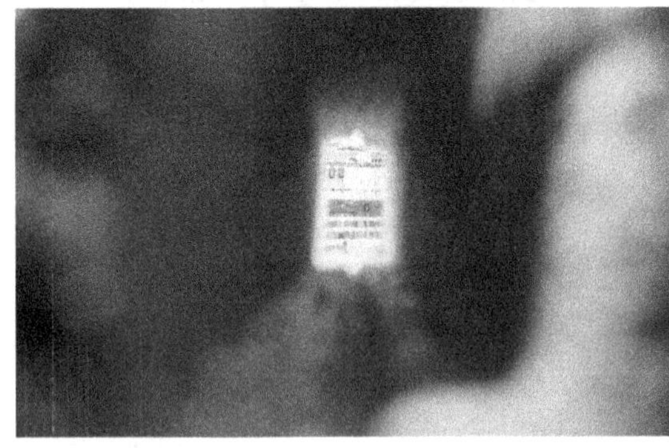

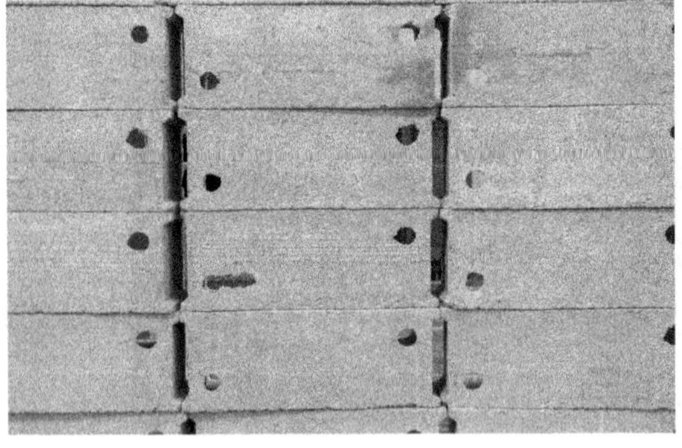

A window can be considered in two ways. At first, we might see a window as an absence of wall, a pure nothingness, a hole; it would just be a wall with a hole: a pierced wall.

Later, given the relatively recent technology of glass (I say 'recent' in regards to the universal history of humanity), we might consider a window as a more or less transparent wall in itself. A glass window, having two faces, also establishes an outside and an inside. Moreover, very often, it reproduces in its shape and structure the orthogonality of the wall, the right angles and the parallel lines of perpendicularity.

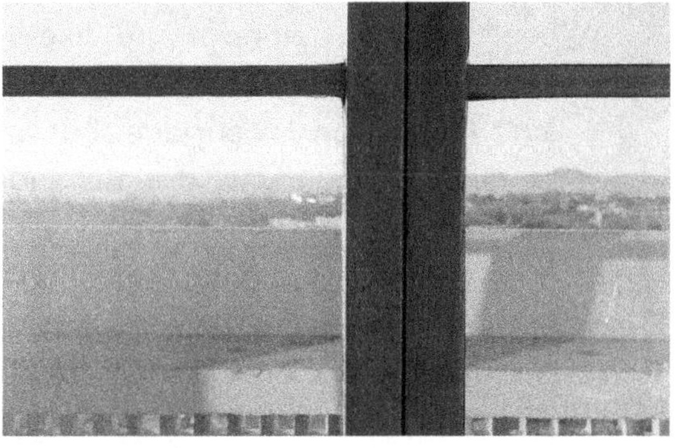

In both ways of considering windows, one thing is certain: no wall, no window. The window apparatus is fully dependent on the pre-existing wall apparatus. A window is fundamentally a modification of a wall. In the first case, the window adds to the wall a very simple optical device: a hole acting as a frame. In the second, it makes some part of the wall transparent, reproducing an equivalent optical device: a glass surface framed by some window jambs.

So if a window is a technical and optical modification of a wall, we can then deduce the following: a window is a non-mobile shield through which one can see, an optical breach in a solid wall, or a transparent wall.

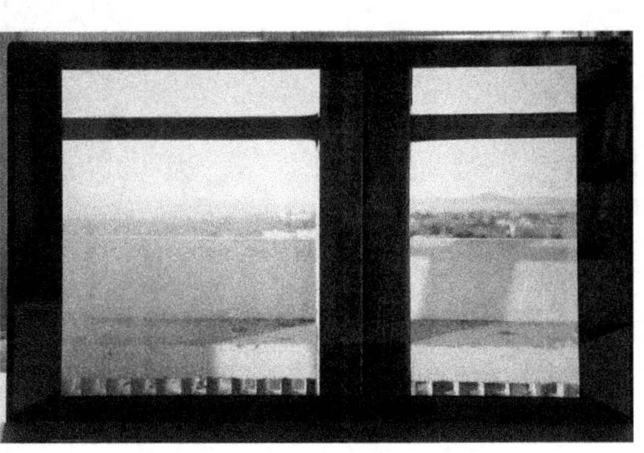

What, then, is a screen? A screen is nothing more than a wall that has been perfected and might even be an elaboration of walls. The screen is the next step after the window, an extension to and multiplication of a window's powers and potentialities, which are themselves based on wall technology.

A screen shows and conceals at the same time. Like a wall, it conceals what is behind it and, like a window, it shows something that isn't literally on its surface, but is beyond, or far away, or—pushing the window potentialities to another level—something that might not even exist at all. The screen also reproduces the orthogonality and perpendicularity of the wall, which was already reproduced by the window. Like a window, a screen gives the feeling of accessing an outside (by 'outside' I mean something that is not literally present in one's own perceptual environment) and multiplies this feeling towards infinite possibilities. It creates (especially with internet and social networks) an inconceivable variety of the 'outside' contents we can access, a terrific increase in what could be seen, heard and done a long time ago through a window.

But—and this is very obvious after the pandemic and the general digitalization of existence—the screen always does so by creating or reinforcing some kind of an inside, some kind of a home, whether this home is my actual home, or a space where I feel safe, or the psychic and homelike bubble I always carry in my pocket with my smartphone. A screen is an elaboration of a wall, relying on the ancestral need for defending an inside from an outside. The screen is our new, universal and omnipresent shield. From walls to screens, we have simply multiplied our ways of shielding and created a 'barbarian' accumulation of walls, confirming Benjamin's saying that "there is no document of civilization which is not at the same time a document of barbarism"[1].

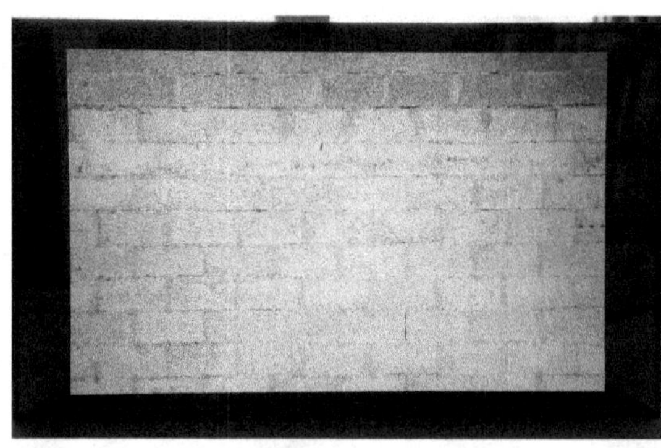

[1] Walter Benjamin, "On the Concept of History", in *Illuminations: Essays and Reflections*, ed. by Hannah Arendt, New York: Schocken Books, 1968, 256.

Aesthetics, art and overprotection

One knows that Western art theory and history have been largely based on the paradigm of the gridded window, starting at least with Alberti's *De Pictura* in 1435. At the beginning of the 15th Century, the invention of the window paradigm forged a new path for visual realism and geometrical perspective. All this has been commented on many times but one sees much less frequently what this paradigm implies in terms of security and distance. Thinking a painting as a window is another way to say that the painter and the viewer always remain safe; maybe they are accessing some kind of outside, but always staying within the shelter of four walls. The painting can certainly 'lighten' the wall and make it almost disappear. The fact remains that, outside the frame, solid walls are still there protecting against external aggressions. A similar analysis could be developed about the elaboration of the notion of 'aesthetic experience' by the end of the 18th century by Immanuel Kant. Through the Kantian dimensions of contemplation and disinterestedness, aesthetic experience—at least as the Occident has built this notion—implies that a basic and bodily security is established; it implies a physical shelter, segregating art and aesthetics from other dimensions of life.

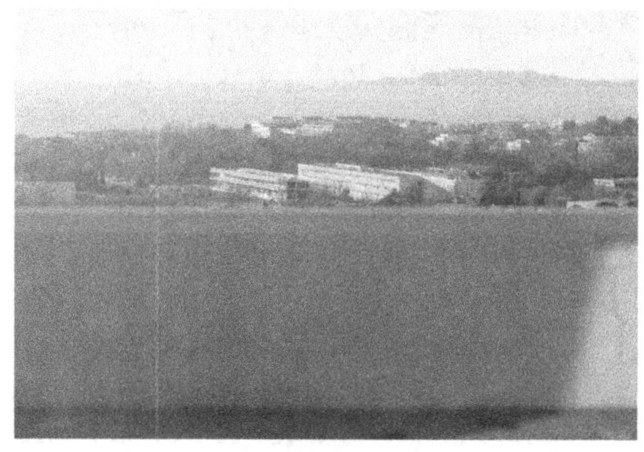

This idea of shelter gave birth to real, physical and architectural constructions. These constructions and apparatuses can be named, in historical order of apparition: black boxes for theatre and performing arts; white cubes for museum spaces and visual arts. I won't repeat here the very long critique of black boxes and white cubes, I would only insist on the fact that modernism didn't really attack these apparatuses. It focused on a more precise figure: it decided to violently attack the window, the illusion that a wall—even if transparent—could represent something else than itself. And it did so in two very different ways.

A formalist version of modernism—
the canonical or Greenbergian
one—decided to go back to the
wall under the window, to block the
window with solid bricks and enjoy
the immanent flatness of 'what is'.
The story says that this process
begins with Édouard Manet (for
instance, with the flatness of his
painting *The Fifer* (1866) and its
abstract beige background blocking any depth, or the dark open
window in *The Balcony* (1868/69)
presenting the inside room in such
an intense backlight that it appears
as a pure obscure surface, or the
same lack of depth emphasized
by the reflective and distorting
effect of a mirror at the back in *A
Bar at the Folies-Bergère* (1882))
and proceeds (let's says through
Kazimir Malevich, Jackson Pollock
and Mark Rothko, if examples are
needed) to the total security of a
panic room devoid of any breach.
Contrasting this formalist and self-
reflexive version of modernism,
another tendency, perhaps more
marginal or peripheral, decided
to perform a very simple action:
it opened the window and simply
jumped out. Having as one of its
ancestors Gustave Courbet—both
the painter of *A Burial at Ornans*
(1850) and an insurgent of the Paris
Commune in 1871—this tendency
might be called 'realistic modernism', despite the vagueness or
the bad reputation of the notion
of 'realism'.

Through the label of 'realistic modernism', I would like to emphasize two features: the factuality of an existing reference or, if representation is avoided, the real presence of the thing itself (for the realistic side)[2], and a constant experimentation on form refusing any idea of transparency or immediate access to meaning (for the modernist side). One work has perfectly epitomized this conjunction of features: *Let Us Now Praise Famous Men*.[3] Nominally devoted to the living conditions of three Alabama sharecropping families in the 1930s, the book explodes all the standards of social reporting. By its unusual length, by its highly complex—not to say messy—construction, by the multiplication of the genres and modes it explores (poetry, narration, description, analyses, facsimile, etc.) and also by the very atypical relationship it imposes between the photographs (by Walker Evans) and the text (by James Agee). *Let Us Now Praise Famous Men* is both a contemporary classic and an artistic monster,

inspiring the current renewal of documentary practices in many artistic fields. And it does so precisely because its formal complexity and constant excessiveness is not performed for its own sake but as a direct result of its subject, as the consciousness of both the necessity and the impossibility of producing an artwork from and in the 'outside'.[4]

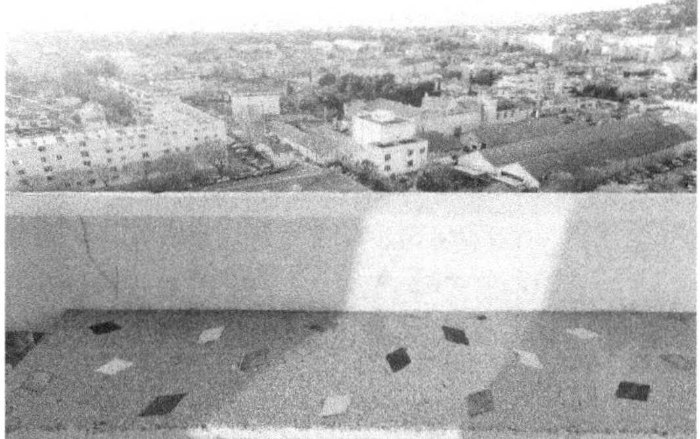

[2] See Frédéric Pouillaude, *Représentations factuelles. Art et pratiques documentaires*, Paris: Le Cerf, 2020.

[3] James Agee and Walker Evans, *Let Us Now Praise Famous Men: Three Tenant Families*, 1st edition with 31 photographs by Walker Evans, Boston: Houghton Mifflin Company, 1941, 2nd edition with 62 photographs by Walker Evans, Boston: Houghton Mifflin Company, 1961. A very complete and annotated edition was released in 2015 as the 3rd volume of James Agee's works: *James Agee: Let Us Now Praise Famous Men*, ed. by Hugh Davies, Knoxville: University of Tennessee Press, 2015.

[4] For a comment on *Let Us Now Praise Famous Men* as an alternative version of modernism, see Jacques Rancière, *Aisthesis: Scenes from the Aesthetic Regime of Art*, chap. 14: "The cruel radiance of what is", London: Verso, 2013.

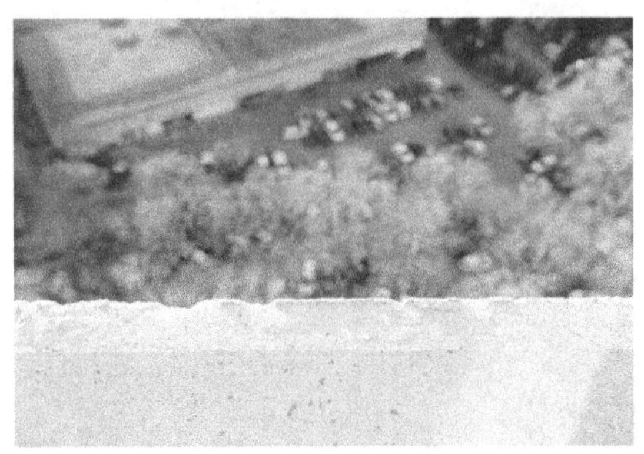

I said that opening the window and jumping out is a simple gesture. That's not true. It can be beautiful, but it implies many risks, especially when the window you jump from is situated very high. James Agee, in his work and his life, crashed to the ground many times. The experience of the 'outside' and its (highly questionable) transformation into a book or an artwork seem to have been bearable only at the cost of chain smoking and alcoholism. The first edition of *Let Us Now Praise Famous Men* in 1941 went completely unnoticed by the critics and was a complete commercial failure and James Agee died of a heart attack in 1955 at the age of 45.

But now, in 2023, what could be a 'realist modernism'? The pandemic has dramatically accelerated the general digitalization of our existences and the current post-pandemic state has conserved many structural features of the crisis. Our windows open less and less easily—not even to mention our double-locked doors—and the screens continue their inexorable invasion.

I recall my initial equations: walls = walls, windows = walls, screens = walls. In this situation fully surrounded by walls, real walls, window walls, and above all screen walls, what could be a 'realist modernism'?

I would suggest that the only gesture that remains available for a 'realist modernist' is bashing one's head against the wall again and again, not knowing exactly if the purpose is to create a breach in the wall or to destroy the head... Like in these two screenshots, respectively borrowed from *Louise-Michel* (Benoît Delépine and Gustave Kervern, 2008) and to *Gegen die Wand* (Fatih Akin, 2004).

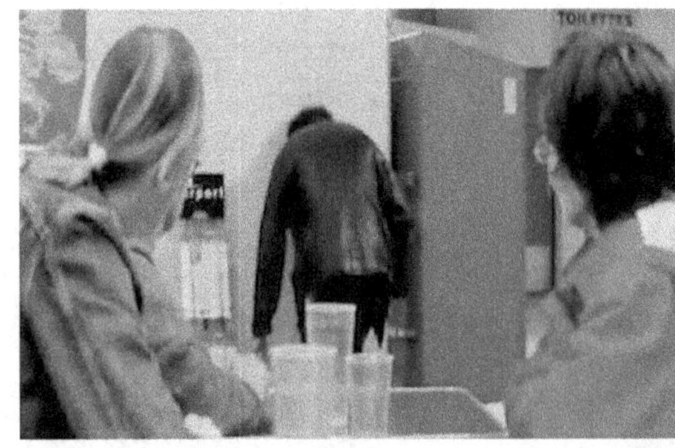

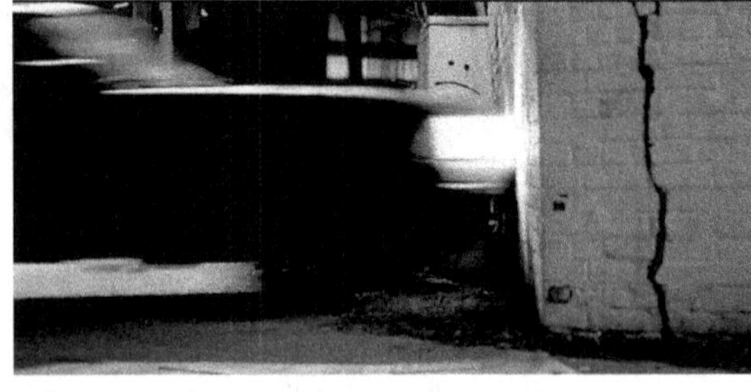

Fig. 14 — Benoît Delépine & Gustave Kervern, Screenshot from *Louise-Michel*, 2008.
Fig. 15 — Fatih Akin, Screenshot from *Gegen die Wand*, 2004.

Following this gesture, the best thing a 'realist modernist' could do, in the current post-pandemic state of pervasive derealization and imprisonment by screens, might be just organizing beautiful nihilistic rage parties...

A Palinode

One could think that, with my argument against screens, windows and walls, I consider self-protection and shielding, in life and more specifically in art, as just bad. That's not true. I remain fully aware of the fact that my own detestation of walls, windows and screens is also the reflection of a privileged position: the position of a white mid-career European male scholar. Considering global inequalities, shields, shelters and walls could be very useful elsewhere, in the right place. Speaking of 'global inequality', one should consider inequality at every level and every scale: of course, and above all, the global North-South inequality, but also the inequality at the scale of a country (for instance, in European countries, where the new slaves of the delivery and logistic industry are serving the new bureaucratic working-from-home class), or at the scale of a city (for instance, in Marseille where I live, with the strong segregation between the northern part of the city—one of the poorest areas of Europe—and the southern part, where the bourgeoisie lives), or even at the scale of a street or a building. Regarding these inequalities, my claim is that black boxes and white cubes, windows and walls, that I quickly disregarded a few lines above, could finally be pertinent as shelter and shielding, not for those who are already overprotected, but for those who are really exposed to systemic violence. But despite all that I've said, I have to declare that I love walls and shields and shelters, when they try to reverse exploitation processes, alleviate inequalities and create safe places for those who really need them.
About screens though, I still have my doubts.

All photographs without caption have been taken by the author.

References

James Agee and Walker Evans, *Let Us Now Praise Famous Men: Three Tenant Families*, 1st edition with 31 photographs by Walker Evans, Boston: Houghton Mifflin Company, 1941.

——— *Let Us Now Praise Famous Men: Three Tenant Families*, 2nd edition with 62 photographs by Walker Evans, Boston: Houghton Mifflin Company, 1961.

Walter Benjamin, "On the Concept of History", in *Illuminations: Essays and Reflections*, ed. by Hannah Arendt, New York: Schocken Books, 1968, 253–264.

Hugh Davies (ed.), *James Agee: Let Us Now Praise Famous Men*, Knoxville: University of Tennessee Press, 2015.

Frédéric Pouillaude, *Représentations factuelles. Art et pratiques documentaires*, Paris: Le Cerf, 2020.

Jacques Rancière, *Aisthesis: Scenes from the Aesthetic Regime of Art*, London: Verso, 2013.

Žiga Divjak

Gejm / The Game

People who have walked across half of the world to escape wars, persecution, violence and crushing poverty, call the last stretch of their route, the stretch that takes them from Bosnia and Herzegovina to a safe destination in the European Union, 'the game'.

The game has no rules, laws don't apply, the powers of the police are limitless, the violence is increasingly brutal, the dangers increasingly more perilous, the possibilities fewer and fewer, and the destination farther and farther away ... Many try several times, even twenty or thirty times; it's a numbers game.

For many, the game is fatal. Available records show that around twenty people have so far lost their lives at our borders.

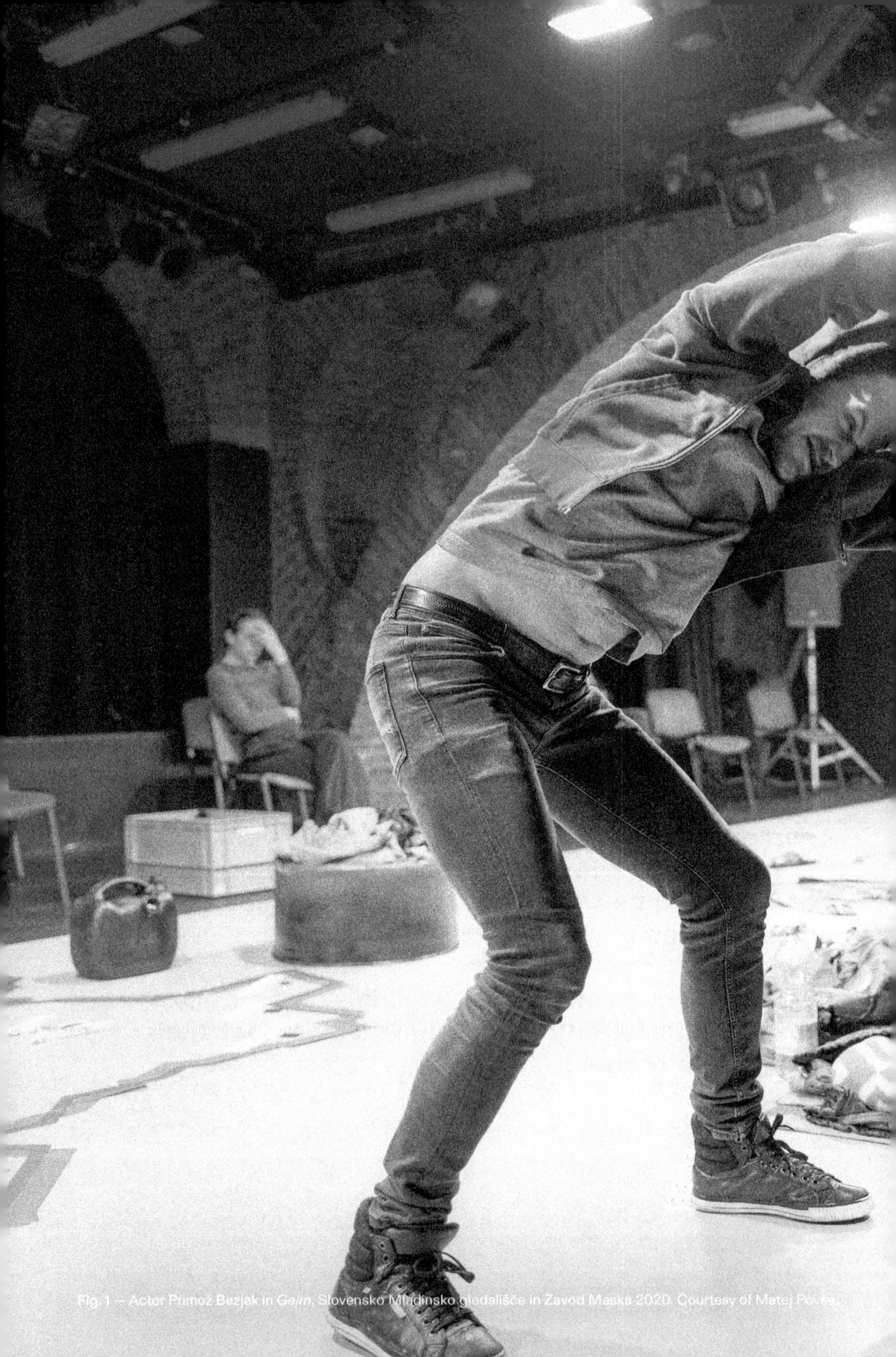

Fig. 1 — Actor Primož Bezjak in *Gejm*, Slovensko Mladinsko gledališče in Zavod Maska 2020. Courtesy of Matej Povše.

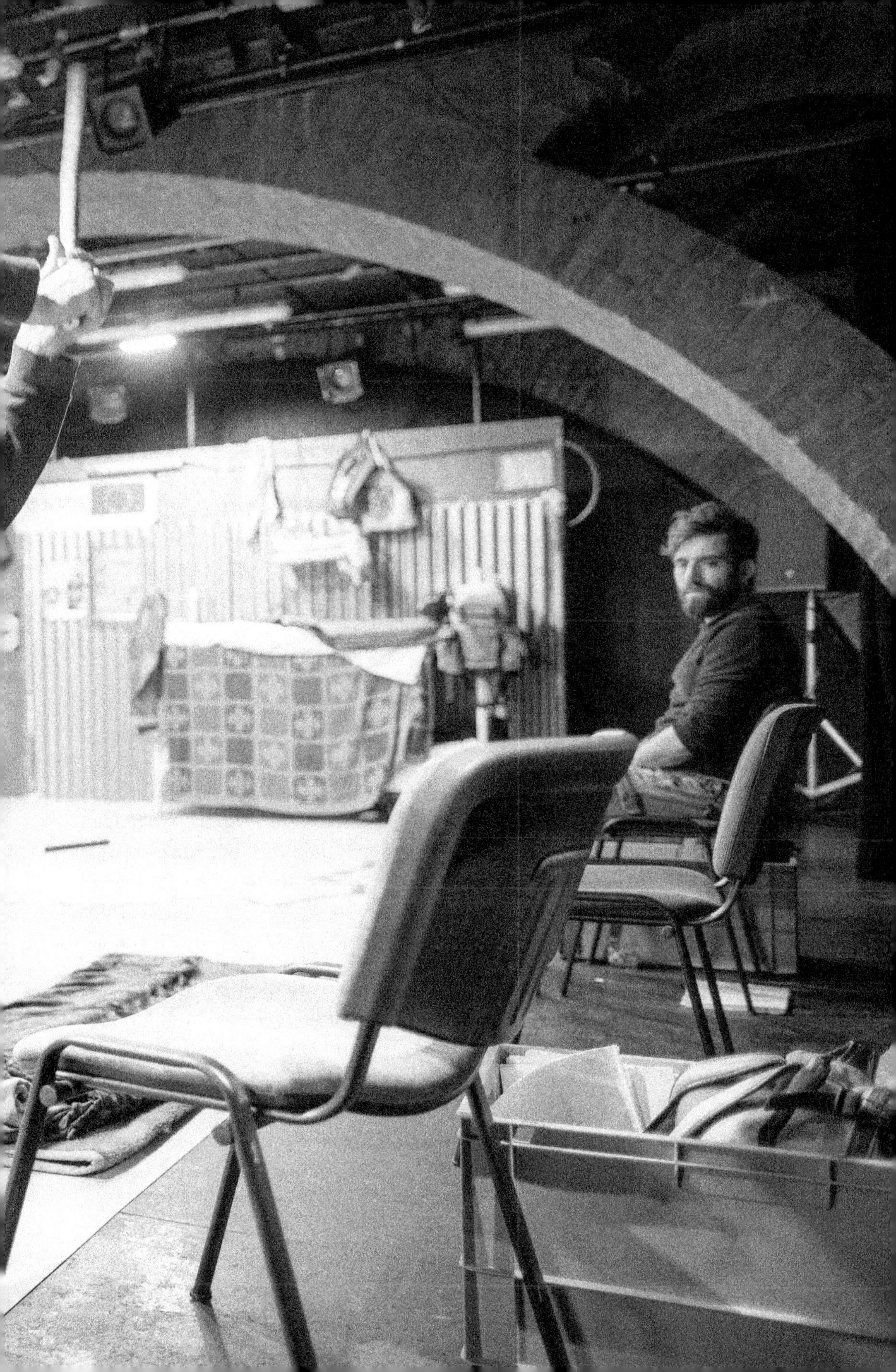

Gejm is a theatre project that problematizes the ongoing illegal practices of police violence on the Balkan migrant route. It is based on reports of 'people on the move' who are stuck in Bosnia and Herzegovina and who say that they have crossed the Slovenian border to claim asylum but were not granted their basic human right to start that procedure. Instead they were illegally returned to the Croatian police and then pushed back to Bosnia and Herzegovina. This illegal process of 'pushing back' is often accompanied by extreme violence and abuse by the Croatian police. There are regular reports of people being beaten by batons, wooden sticks, iron bars and chains. People have been kicked, thrown to the floor, undressed, have had their belongings taken from them, their passports burned and telephones destroyed. In winter they are regularly doused with cold water or forced to undress and then thrown into vans with the air conditioning on maximum. In summer they are thrown into vans without windows or ventilation and are left for hours in the sun. They are forced across rivers even if they don't know how to swim. They are bitten by police dogs. A number of reports that describe in detail the extreme violence that people on the move experience and the denial of the right to claim asylum that they face daily, show us that these are not isolated incidents but a standard procedure, in which the authorities of two European Union member states make arbitrary decisions to whom the laws, human rights and regulations apply and to whom they do not. This is a situation that should have been eradicated long ago.

The performance is staged so that the performers and audience sit together on both sides of a long narrow rectangle grey floor with a makeshift map on it, that stretches from Bosnia and Herzegovina through Croatia and Slovenia to Italy. The map features rivers, borders and names of certain places. On the Bosnian side of the map the set is divided by a replica of a wall with a bed from the migrant centre in Velika Kladuša in Bosnia and on the Italian side there is a metallic board showing the principle of non-refoulement.[1]

The performance has a three-part structure. The first part is very informative. Actors explain the legal obligations of Slovenia towards foreigners that claim asylum and introduce the statistical background to the testimonies that follow in the second part as well as some of the official responses of the state authorities. The second part is composed of

---

[1] Non-refoulement is a fundamental principle of international law that forbids a country receiving asylum seekers from returning them to a country in which they would be in danger of persecution.

chronologically ordered confessions of people on the move who have experienced violence and the denial of their right to claim asylum in Slovenia. All confessions have a very formal introduction that states the date and place of the event, the number of people involved, their nationality and the violence inflicted. This introduction gives us an investigative and formal framework for the more personal testimonies that follow. The testimonies are based on reports from NGOs working on the Croatian-Bosinan border that systematically document pushbacks. During the process of making the performance, we transformed these reports into first-person confessions. Actors don't interpret the confessions in a dramatic way, but rather present them with compassion and dedication. After each confession, an object is placed on the map where a pushback has taken place, a small action takes place and a paper report of the event is placed on the metallic board with the principle of non-refoulement written on it. During the performance, the floor is slowly covered with the traces of previous testimonies and the non-refoulement text is covered with reports that show Slovenian abuse of it on the Balkan migrant route. The third part is the shortest and it is composed of audio recordings of people that managed to claim asylum in Slovenia and are now suffering uncertainty about their legal status in Slovenia because the procedures are extremely slow and there is no certainty about how will they be resolved. People escaping violence meet extreme violence and are then welcomed by slow violence.

What follows are excerpts from the text. I have included the first part of the performance for an easier understanding of the context and three testimonies of the people on the move from the second part. The names are the names of the actors in our performance.

Excerpts from the text:

Part I:

<u>Vito:</u> As a party to the Geneva Convention and a member of the European Union, the Republic of Slovenia is required to provide international protection (asylum) to those persons who are not guaranteed such protection in the country of their nationality or permanent residence.

    <u>Maruša:</u> A foreign citizen or a person without citizenship who believes they are systematically persecuted in their country of origin because of their political beliefs or because of their religious, racial,

national or ethnic affiliation can apply for international protection. Anybody believing that their life and freedom would be endangered upon their return to their country of origin, or that they could be subjected to torture, inhumane treatment or punishment may also apply for such protection.

<u>Sara:</u> Foreigners discovered crossing a border irregularly are processed by the police for illegal crossing of the state border. If they apply for international protection, the police carries out a registration process after which they are transferred to the asylum centre where they can later officially apply for international protection. If they do not apply for international protection, the police starts the process of their return, as well as fining them for illegal crossing of the border. The key element, which dictates the procedure according to which the aliens will be processed, is thus the moment in which the person expresses the intent to apply for international protection.

<u>Primož:</u> The right of international protection is a fundamental human right, based on the right to live, prohibition of torture and inhumane treatment, and the principle of non-refoulement.

<u>Matej:</u> In June 2018, reports surfaced about refugees who lived in makeshift shelters in Velika Kladuša and Bihać and claimed that they had crossed the Slovenian border and tried to apply for asylum. When confronted with the Slovenian police, their pleas were ignored, and instead of being taken to the asylum centre, they were returned to Croatia, and from there to Bosnia and Herzegovina.

<u>Vito:</u> Numerous testimonies of foreigners that they didn't have the possibility to state their intent to apply for international protection during the police procedure are corroborated by the NGO reports and official statistical data.

<u>Sara:</u> According to the data from the Ministry of the Interior of the Republic of Slovenia, 371 persons of the 379 processed expressed the intent to apply for international protection at the police station in Črnomelj in May 2018, while in June of the same year, only 13 of the 412 processed did. In a single month the number of people applying for international protection dropped by 95%. This trend continued in the months that followed.

<u>Matej:</u> The Human Rights Ombudsman's report warned of the shortcomings of the police procedures. In it, they say that a negligible number of the officially recorded cases intended to apply for international protection at the Črnomelj police station [...] in the Ombudsman's opinion, this indicates the seriousness of the accusations that there may have been irregularities in some police procedures, including the incidents of pushbacks.

Primož: Forced returns without appropriate procedures (known as push-backs) are illegal forced operations in which the authorities prevent people from entering a country or return them to a country from which they came, and strip them of the possibility to apply for asylum.

Vito: After police procedures have been completed, the individuals are returned through so-called informal procedures, in which aliens are not issued with a formal order and they have no right to appeal or access to free legal aid.

Maruša: The fact that their returns are based on the agreement between Slovenia and Croatia on readmission does not make the procedures less unlawful—the so-called pushbacks cannot be legalised.

Sara: Such informal procedures are all the more worrisome because of the reports about police violence against migrants in Croatia and the humanitarian crisis in Bosnia and Herzegovina.

Maruša: Foreigners there live in conditions that due to the lack of housing, security, basic living necessities and poor conditions of hygiene, are not compatible with the standards of Article 3 of the European Convention on Human Rights, which prohibits torture.

Sara: The website of the Slovenian Police, in the section on "Tasks and duties of Slovenia's police related to illegal migrants" states that:

Vito: "Foreigners are never forcibly returned to countries [...] where they could be subjected to torture or inhuman or degrading treatment. Such forcible return is clearly forbidden by the Aliens Act."

Maruša: The Ministry of the Interior responds to the reports about the violence of the Croatian police towards migrants that Slovenian police returns to Croatia:

Sara: "[...] Based on individual reports from media and the statements of migrants who pursue their own, different interests, we cannot confirm that Croatian police violates international conventions of human rights."

Matej: The foreigner's testimonies and reports show that not even unaccompanied minors, a particularly vulnerable group that must be provided with particular procedural guarantees in legal proceedings, are exempt from the informal return processes.

Maruša: The General Police Directorate issued the following statement to Amnesty International and the media:

Primož: "We consider the statements about so-called pushbacks to be unsubstantiated. The Slovenian Police, despite the increased number of irregular crossings on the border with the Republic of Croatia, carries out its tasks professionally and legally and in the course of its work fully respects the rights of aliens, including the right to international protection."

Vito: In 2018 the police recorded 9,262 irregular border crossings and 4,678 stated intentions to apply for asylum.

Sara: In 2019 the police recorded 16,099 irregular border crossings and 4,991 stated intentions to apply for asylum.

Matej: Despite the 74% increase in the number of illegal crossings, the number of stated intentions only increased by 7%.

Maruša: The number of people returned to Croatia increased by 136%.

Matej: By 15 December 2019, the Republic of Slovenia erected 189,835 metres of temporary obstacles on the border with the Republic of Croatia. Of these, 115,685 metres are razor wire and 74,150 metres are panel fence.

Part II:

Primož: 27 July 2018

Near Jelšane, Slovenia
7 persons, aged 17 to 28, from Syria
Minors involved
Violence used: exposure to extreme temperature during car ride, reckless driving, destruction of documents, theft of personal belongings, pushing people to the ground, beating with batons and fists, threatening with guns, gunshots
Intention to apply for asylum in Slovenia expressed

We walked for three days and three nights, non-stop. Non-stop. We took minimal rests so that we could get to Slovenia as soon as possible. After three days, we managed it. But soon after the border, in a forest near Jelšane, the Slovenian police caught us. We told them we were from Syria and that we needed asylum. They didn't listen to us, they just took us to the border and passed us over to the Croatian police. The Croatians locked us up in a white van without windows. It was mad hot, we could barely breathe. After half an hour of driving I started getting dizzy, I started banging on a small window that was between us and the driver, I asked them if they can turn on the ventilation. *"Please. Open window. Please, air, oxygen, please."* They didn't open anything, just yelled back, *"Fuck you, no oxygen."* And then they braked suddenly, so that we all flew forward. They drove like this on purpose, so that we would get really shaken. Constantly accelerating, braking, accelerating, braking, and taking the bends in a way that made us fall all over each other. Once we got to the Bosnian border, the cops took away whatever we had, phones, money, papers. They took my 200 Euros, and from my friend, 300. They broke our phones with a metal rod. They checked our papers and talked to each other in Croatian. One cop ran away and returned with a gasoline canister, poured a little gasoline on the ground and lit a fire. The cop who held our papers started tossing them into the fire. Passport after passport. I was screaming, *"please, no, please no"*, and he was looking into my eyes laughing and just continued to throw documents into the fire. They started yelling, *"Go back to Bosnia, go back."* They started hitting us with batons and kicking us. They started shooting into the air and the ground. And we just ran. We ran like crazy, we ran until we could no longer hear the shots. A friend who got it the most went to hospital in Kladuša, but they said to him, *"Sorry, we cannot do anything for you."*

<u>Sara:</u> 26 October 2018

Slovenian–Italian border
20 persons, aged 19 to 30, from Pakistan
Violence used: beating with batons and fists, insults, destruction of personal belongings
Intention to apply for asylum in Slovenia expressed

We started off in Bihać, crossed Croatia and continued into Slovenia and after seven days we finally arrived. We arranged with smugglers to pick us up in some forest. They didn't tell us the exact hour, just where we had to be. We waited for them for five days. We ran out of food and water ... We were knackered from walking, from hunger, waiting, from everything ... After five days, a van finally showed up. We'd arranged for two vans and we said that not all twenty can go into one van. But they said that that was it, that if we wanted to, we should squeeze in, and if not, buh-bye. We had no choice and all twenty somehow crammed inside. We were driving, and when we were very close to the border with Italy, the Slovenian police stopped us. They took us to some meadow, and when the van opened, they shouted, *"You come out. One by one."* They opened the van door and pulled us out one by one. When I was waiting in the closed van, I didn't see anything, I just heard the screams of the people who exited before me. I knew that any minute now it would be my turn. I was scared like shit. The door opens, they grab me, pull me out, the direct light straight into my eyes, I can't see, and they're all wearing black, so that I don't even know where it's coming from, it's just pouring from all sides. One group of cops was standing by the van, one a little further away, and one a bit further still. And I was watching how two policemen, who were holding a man, knocked him to the ground and yelled, *"Italia?! If you want to go to Italia, go to Italia!"* They let him go, and the man started running like hell, but the second group of policemen caught him immediately, they laughed at him,

"No, no, you go to Bosnia!" They knocked him to the ground again and they beat him again. And when the second group of policemen was done with us, the third one caught us. And we got our third beating. I couldn't escape anywhere, they were everywhere. One of us was yelling, *"My arm is broken, my arm is broken!"* But they didn't stop beating him. And the worst thing was that they were laughing all along. That they were laughing while they were beating us, they were enjoying it. They took our bags, phones, money, chargers and forced us back to Bosnia. Everything hurt, my entire body. I could feel how the blood was coming from the inside. I remember that I suddenly just collapsed … And I was just lying there … Alone. I was lying like that for a long time. Once I pulled myself back together, more or less, I started thinking how can I now call my friends, how can I get to Kladuša … My legs hurt so much they shook all by themselves. Somehow I dragged myself to some road. I saw a man, asked him for some water, and he gave it to me. Then he went. I watched him enter a bar. I stood there for a while, then I went.

<u>Matej:</u> 8 November 2018

Vinica, Slovenia
19 persons, aged 16 to 30, from Afghanistan
Minors involved
Violence used: beating with batons and fists, theft and destruction of personal belongings
Intention to apply for asylum in Slovenia expressed

We started somewhere between Velika Kladuša and Bihać. We walked for five days across Croatia and on the sixth day we crossed the border with Slovenia, by crossing the river. We weren't the best swimmers, but we had plastic garbage bags with us, and we blew them up and tied them, so that they floated a bit and we held onto them. When we got to the Slovenian side, somewhere near Vinica the Slovenian police caught us. They took us to the police station. In our group were two boys, aged 16 and 17, and they clearly stated that they would like to apply for asylum in Slovenia. And they put it into the form, too, that their end destination was Slovenia. But the cop simply crossed out what they wrote on the paper, and wrote Italy himself. And they said, *"No, no, mister, please. Minors, we minors."* And the cops just said, *"No minors in this group."*
The next day they passed us over to the Croatian police around ten in the morning. The Croatians put us in a van, without food, without water, and we were in this van until half past eleven at night, when they took us and three other vans towards the Bosnian border. Around three a.m. we

stopped on a gravel road. The cops opened the door. They had strong headlights on their helmets, and they pointed them directly into our eyes. They were standing in two long rows down the hill. At the top of the hill, there was a huge barrel of water, which they emptied, so that it was all soggy and slippery. They opened the door, three of us have to go out and they closed the door. We had to go between two rows of cops, while they beat us, pounded, kicked … And then again, they open the door, three out, they close the door, pounding, beating, kicking, open the door, three out, close the door … And you run between those two rows of cops so that you'd get out of the tunnel as quickly as possible, the tunnel in which everybody's kicking you pounding on you, beating you, and of course you slip and fall, and when you fall, they kick even harder, they hit even harder, with batons, and scream, *"Go, go, go!"*

And you get up, you slip, you fall, harder. *"Go, go, go"*, you get up again, you fall, *"go, go, go."* Beneath the hill is a forest and the Bosnian border. I barely dragged myself down the hill, and when I got to the forest I just collapsed. For ten minutes, I just sat and breathed.

In the other van was a family: father, mother and a child. They didn't beat the mother and the child. The father, yes.

When we went through the forest and got to the Bosnian side, we met a man who said he could take us to Velika Kladuša, but for ten Euros a person. There were five of us, and all we had hidden away was twenty Euros, but the man said it was fine and took us.

GEJM / THE GAME
Directed by: Žiga Divjak
Cast: Primož Bezjak, Sara Dirnbek, Maruša Oblak, Matej Puc, Vito Weis
Featured on the recording: Hamza Aziz, Zaher Amini, Khalid Ali, Behnaz Aliesfahanipour
Research assistant: Maja Ava Žiberna
Dramaturgical collaborator: Katarina Morano
Set design: Igor Vasiljev
Costume design: Tina Pavlović
Music and sound design: Blaž Gracar
Speech advisor: Mateja Dermelj
Lighting design and stage manager: Igor Remeta
Production and stage manager: Tina Dobnik
Assistants director: Ana Lorger, Nika Prusnik Kardum
Co-production: Mladinsko Theatre and Maska Ljubljana

The text of the performance is based on testimonies from the Border Violence Monitoring Network, see database https://borderviolence.eu/, accessed 23 February 2024.
Premiere: 10 June 2020

Cikacé Lestine and Sandra Umathum

Hands Up!
On the Inequalities of a Global Bodily Vernacular

Two hands held up with palms facing out is a gesture everyone is familiar with. We know it from films, from literature and media coverage. We've known it since childhood—from role-playing games, from television or children's books—and already by then we learned that this gesture should be able to ward off threat and attack. The gesture demonstrates that a person is not carrying arms and that at this very moment, they are posing no danger—and the demonstration is emphasized by the cessation of movement; the standstill of the body it often accompanies. Hands raised into the air can also be a sign for surrender, for a person being ready to be removed or even arrested. It is a gesture that is, in other words, part of an agreement, conveyed by the command, "Hands up!" and the threat, "Or I'll shoot!" According to this agreement, the lifting of the hands is the condition for not firing, and is therefore dependent on the reliability of the person holding the gun not to carry out violence while the hands are lifted. If the agreement is intact, the raised hands cause a shielding effect that, by preventing a shot, ensures the integrity of a body and possibly the preservation of a life.

The US-based Kenyan author, researcher and blogger Keguro Macharia calls the hands up gesture and its inherent aspect of shielding a "global bodily vernacular"[1]. It means the same everywhere. Yet neither does it guarantee protection in all contexts nor does it protect all bodies to the same degree. The recurring violations of this global bodily vernacular give a very clear picture of both the situations in which the shielding effect of raised hands is suspended (e.g. in wars, in mass shootings or in killing sprees) and of the bodies that can rely on the shielding effect of the raised hands less than others. This distinction between bodies; respectively the

[1] Keguro Macharia, "Hands up, don't shoot" (15 August 2014), https://gukira.wordpress.com/2014/08/15/hands-up-dont-shoot/, accessed 15 August 2023.

exposedness of bodies to different degrees of vulnerability are nothing other than one significant manifestation of discrimination (race, ethnicity, gender identity, class, religion, disability etc.) that is confirmed by numerous examples around the world. In the following, we will narrow the focus primarily to the US American context, where in recent years the hands up gesture has played a central role in debates around the unequal right to self-defence and where the repeated violations of this gesture's shielding effect by police officers are intrinsically intertwined with the Black Lives Matter movements.

In the US, the greatest cause of civilian death by the state results from police officers' use of firearms. According to the *Mapping Police Violence* database, the number of Black people shot and killed since 2013 is nearly three times greater than the number of white people.[2] On the basis of this data the sociologist Reed T. DeAngelis points out that Black victims, "were less likely than their White peers to [...] be armed at the scene of their killings, and more likely to flee the scene."[3] The data do not provide any information about how many of the people that were killed tried to ward off the gunshot by raising their hands. In most cases, however, it includes a brief description of the situation and the officer's reason for firing a shot. Almost all reasons are related to the officer's right to self-defence or the defence of others.[4] But how to evaluate the level of (real) danger in a split second? And what level of danger and risk will justify deadly force?

> The officer approaches the driver's door and taps the window. Khalil cranks the handle to roll it down. As if we aren't blinded enough, the officer beams his flashlight in our faces.
> "License, registration, and proof of insurance."
> Khalil breaks a rule—he doesn't do what the cop wants. "What you pull us over for?"
> "License, registration, and proof of insurance."
> "I said what you pull us over for?"
> "Khalil," I plead. "Do what he said."

---

[2] See Mapping Police Violence, https://mappingpoliceviolence.org, accessed 15 August 2024.
[3] Reed T. DeAngelis, "Systemic Racism in Police Killings: New Evidence From the Mapping Police Violence Database, 2013–2021", *Race and Justice*, 0(0) (2021), https://journals.sagepub.com/doi/10.1177/21533687211047943, accessed 15 August 2024.
[4] See Mapping Police Violence, https://mappingpoliceviolence.org/?year=2024&location=the+U.S.&race=people, accessed 15 August 2024.

Khalil groans and takes his wallet out. The officer follows his movements with the flashlight.

My heart pounds loudly, but Daddy's instructions echo in my head: *Get a good look at the cop's face. If you can remember his badge number, that's even better.*

With the flashlight following Khalil's hands, I make out the numbers on the badge—one-fifteen. He's white, midthirties to early forties, has a brown buzz cut and a thin scar over his top lip.

Khalil hands the officer his papers and license.

One-Fifteen looks over them. "Where are you two coming from tonight?"

"Nunya," Khalil says, meaning none of your business. "What you pull me over for?"

"Your taillight's broken."

"So are you gon' give me a ticket or what?" Khalil asks.

"You know what? Get out the car, smart guy."

"Man, just give me my ticket—"

"Get out the car! Hands up, where I can see them."

Khalil gets out with his hands up. One-Fifteen yanks him by his arm and pins him against the back door.

[...]

"You ain't gon' find nothing," Khalil says.

One-Fifteen pats him down two more times. He turns up empty.

"Stay here," he tells Khalil. "And you," he looks in the window at me. "Don't move."

I can't even nod.

The officer walks back to his patrol car.

My parents haven't raised me to fear the police, just to be smart around them. They told me it's not smart to move while a cop has his back to you.

Khalil does. He comes to his door.

It's not smart to make a sudden move.

Khalil does. He opens the driver's door.

"You okay, Starr—"

Pow![5]

The use-of-force policy of the US Justice Department states that the use of deadly force is justified under conditions of extreme necessity only. In one paragraph it says that "[a]n officer may use deadly force to protect

[5] Angie Thomas, *The Hate U Give*, New York: HarperCollins Publishers, 2017, 21–23.

himself/herself or others from what he/she reasonably believe [sic] would be an imminent threat of death or serious bodily injury."[6] One of the main problems starts here, by declaring the officers' subjective assessment as the criterion for classifying actions and behaviours as threats. Legally, it means the 'reasonable belief' of an officer that their own life or the lives of others were in danger is prioritized over the real threat posed by an action or behaviour. Yet the gesture of reaching into a pocket or into the glove compartment that many films, novels or witness cell phones depict as the trigger for deadly force is often just the consequence of an officer's request to see a document. The alleged refusal to comply with a police officer's command has time and again turned out to be just the inability to do so: There are people—and these are not rare exceptions—who get shot, because they are deaf and cannot hear the verbal police orders or because they experience a mental health crisis and fail to follow instructions. Between 25 and 50% of people killed by the police are disabled. And then there are people who get shot even though they raised their hands into the air.

In the US, the average length of core basic police training is less than 22 weeks,[7] "with an emphasis on weapons and tactics and too little focus on decision-making, communications and other critical thinking skills that officers use every day."[8]

In many cases, 'citizen camera witnessing'[9] has proven to be essential in challenging police justification for the killing of citizens. In France, for example, Nahel Merzouk, a teenager of North African descent was shot dead in his car during a police intervention in June 2023. Without questioning it, the media spread the police officer's version: that he had decided to shoot because the young man was about to run him over—

[6] See UCLA Police Department, "Use of Force", https://police.ucla.edu/other/use-of-force, accessed 15 August 2024.
[7] "In comparison, police recruits in Japan get between 15 and 21 months of training. Police in Germany get 2.5 years of training. And in Finland, police education takes three years to complete." Jack Date, "Why police training in the US falls short compared to the rest of the world: Report", in *ABC News* (15 February 2023), https://abcnews.go.com/US/police-training-us-falls-short-compared-rest-world/story?id =96727748#:~:text=A%202018%20Justice%20Department%20study,or%20less%20than%20 22%20weeks, accessed 15 August 2024.
[8] Date, "Why police training in the US falls short compared to the rest of the world".
[9] See Kari Andén-Papadopolous, "Citizen camera-witnessing: Embodied political dissent in the 'age of mediated self-communication'", in New Media & Society, 16(5) (2014).

a version that thanks to the publication of a video portraying the scene—could be proven wrong.[10]

Taking pictures, recording incidences and 'shooting (back)' with cameras are important and effective means against the crimes of police officers. It is, as Kari Andén-Papadopoulos, professor in Media and Communication Studies at the University of Stockholm, states, a form of "embodied political dissent in the age of mediated mass self-communication"[11]. Attempts to put a stop to citizen camera-witnessing even by law, only underlines the effectiveness of the pictures and videos participants or bystanders produce. In 2021, the French government tried to pass a bill to ban filming police officers and disseminating photos or videos of them "with intent to harm"[12]. In the end, the law was judged unconstitutional and then rejected.

Beyond the legal, social and symbolic frames around the hands up gesture, the global understanding of it first and foremost stems from the ethical dimension of the relationality it creates. An unarmed person who raises their hands in front of someone holding a weapon pointed at them induces a very specific constellation with another human being—a constellation that is often face-to-face. The philosopher Emmanuel Lévinas theorized the encounter with the face of the Other as an initial and essential ethical moment. According to Levinas, a face-to-face encounter is a fundamental experience of alterity, as it confronts us with the nakedness and the extreme vulnerability of a face directly calling for our responsibility towards them. The face can also be seen as the mediator of the relationship to Otherness and the key to intersubjectivity. It is, *in fine*, "what forbids us to kill"[13]—which might explain why in many cases people are being shot in the back or with their faces or eyes covered. Lévinas underlines that this ethical relationship exists beyond any cultural or social context. It is a primary sensitive experience. Therefore, to shoot when hands are raised is more than the violation of an agreement and more than the betrayal of the shielding effects it is supposed to imply. It is a

---

[10] See Antoine Albertini, "Clashes erupt in Paris suburbs after police officer kills 17-year-old driver", in *Le Monde* (28 June 2023), https://www.lemonde.fr/en/france/article/2023/06/28/tensions-erupt-in-paris-suburb-after-police-officer-put-in-custody-over-death-of-17-year-old_6038689_7.html, accessed 15 August 2024.

[11] Andén-Papadopolous, "Citizen camera-witnessing".

[12] Reporter without Borders (RSF): "France: As it stands, ban on filming police 'with intent to harm' would threaten press freedom", in *Reporters without Borders* (6 November 2020), https://rsf.org/en/france-it-stands-ban-filming-police-intent-harm-would-threaten-press-freedom, accessed 15 August 2024.

[13] Emmanuel Lévinas, *Ethics and Infinity: Conversations with Philippe Nemo*, Pittsburgh: Duquesne University Press, 2011, 86.

wilful killing, which is an infringement against humanity. This is why it is so necessary to continue to be attentive to the contexts in which this gesture has become inefficient and in which it has failed to protect one's life. Which bodies could not be protected by this gesture? Whose humanity has been denied? Whose vulnerability, integrity and dignity have been negated? Whose bodies have, in doing so, been othered?

"Blackness is", as Keguro Macharia puts it, "the great alchemy of social relations: it transforms hands reaching into pockets into weapons of mass destruction, wallets and brooms and keys and phones into machines whose wielders must be destroyed, proximity into justification for violence and murder."[14] The systemic and structural racism in police power and police killings sits exactly here: in the production and reproduction of distinctions between (groups of) people, in the applications of double standards, in the difference in responses to the raised hands, and thereby, in the regulation of the unequal vulnerability of bodies.[15] "[B]lack life forms", Keguro Machiaria says, "do not have access to vernaculars of the human, no matter how global the circulation of those vernaculars."[16]

Anusha Kedhar, scholar and practitioner of dance, describes the way the hands up gesture has become part of the black body's habitus.[17] In anticipation of a possible face-to-face encounter with the police in a society where "the presence of black bodies in public spaces is seen as de facto threatening"[18], young Black people are taught how to behave in such encounters by their parents. The hands up gesture is and keeps on becoming "part of the black body's repertoire of survival"[19]. However, young Black people have to learn a gesture that does not even guarantee the protection of their lives. Blackness is specifically the element that turns this gesture into a potentially "failed sign", as Kedhar says: it transforms

[14] Macharia, "Hands up, don't shoot".

[15] As the case of Tyra Nichols, a Black man who was killed by five Black police officers, shows: racism does not only happen to Black people, "it also happens through them", as Theodore R. Johnson writes: "Blacks and whites receive the same narratives and images that perpetuate [...]." Theodore R. Johnson: "Black-on-Black Racism: The Hazards of Implicit Bias. How the politics of respectability twists society", in *The Atlantic* (26 December 2014), https://www.theatlantic.com/politics/archive/2014/12/black-on-black-racism-the-hazards-of-implicit-bias/384028/, accessed 15 August 2024.

[16] Macharia, "Hands up, don't shoot".

[17] Anusha Kedhar, "Hands up! Don't Shoot!: Gesture, Choreography, and Protest in Ferguson", in *The Feminist Wire* (October 6, 2014), https://thefeministwire.com/2014/10/protest-in-ferguson/, accessed 15 August 2024.

[18] Kedhar, "Hands up! Don't Shoot."

[19] Kedhar, "Hands up! Don't Shoot."

"this universal gesture of submission into a gesture of guilt, criminality and culpability"[20].

> "Blackness becomes the break in this global bodily vernacular, the error that makes this bodily action illegible, the disposability that renders the gesture irrelevant."[21]

The US-American television series *Atlanta*, created by Donald Glover, is set in a universe incredibly close to ours, but with unsettling and cynical twists that provoke reflections on the society we live in. The ninth episode of the third season ("Rich Wigga, Poor Wigga") deals with the question of structural racism and the way it interplays with police violence. The story follows a light-skinned, mixed-raced teenager Aaron (Tyriq Withers), who gets into a fight with Felix (Tireny Oyenusi), a Black student from his high school, after both were denied a scholarship to college that was offered to Black students only. For different reasons, both of them were considered "not Black enough" by the school board. After chasing each other with home-made flamethrowers, Felix finally manages to pin down the unarmed Aaron by standing on a wall, before Felix then gets shot by a police officer. Aaron puts his hands up in the air and turns towards the police officer. While unfolding the complexity of Black experience and the Black bodies' entanglement in multiple dimensions of oppression and privilege, this episode also shows how in certain moments the most immediate, shallow perception of a situation is the only thing that counts. In this case, the racist bias related to skin colour (one is read as Black, the other one as White, one as a potential danger, the other one not) becomes effective and threatens Felix's life without even giving him the chance to raise his hands up before he gets shot. The episode ends in a bittersweet, cynical plot twist: when he is carried away by the ambulance, he is granted the money for the scholarship with the reasoning that "getting shot by the police is the Blackest thing anybody can do".

Many have pointed out that in the US the history of white supremacy and Anti-Blackness continues and is thus continuously updated in police operations—and not least in the assessments by numerous officers who set the level of danger to their own lives or the lives of others so

[20] Kedhar, "Hands up! Don't Shoot."
[21] Macharia, "Hands up, don't shoot".

high that the use of lethal firearms seems justified. But many of these assessments and the actions that proceed from them neither look like the result of objective examinations nor do they appear to be reasonable belief. Rather, they represent a long-rehearsed and practised behaviour that scholar and director Lindsay Livingston described as the repetition of "previous choreographies of engagement"[22]. What is repeated is in fact more than the previous choreographies of engagement. Every repetition is—as the German word for repetition (*Wiederholung*) implies—a bringing back (*Wieder-Holung*) of the disparity between cause and effect. Every repeated disparity cements its racist (or discriminatory) structure and grounding. Every repeated disparity strengthens the belief in the rationality of this treatment. And every repeated disparity consolidates the threat to people who are to be confronted with this disparity because of their skin colour (or their class, their religion, their gender). Against this backdrop, what form of self-defence can the hands up gesture still claim, if innocence and vulnerability are suspected of not being an option?

"Gestures carry calls"[23], performance scholar Rebecca Schneider writes. They allow a response to happen. They allow responsible responses to happen. They allow responses to happen that change and challenge the dominant narrative.

In popular culture the recurring presence of scenes picturing violent encounters between Black citizens and policemen, sometimes with dramatic outcomes, echoes Anusha Kedhar's notion of the lifted hands as a gesture of the Black body's repertoire and reveals how much it has become widely acknowledged as part of the Black experience. Fictional artworks cannot be taken as proofs of reality, of course. Nonetheless, they mirror and reveal the collective imaginary and the rooted fear around police violence, a violence that is based on facts. Like the movie *Queen and Slim* (2019) by Melina Matsoukas and Lena Waithe, in which Slim (Daniel Kaluuya) drives Queen (Jodie Turner) back to her place after a failed first Tinder date, when they get stopped by a police officer because Slim switches lanes without signalling. The police officer is aggressive

[22] Lindsay Livingston, "Good [Black] Guys With Guns: Performance and the Anti-Black Logic of US Gun Culture", in *Lateral. Journal of the Cultural Studies Association*, Issue 9.1 (Spring 2020), https://csalateral.org/forum/gun-culture/good-black-guys-with-guns-livingston/, accessed 15 August 2024.
[23] Rebecca Schneider, "That the Past May Yet Have Another Future: Gesture in the Times of Hands Up", *Theatre Journal*, Volume 70, Number 3 (2018).

from the start of the intervention and seems to enjoy the power play and his unjustified checking of the car. Slim knows that complaining is not an option and that not responding is the best response.

> Police Officer: License and registration.
> *Slim reaches for his wallet.*
> Slim: I'm grabbing my wallet.
> Police Officer: I can see that.
> Queen: *(under her breath)* Well, y'all like to shoot first and ask questions later.
> [...]
> Queen: I can't believe this shit.
> Slim: Just chill.
> *She doesn't like being told what to do.*
> Queen: Excuse me?
> Slim: I told you to chill out.
> Queen: I have a right to be angry.
> Slim: I ain't tryna die tonight.[24]

It is Queen, the female character, who responds to the officer with defiance. Later, when the situation escalates and the officer pulls his gun and points it at Slim, she again refuses to surrender to fear. Indeed, she is an attorney. She knows her rights, so instead of blindly obeying the officer she decides to reach for her phone and film the scene.

> Police Officer: Ma'am if you don't get back in the car I'm gonna have to arrest you too.
> Queen: I'm happy to get back in the car, but would you mind telling me why you're arresting him?
> Police Officer: Get back in the vehicle now!
> Queen: I'm reaching for my cell phone—
> Police Officer: Keep your hands where I can see them!!
> Queen: I have the right to record this arrest.
> *Queen REACHES in her pocket. Officer Reed AIMS HIS GUN AT HER and FIRES OFF TWO SHOTS. BOOM! BOOM!*[25]

Queen and Slim are realistically portrayed as being aware of a society where violence towards Black bodies is omnipresent, repetitive and

---

[24] Lena Waithe, *Queen & Slim* (Screenplay), https://thescriptsavant.com/movies/Queen_&_Slim.pdf, accessed 15 August 2024.
[25] Waithe, *Queen & Slim*.

abusive. They are conscious of the danger they find themselves in. We the viewers know what may happen and they know it as well. And we know that they know: "Just as [Slim] starts to pick up speed. He hears a horrifying sound. WOOP WOOP. Every black person's worst nightmare."[26] The threat of (sudden) police violence has become common knowledge. It is all the more remarkable to have a victim depicted as not 'passive', as not obedient and extremely cautious. Queen's attitude may seem 'aggressive' towards the officer, who is entirely unprepared to de-escalate the situation. Yet she is only exercising her rights—which also is a reminder that this kind of response does not justify being shot.

Representations in popular culture are tricky. Is it better to show reality (at the risk of repeating the same narrative over and over again), or to create new narratives (as utopian as they may be)? Jordan Peele, the director of *Get Out* (2017), was confronted with this very question.[27] After having been trapped by his girlfriend's family into a covert racist human trafficking network, the young Black protagonist Chris (Daniel Kaluuya) tries to escape their house. In the first version of the closing of the film, the police arrive as Chris is strangling his girlfriend in an attempt to end her life before she murders him. He gets up, his hands up in the air, while the two police officers point their guns at him. He then gets arrested and unjustly sent to prison, where he finds himself surrounded by other Black men. But Peele decided to change the outcome of the movie. In a context where society was becoming more and more aware of police violence, he felt that people "needed a release and a hero"[28]. In the new ending, Chris cannot bring himself to kill his girlfriend. As he hears a patrol car arriving, he puts his hands up in the air, looking desperate, while she tries to call for help, knowing she will be taken to be the victim. At this very moment, the two characters as well as the audience know perfectly well what will happen if a policemen gets out of the car. But it is not a policemen who gets out of the car. It is Chris' friend, a TSA (Transportation Security Administration) officer, who comes to rescue him and together they escape. The decision to change the end is significant: it introduces another narrative because, as Peele puts it, "people needed a release [...]"[29], from these endings both in movies and in real life.

[26] Waithe, *Queen & Slim*.
[27] See Jordan Peele: "Commentary on Alternate Ending",
https://www.youtube.com/watch?v=JUMGzioWST4, accessed 15 August 2024.
[28] Peele: "Commentary on Alternate Ending".
[29] Peele: "Commentary on Alternate Ending".

On the 9th of August 2014, Michael Brown, a Black 18-year-old, was shot dead by a white police officer in Ferguson, Missouri. The first testimonies stated that the young man had his arms up and begged the policeman not to shoot. In the following weeks many witnesses changed their testimonies, and although the investigations could not conclusively determine what had really happened—whether Brown had raised his hands and whether or not the policeman had fired six times(!), out of 'pure' self-defence—shortly after this incident "Hands up, don't shoot" became a rallying cry. And with it the embodied gesture evolved as the symbol of national and also international protests against police brutality towards unarmed Black people, thus outgrowing the reference to this sole case.

In the context of these protests, the gesture expanded its meaning. Its reiteration became a sign for solidarity with Brown and other victims. It became a denunciation of police brutality towards minorities. It became a joint choreography demonstrating, as Kedhar puts it, "non-cooperation with an unjust and racist state"[30]. It became a reminder of the fact that in white spaces, Black bodies can never rely on being presumed innocent and that for Black persons, raised hands do not reliably serve as a shield (which is why it ultimately makes no difference whether Brown and the many others had or had not raised their hands). The reiterated gesture transformed itself into a political strategy for demanding change and for stopping the mistreatment of minorities. It shifted its meaning from a representation of surrender and subjection to an act of power and defiance, from being a response to a call: a call to fight, to resist, to precisely not surrender—a call that challenges and provokes a response from the police, from the government, from the public. It became, as Rebecca Schneider says, "a call to a different future"[31].

Yet there were people who refused to raise their hands during these protests. As this gesture had proven to be ineffective in contexts of structural racism, not putting one's hands up became in itself an act of resistance. Became a sign of refusal to reperform a gesture which has so often been disrespected and therefore unable to function as the shield it should actually function as.

[30] Kedhar, "Hands up! Don't Shoot!"
[31] Rebecca Schneider and Lucia Ruprecht, "In Our Hands: An Ethics of Gestural Response-ability. Rebecca Schneider in Conversation with Lucia Ruprecht", in *Performance Philosophy* 3, No. 1 (2017), https://www.performancephilosophy.org/journal/article/view/161/173 , accessed 15 August 2024.

References

Antoine Albertini, "Clashes erupt in Paris suburbs after police officer kills 17-year-old driver", in *Le Monde* (28 June 2023), https://www.lemonde.fr/en/france/article/2023/06/28/tensions-erupt-in-paris-suburb-after-police-officer-put-in-custody-over-death-of-17-year-old_6038689_7.html

Kari Andén-Papadopolous, "Citizen camera-witnessing: Embodied political dissent in the 'age of mediated self-communication'", in *New Media & Society*, 16(5) (2014), 753–769.

Jack Date, "Why police training in the US falls short compared to the rest of the world: Report", in *ABC News* (15 February 2023), https://abcnews.go.com/US/police-training-us-falls-short-compared-rest-world/story?id =96727748#:~:text=A%202018%20Justice%20Department%20study,or%20less%20than%2022%20weeks

Reed T. DeAngelis, "Systemic Racism in Police Killings: New Evidence From the Mapping Police Violence Database, 2013–2021", *Race and Justice*, 0(0) (2021), https://journals.sagepub.com/doi/10.1177/21533687211047943

Anusha Kedhar, "Hands up! Don't Shoot!: Gesture, Choreography, and Protest in Ferguson", in *The Feminist Wire* (October 6, 2014), https://thefeministwire.com/2014/10/protest-in-ferguson/

Emmanuel Levinas, *Ethics and Infinity: Conversations with Philippe Nemo*, Pittsburgh: Duquesne University Press, 2011.

Lindsay Livingston, "Good [Black] Guys With Guns: Performance and the Anti-Black Logic of US Gun Culture", in *Lateral. Journal of the Cultural Studies Association*, Issue 9.1 (Spring 2020), https://csalateral.org/forum/gun-culture/good-black-guys-with-guns-livingston/

Keguro Macharia, "Hands up, don't shoot" (15 August 2014), https://gukira.wordpress.com/2014/08/15/hands-up-dont-shoot/

Mapping Police Violence, https://mappingpoliceviolence.org; https://mappingpoliceviolence.org/?year=2024&location=the+U.S.&race=people

Jordan Peele, "Commentary on Alternate Ending", https://www.youtube.com/watch?v=JUMGzioWST4

Reporter without Borders (RSF), "France: As it stands, ban on filming police 'with intent to harm' would threaten press freedom", in *Reporters without Borders* (6 November 2020), https://rsf.org/en/france-it-stands-ban-filming-police-intent-harm-would-threaten-press-freedom

Rebecca Schneider, "That the Past May Yet Have Another Future: Gesture in the Times of Hands Up", *Theatre Journal*, Volume 70, Number 3 (2018), 285–306.

Rebecca Schneider and Lucia Ruprecht, "In Our Hands: An Ethics of Gestural Response-ability. Rebecca Schneider in Conversation with Lucia Ruprecht", in *Performance Philosophy* 3, No. 1 (2017), 108–25, https://www.performancephilosophy.org/journal/article/view/161/173

Angie Thomas, *The Hate U Give*, New York: HarperCollins Publishers, 2017.

UCLA Police Department, "Use of Force", https://police.ucla.edu/other/use-of-force

Lena Waithe, *Queen & Slim* (Screenplay), https://thescriptsavant.com/movies/Queen_&_Slim.pdf

What it Takes: A Life in Activism

Sophia New

As part of the Research Week in 2022 at the HZT-Inter-University Centre for Dance Berlin we are looking into different practices and contexts in which bodies turn into shields, either by choice or by force. In the following conversation we will explore your experience as an eco-activist, particularly some of the body-based strategies that you have been sharing with us in your workshop in the last few days. You have also brought a collection of images to share with us that act as a mnemonic trigger for actions that you were directly involved in or knew very well.

Hanna Poddig

Thanks for inviting me. Let's start with a photo from the Hambach Forest Occupation, circa 2014, which has recently become the most well-known forest occupation in Germany. In this context, many people were sent to prison for their acts of resistance in the forest. Some of them because they refused to give their ID, which is illegal in Germany. This act of resistance was not that common before the actions in Hambach Forest and the protests of *Ende Gelände*.[1] People would refuse to give their IDs by, for example, putting glue or glitter on their fingers to avoid fingerprints being taken, or they would not say anything that might inform the cops which languages these people speak. These practices have resulted in prison sentences, and part of the work around the Hambach Forest Occupation included solidarity work for them.

[1] Ende Gelände started in 2015 and is a grassroots organization consisting of climate activists from the anti-nuclear and anti-coal movements, who believe in using direct action and civil disobedience.

Sophia New
Can you tell us a little bit more about the things that were constructed for specific actions?

Hanna Poddig
At times we have used large wooden tripods, as a construction to block things. For example, we put them on top of a caravan that someone had taken the roof off, then dug a hole and sank it into the ground to block the building of a slaughterhouse. Inside the caravan they built a concrete lock-on construction and on top of this construction they put the tripod. In this way, it's possible to combine many different types of direct action to try to stop the construction of a slaughterhouse.

Sophia New
So basically it's a delaying tactic, a strategy to actually make it difficult to just roll off a caravan by making it heavier and more cumbersome.

Hanna Poddig
Sometimes the success of these blocking actions is not to prevent eviction in that actual location, but to make decision-makers who plan something in other places understand that it will be a lot of work to get rid of these people and that they should reconsider their plans. For example in 2020, a group of around 20 people including myself went to a site where there were plans for a liquid gas terminal in Brunsbüttel, an industrial harbour town in northern Germany. We put up two tripods and said, if you really start constructing here, we will come back. Then one year later *Ende Gelände* went there to do a mass action against a large terminal and now it seems that because of one of the mass actions the investors said they were pulling out. This project will probably not be realized in Brunsbüttel. Of course, we can't be sure that they won't find another site, but then it's years of delay. And hopefully in the intervening years, gas won't be seen as a good solution any longer, but as the dirty fossil fuel that it is. We also use tunnel systems. Some of the tunnels are really, really small you can't turn around inside them and they go deep underground. One such tunnel was dug six metres beneath the ground in Hambach Forest to make it more difficult to evict the forest occupation. It was cleared in 2012, and there was a person inside, down in a 'room' at the end of the tunnel system. I think it was 14 metres in length. The idea came from the UK, where people had built tunnel

systems before to protect the forests. As far as I know, it is the biggest tunnel of its kind that has ever been dug in Germany.

Sophia New

In the workshop you told us about what it's actually like to go to these sites. It was interesting to hear your experiences about them and that the police sometimes didn't really believe that somebody was down there. How do you decide what information to give to the police, and when to withhold information? How did someone eventually convince the police that there was someone in the tunnel?

Hanna Poddig

I think it's a very personal decision—the decision of the person going into this tunnel system, which I would never ever dare do. I think it's up to this person to speak in advance with the people supporting them about the information they give and about how to communicate it. As the police did not believe that there was really someone in there, the activist supporters started a huge media campaign to try to make the media focus on the police not believing and thereby endangering this person's life. It is always a difficult decision. How long can a blockade or an action stop an eviction or lead to more media interest? And when do we focus on safety? Over the years, we have done many of these blockades with the tripods and then we had the feeling that we were always doing the same, so we had to do something else.

Sophia New

That's another interesting thing: trying to find new strategies once something becomes recognizable by the police; by switching tactics.

Hanna Poddig

It's a challenge for big campaigns to say, now it's over, it's enough. I think it would be a great sign for the activist community to say, okay, for some years this was the right answer to the political situation but now we stop doing it. If you use certain strategies over and over again, you'll always have the problem that some people might decide to join other campaigns. But there are also new people who still believe in the 'corporate design' and the 'brand' that you created years before!

In the next image (Fig. 2) we see a combination of different types of action. Inside this tower, there was a lock-on action to defend some

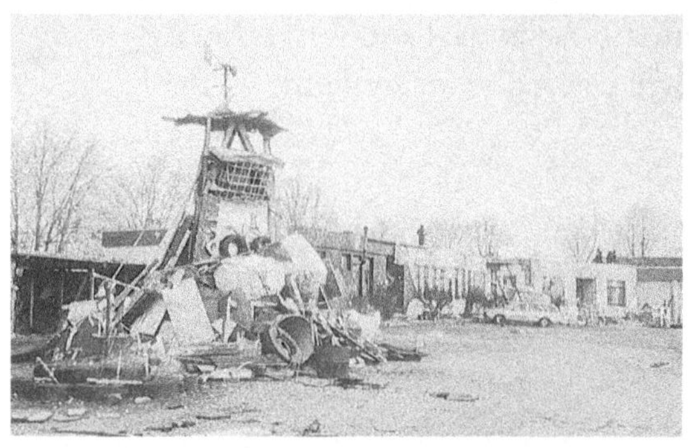

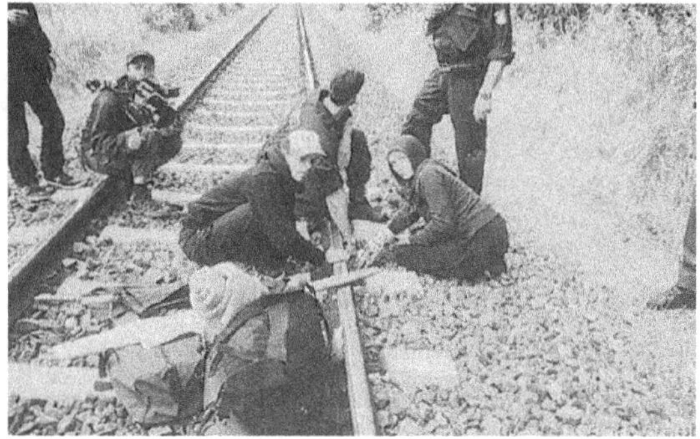

Fig. 2 — 'Pipe dream factory', Flensburg, 2016. Courtesy of Pay FeinFrisch.

Fig. 3 — Locking on to stop the transport of uranium, somewhere on the train route between Münster and the uranium enrichment facility in Gronau, 2012. Courtesy of aaa-West.

occupied houses in the northern German city of Flensburg. You can see that these houses were not really attractive—and by building this tower of trash, we created a symbol that was much more iconic than these boring houses. Many occupations and movements create their own kind of resistance architecture: sometimes it is useful, sometimes it is easy and cheap to build, sometimes it is a colourful and creative piece of art. To destroy this tower, the people that were inside of it had to be taken out first, the lock-on removed and then the tower, which was kind of difficult for the cops. The next image (Fig. 3) shows a lock-on action in 2012, where you can actually see the lock itself, or at least the construction that we use. There's a metal tube and we are locked together inside this metal tube.

Sophia New

In the workshop you said that there is a kind of two-step system. There's a concrete block underneath the rail that's been put there by somebody else years before so that you're actually installing yourself under the rail to another kind of concrete block, making it more difficult.

Hanna Poddig

Not in this specific case, but in some other cases.

Sophia New

We also heard that there are actually saws that have been developed to cut people out of cars, which means that you can be cut out of something like this. It just cuts through the metal and stops before you get to the skin.

Hanna Poddig

Which is, of course, great that the special forces of the police have this equipment now. But on the other hand, it means that they are professionalized. And in this case, it only took them half an hour to get rid of us. So this would be a reason to use concrete, because at more or less exactly the same site some years later, in 2017, people locked on to concrete and it lasted 15 and a half hours. That's a huge difference. The, let's say, 'normal' lock-on actions are cleared pretty fast. So most of the delay of this kind of action is the time waiting for the special forces.

Sophia New

And was that also the case in this particular action? Because you said that you had to act very quickly because you knew the helicopters were over-head, and if they would spot you, then they would stop the action. Did you have to choose a different spot than the one you had planned?

Hanna Poddig

No, we went exactly to the spot where we wanted to go to. If you only have this one metal tube, you definitely have to go to exactly that spot and sometimes you even have to search for it. That's kind of funny because those who prepare it are not the ones who do the lock on action in the end. So you get some fancy notes which say, there's a tree and from there you have to go ten meters, then on the other side there's a particular sign at least there was five years ago when we put it there.

You might all know those pictures of *Ende Gelände*, of people inside an open cast coal mine, stopping these huge diggers, which are the biggest movable machines on earth. But these actions do not come out of nothing. They are results of activists trying to work out if it is possible to squat a digger without the protection of a mass action backing them up. Sometimes these small group actions fail but sometimes they are the prototype for mass actions. And this is what we can see here. This was 2013, the year before *Ende Gelände* started. It's a small group playing Zamba music and having a picnic on the digger.

This is another photo of the Hambach Forest Occupation to give you an impression of what tree houses like this

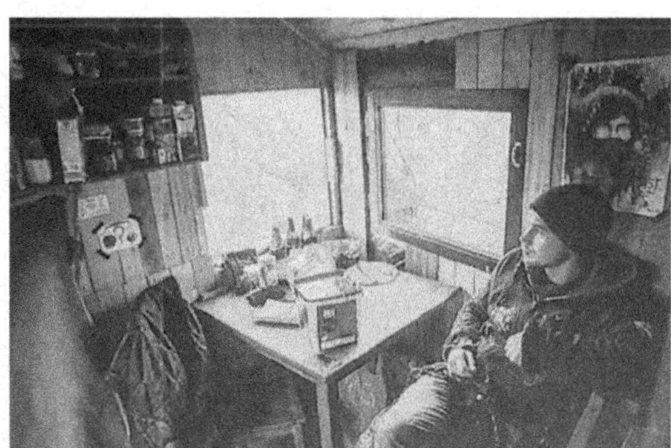

Fig. 4 — Tree House, Hambach Forest Occupation, 2016. Courtesy of Pay FeinFrisch.

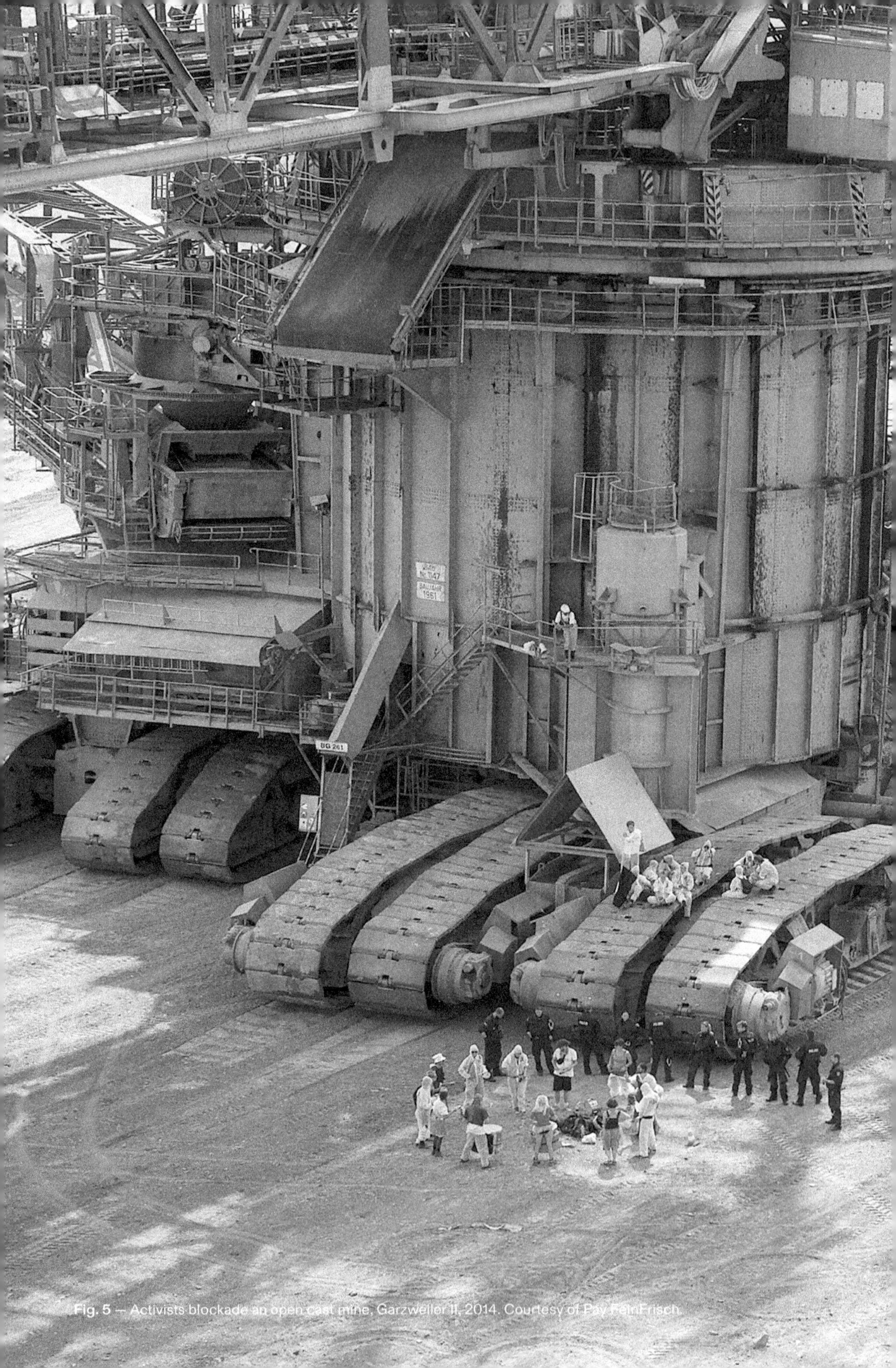

Fig. 5 — Activists blockade an open cast mine, Garzweiler II, 2014. Courtesy of Pay FeinFrisch.

look like from the inside. It's really a cosy little home. Well, it was. This one was destroyed. But then rebuilt.

Sophia New

Do you happen to know if people in the Hambach Forest Occupation actually considered that they were really using their bodies as human shields for the trees?

Hanna Poddig

Yes, definitely. I think in the forest this is even more obvious than when squatting an airport for example, because if you are sitting on a concrete construction or on a road, you do not feel this close connection. But if you are chained to a tree or if you are living on a tree and living with this tree, you definitely have this feeling of using your body to protect another living being. I mean, all these trees had names. People really had a close connection to them.

With the last picture I want to go back to a small action to avoid the impression that you have to build a tree house to be an activist. First of all, you do not have to be an activist at all and secondly, you can do things without building tree houses. This is one example. There is a form of street theatre I really like. It's called Mars TV. You have to wear stupid outfits; that's part of the game. You are a journalist from Mars trying to find out why there is so much weird stuff happening on this planet. Because on Mars, there's no such thing as the military, there's no such thing as a nuclear industry, there's no such thing as borders or money. And as someone from Mars, you don't understand why people do not resist all this. You can ask whatever naive questions and people tend to give really great answers.

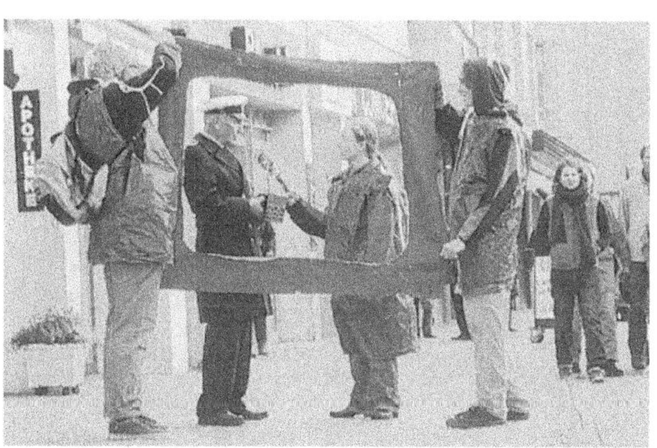

Fig. 6 — Mars TV, Flensburg, 2010. Courtesy of Pay FeinFrisch.

Sophia New

Thank you so much. That gave us a fascinating insight and it was really great to hear about the strategies behind of all of those images. The thing that I've been thinking about is that with human shielding, there always comes this idea of protection. I'm curious to know: to do this kind of work,

I imagine that you also have to be careful to protect yourself and protect others. So how do you actually go about that in your work?

Hanna Poddig

A good friend of mine once said that he could imagine doing lock-on actions because as soon as you are chained to whatever, you don't have to make any decisions and you are not responsible for someone else. But he said that he cannot ever imagine being the person supporting lock-on actions: to be the person deciding how to take care of others in a situation where you might be the next one arrested, where you know that opening your mouth might lead to being taken away from the person you should be supporting. Having this in mind, we just all have to find our position within all this where we feel comfortable. I think that's something you can find out through experience and by talking to each other. One of the things you should definitely address before doing an action is anxiety, because we all are afraid but we try to find a way to handle it and to help each other. That's something we always have to work on.

This text is the result of an interview carried out on 12 January 2022 in the context of the Shielding Research Week in Studio 14, Uferstudios, Berlin.

Diego Agulló

Invoking the Shielding Powers of the Body.
Tales of Animal Spirits in Speculative Folk Dances

1.
The *Turtle* Dance: A Ritual of Shielding

I was 7 years old when I witnessed for the first time the *Turtle* dance for the first time. As I did every summer, I spent my vacation with my grandparents in a town by the sea in the north of Spain called Santoña. At that age I was still too shy to hang out with the local kids, so I used to follow my grandmother everywhere. Her name was María Zabala and she was an extremely energetic person, always in a very good mood. Her laughter was so loud that strangers in public spaces would turn around to check whose laughter it was. Thanks to this, she became very popular in that town, especially among a very peculiar group of local women of the same age. They used to meet every day and I cannot recall any occasion when a man would be included in their circle. I remember they used to dress in a picturesque manner wearing too many layers of some kind of traditional clothing and they all wore necklaces of turtle shell. I used to spend a huge amount of time observing and listening to them. They would do normal things, such as playing cards together or going for long walks along the coast; nothing extraordinary to my eyes, except for that one night every summer when they would invoke the spirit of the turtle by dancing around the fire.

Because of my tender age, I was allowed to join the ritual. My memories are blurry and vivid at the same time. It was the first time that I participated in a pagan ritual of that kind. It was performed at night by the dunes between the sea and the forest. I can clearly remember them dancing but I can hardly say what happened before that or afterwards. The dance could be described in the following way: One person at a time danced around the fire, while the rest of the women stood in a circle creating rhythms with turtle shell shakers. It was a slow dance characterised by a meandering

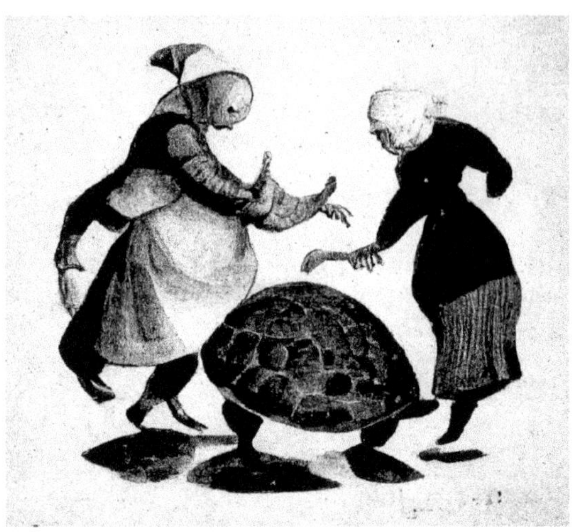
Fig. 1 — Illustration of two women performing the *Turtle* dance.

movement of big steps from side to side. Their legs were wide and their arms stretched up towards the sky. The woman dancing around the fire would keep staring at the sky for the entire time. The movement pattern was rather monotonous but quite hypnotic. Since it was a solo dance, they would have to take turns to step into the centre of the circle. The person who finished the dance around the fire would let out a yell, run straight into the sea and return to the group after having plunged into the dark waters.

I believe that the effect of the ritual was to have the spirit of the turtle embrace the dancer, creating an invisible shield around the body as a symbol of protection. In my memories a huge turtle was present during the ritual but today I am completely sure that this vision might have been the result of a hallucination created by the state of ecstasy of the women around me.

This is a type of childhood memory in which, at that time, I didn't question its extraordinary nature and I simply accepted that what I saw was normal. It was only many years later that I started to realize that maybe I had witnessed something extraordinary. Unfortunately, my grandmother had already passed away by then and I wasn't able to ask for more details about those exceptional experiences. About 35 years later, I decided to return to that village at the same time in the summer and tried unsuccessfully to find any sign of the ritual. Nobody seemed to have heard about it.

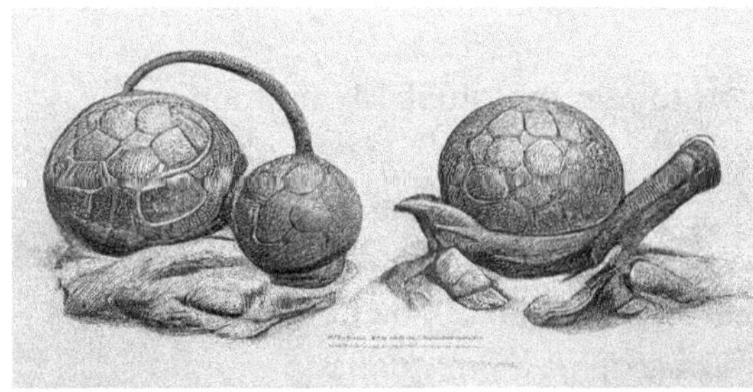
Fig. 2 — Engraving of percussion instruments used during the ritual.

I visited most of the libraries in that region searching for evidence of pre-Christian rites involving turtles. Unfortunately, I didn't find any written record of such a practice until the final evening when I went to eat something at a local place and hanging on the walls of a grubby tavern in the village of Berria (Cantabria), I found the treasure of a collection of visual testimonies of the *Turtle* dance: one engraving from the 18th century showing two women dancing with an enormous turtle, another engraving representing the turtle shells used as a percussion instrument during the ceremony and a series of old daguerreotypes from the beginning of the 20th century showing a group of women performing the *Turtle* dance in a forest in Northern Spain. This visual evidence proved to me that what I saw in my childhood was not just a sporadic event in time but rather a practice that belongs to an old occult tradition that was mysteriously absent from popular knowledge and was most probably transmitted down the generations by a few chosen ones. The owner of the tavern claimed that the images belonged to his mother, and he decided to hang them as decoration without knowing exactly what they represented. It was obvious that his mother had never revealed the *Turtle* dance to her son. I feel extremely lucky to have participated in such a ritual and I believe that the protective spirit of the turtle has accompanied me ever since, shielding me from life's adversities and misfortune.

The turtle is a perfect example of an animal that embodies the idea of shielding. It is a reptile whose body is characterized by having developed a shell from its rib cage. The shell is composed of two parts: the upper part called a 'carapace' and the underside called a 'plastron', they serve to protect the animal and provide shelter from the elements. The carapace appears in several cultures as a symbol of good luck and protection from evil and witchcraft.

The shield is incorporated into the body through a development of the bone structure. Actually, in most vertebrates the rib cage already serves as in most vertebrates a shield for the internal organs. What is special about animals like the turtle is that the rib cage has expanded outside the body and has

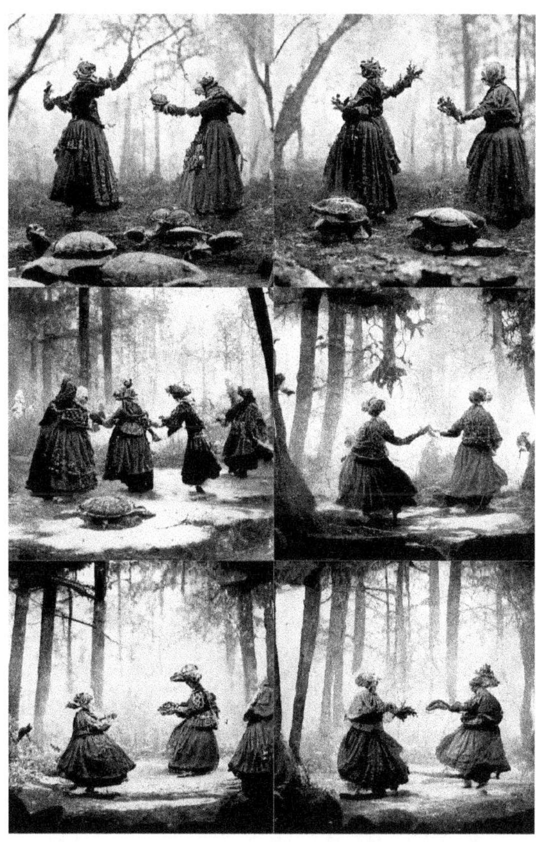

Fig. 3 — Six daguerreotypes of a group of women dancing the *Turtle* dance in a forest.

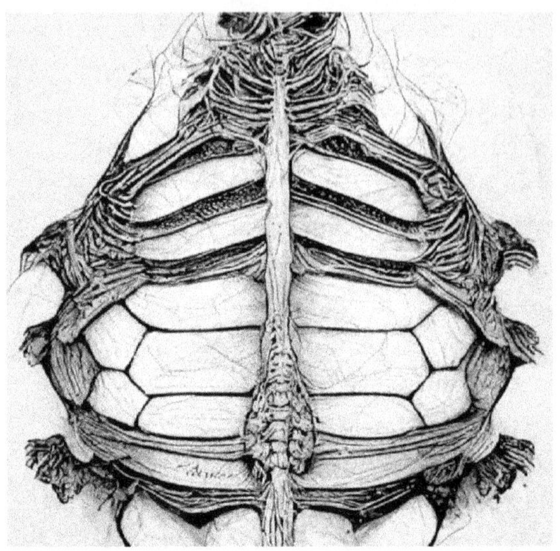

Fig. 4 — Detail of a turtle shell.

become its outer layer, replacing the skin and offering much stronger protection.

It is well known that turtles and tortoises have played important roles in many different cultures as symbols of longevity, stability, and wisdom. In regard to the ritual in which I participated in during my childhood, I came to the conclusion that its main purpose was to invoke the spirit of the magic turtle by asking for protection from misfortune, evil influences and illness. It is an example of a ritual performed in order to receive shielding qualities from an animal spirit. The dance provided spiritual protection. Since that time, I believe that a dance can be a shield.

2.
The Body as Projectile

La Danza del Topetazo

After that journey to the north of Spain where I searched for evidence of the existence of the *Turtle* dance, I felt an uncontrollable urgency to start a long term research to look for other folk dances in Spain that invoke an animal spirit in order to shield the participants from danger.

The next shielding ritual I came across during my journey to Spain is performed in the mountains of the Sierra de Gredos and is called *La Danza del Topetazo* (The Bump Dance). *Topetazo* is a Spanish word used to designate the precise

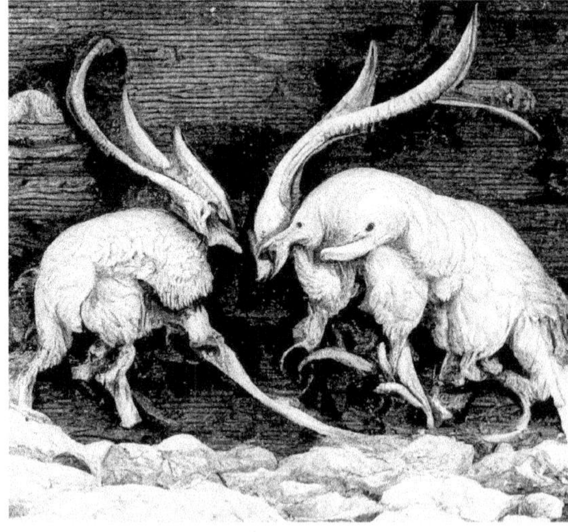

Fig. 5 — Illustration from a 18th century encyclopedia of two ibex showing the moment before their cephalic shields impact against each other.

moment when two horned animals butt their heads together. The animal spirit invoked in this folk dance is the ibex, also known as the wild goat. As with the turtle, the body of the ibex is protected by an extension of the bone structure, to be more precise, a 'cephalic shield' that protrudes from the skull of the male ibex. These are two large curved horns that consist of a covering of keratin and other proteins surrounding a core of living bone. These function as protection but are also for attack, they are cells of the body that have become weapons. The male ibex takes part in agonistic behaviour because dominance is required to gain breeding rights. The male ibex is an animal that uses its body as a projectile. In order to attack, it throws itself into the air to impact against another body with its horns.

La Danza del Topetazo is a folk-loric dance that ritualizes the battle between two bodies that compete for power. The dance became popular in Spain after the great painter Goya captured it in a series of engravings (see Fig. 6). The location of the ritual is a cave in a mountain, and it takes place during the sunrise. In this way, the time of the ritual is defined by the time that the sun beams gradually enter the cave filling it entirely with light. The two dancers wear a wool and leather tunic and a mask that incorporates a helmet with two ibex horns attached to it. The beginning

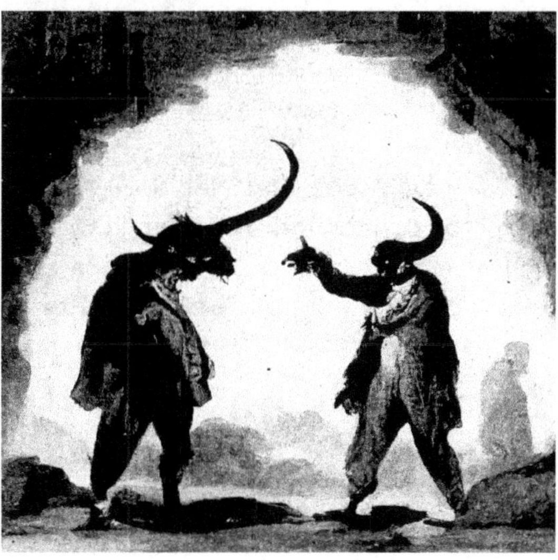

Fig. 6 — Etching attributed to Goya's series *Los Disparates* depicting *La Danza del Topetazo* (1799).

of the ritual symbolizes the prelude to the battle with the two warriors engaging at a distance without coming into bodily contact. It is an exchange of gestures during which they taunt each other as they slowly circle one another. The sound of a bass drum beats the rhythm and heightens the tension of the scene. Gradually the circles become smaller, and they start to engage in a rhythmical pattern of steps as if they would jump in the air. At this moment the horns point towards each other until one dancer decides to jump and throws his body into the air to impact against the horns of his partner producing a sound that synchronises with the beat of the percussion. A skilful dancer knows exactly when to butt heads and how not to hurt himself or his partner while performing this dance. It has more of symbolic power than being a real fight.

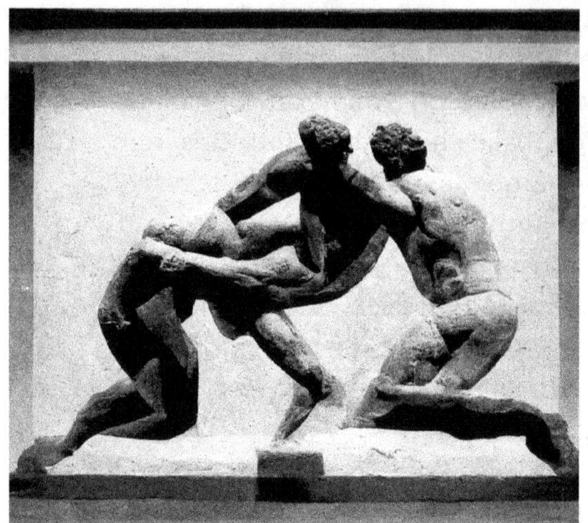

Fig. 7 — Greek sculpture from the archaic period representing Greek dances. Private collection.

The Intimate Affinity between Dance and Danger

While witnessing the *Topetazo* dance, what impressed me most was the fact that the body was used as a projectile. This reminded me of ancient Greek dances and how, thanks to my fascination with the etymology of words, some years ago I had discovered something marvellous: 'dance' in Greek literally means 'to throw one's body'. The Greek root for dance is *ballein*, which means 'to throw so as to hit' and it is also the root of words such as: ballet, devil, problem, ballistics and bullet. These semantic connections between 'ballet' and 'bullet', 'devil' and 'problem' reveal a secret affinity between 'dance' and 'danger' and the resulting necessity of shielding the body from it. In this light, shielding belongs intrinsically to the action of dancing as a direct consequence of it.

In those athletic dances from ancient Greece bodies were coming forcefully into contact, colliding and impacting with each other, the body of the dancer literally becoming a 'bullet'. Since 'ballistics' is the science that studies the movement and behaviour of projectiles in space, we can immediately see the close affinity between choreography and ballistics. This makes us consider the affinity between dancing and fighting, dancing and martial arts, choreography and war. Shielding appears as a necessary process in the context of dance. Dance can be your weapon but dance can be your shield too.

3.
The Embodiment of Danger

La Abonanza and *La Pedrá*

Inspired by the etymology of dance, I started to research what is the intimate affinity between dance and throwing projectiles at 'bodies without shields' or, in other words, how dance can be the embodiment of danger when exposing oneself to the threat of flying objects aimed at the body. The absence of a shield implies finding alternative ways to protect oneself from impact for example, by turning the dance itself into a shield. My next research question became the following: Does a body instinctively have the somatic knowledge to protect itself from projectiles without using a physical shield?

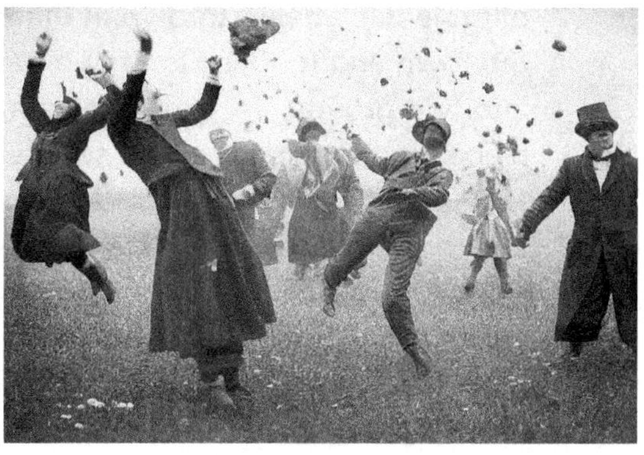

Fig. 8 — *La Abonanza*. Photograph from the fields of Cercedilla.

I found in Europe several folkloric events in which participants throw different types of projectiles at each other. For example, in *La Tomatina* festival in Valencia the participants throw tomatoes in a one-hour tomato fight. In Italy there is the Carnival of Ivrea during which people throw oranges at each other. When I moved to Berlin in 2005 to Berlin, I also witnessed the *Gemüseschlacht* at the Oberbaumbrücke in which every year, people from Friedrichshain and people from Kreuzberg throw vegetables at each other. But the most inspiring ritual I encountered was in Cercedilla (Sierra de Guadarrama, Spain). It is called *La Abonanza*. Its animal spirit is the cow, or to be more precise, the cow's shit. It consists of villagers of all ages throwing cow shit at each other as a ritualized way of fertilizing the fields. The soil gets fertilized by the tumult of people throwing shit at each other and the intensity of the battle mixes the cow shit with the soil of the field.

La Abonanza later developed into a game called *La Pedrá*. This game is the result of replacing the cow shit with a handmade leather ball stuffed with horsehair and roots, the impact of which on a body is much more painful than the cow shit. Liberated from the fertilizing function, the game focuses exclusively on how the participants demonstrate their mastery of 'body shielding' when exposing themselves to the danger of hundreds

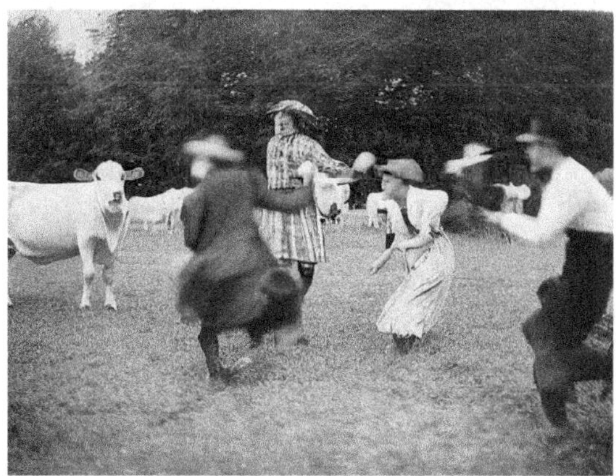

Fig. 9 — *La Abonanza*. The inhabitants of Cercedilla with the cows.

of projectiles being thrown at them. It takes place in the main square of the town and it consists of two parts. First, the participants are divided into two groups. The first group, around 10 people, are blindfolded and placed in the middle of the square. The second group, between 50 and 100 people, throws hundreds of balls at the blindfolded bodies. There are certain guidelines to follow: The balls must be thrown with enough force (the impact on the body has to be painful) but they can be thrown at any body part; the only requirement is to keep a certain distance between the person who throws and the person who is blindfolded to avoid throwing from close range. People can throw as many balls as they wish for 10 minutes until a trumpet sound indicates the transition to the next part. In the second part the people stop throwing projectiles and the 10 blindfolded dancers keep moving, exploring, for at least ten more minutes the resonances that have been embodied during the first part for at least ten more minutes.

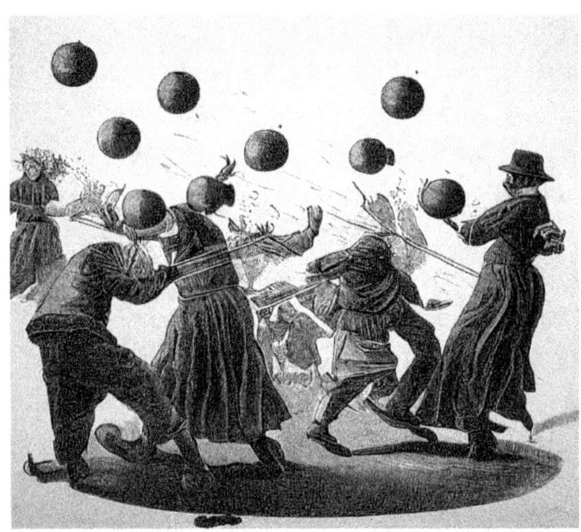

Fig. 10 — Cartoon from *La Gazeta de Guadarrama*. Local newspaper in Cercedilla, documenting *La Pedrá*.

Transforming Negativity into Affirmation

I realized that my main interest was not the actual throwing of the projectiles but afterwards, when the 10 participants kept moving, embodying the previous attack. This embodiment becomes an affirmative force; dancing without resentment, without anger and channelling out all the negative emotions. The throwing was internalized so that the external driving force became internal, producing a sensation of empowerment. The dance is now independent from the attack. This 'affirmative dance' is an expression of shielding oneself from the negative effects of an attack. The participants manage through this dance to transform (a catharsis) the negativity of life into an affirmative joyful celebration of life.

During my residency at Cercedilla, I was trained by a group of locals in how to participate in this ritual. They instructed me in the different ways of shielding myself when the ball is thrown at me:

The primary strategy is provided by instinct through the fight-or-flight response that produces physiological changes that give the body more strength and speed.

Shielding the nervous system from panic by maintaining a deep relaxation in the body helps to prevent the fear of not knowing when the projectile will impact.

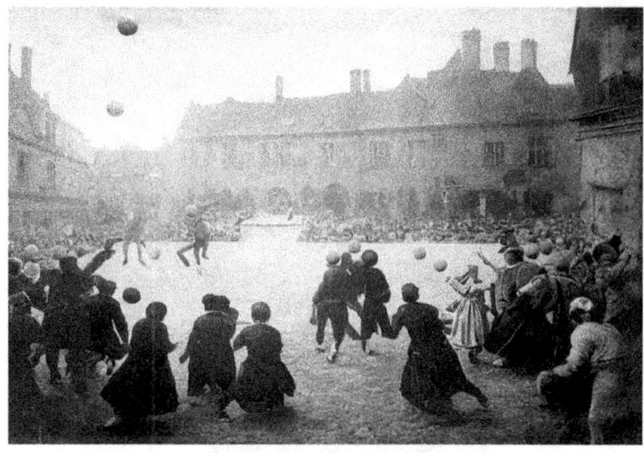

Fig. 11 — The main square in Cercedilla where *La Pedrá* takes place every year.

The body also shields itself instinctively by folding itself towards the inside in order to protect the front which is more fragile. This can develop into laying down on the floor in foetus position, covering one's own head and front of the body so the back of the body functions like a shield or body armour.

Arms also function as shields covering the most vulnerable body parts such as the face or genitalia.

Another tactic is to become a difficult target by being faster than the person throwing. Speed is a practice of shielding when you move faster than the projectile.
Gradually a dance emerges from combining all these tactics.

4.
The Permeable Shield

The *Pongo* Dance and the Jellyfish

At this point in my research I asked myself what a folkloric dance would look like, if the animal invoked during the ritual would not be a vertebrate and shielding the body would not imply a rigid and impenetrable structure provided by shells or horns but rather a flexible and permeable body. I found the answer to my question during my continued visits to Tenerife in the Canary Islands where the jellyfish is the symbol of protection in a pagan folk dance called the *Pongo* dance.

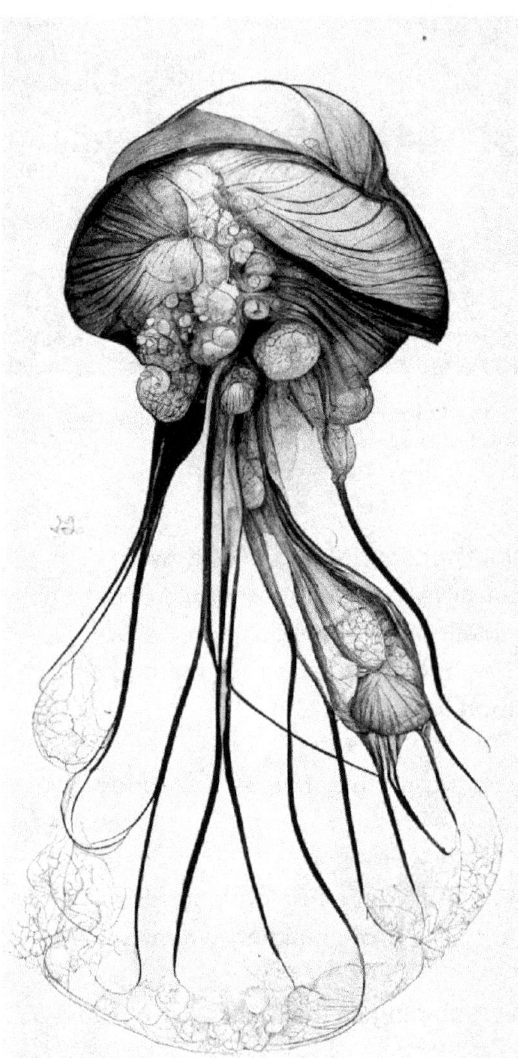

Fig. 12 — Illustration of *Pelagia noctiluca*.

The shielding powers of the jellyfish are the qualities of transparency, flexibility and poisoning. As an invertebrate animal, the jellyfish is characterized by its hydrostatic skeleton. The body is gelatinous and composed of an umbrella-shaped bell and a set of stinging tentacles. The bell is a transparent jelly-like matter that can pulsate to provide propulsion. Besides stinging toxins in the tentacles, the jellyfish protects itself by being transparent, or in other words, by not being seen or appearing to be empty.

Based on the shielding powers of the jellyfish, the *Pongo* dance is a dance with a martial aspect, so people from all generations learn self-defence by practising folk dances. The dancers gracefully pulsate their bodies vertically up and down as if the air has transformed into liquid and the dance is being performed under water. They transmit the sensation of floating on air. The dance is performed on the beach to the sound of a drum and all the participants wear a hat in the shape of a jellyfish. The purpose of the dance is to distract the other dancers with different arm gestures so that their jellyfish hats can be removed. In order to prevent that, the dancers need to protect their hat with a movement of the arm called the *Pongo.* Instead of resisting or repulsing the partner, the arm rolls back following the direction of the opponent's arm without any resistance and yielding to the emptiness which can make the opposing dancer lose their balance and fall. Protection is not associated with resisting an attack but rather to saying *yes* to it, accepting the opponent's force and redirecting it into the emptiness. It is the art of 'soft shielding'. It is a very playful dance that also becomes a game that people learn to play from childhood. In some parts of the island there are local competitions where people compete to steal the hat without losing balance.

What is interesting about the *Pongo* is that *shielding* is practised without resistance. It requires learning how to place the body at the right angle in relation to your partner and to the ground. As a consequence, you feel rooted, as if your body was ingrained into the ground. This rooting enables you to yield to your partner's attack, letting the force pass through you without destabilizing you. The requirement is to be centred and to hide your centre, not revealing to your opponent where that centre is. When you resist or meet force with force, you lose balance and immediately expose your centre to your opponent.

Keeping Oneself Open to Alterity

What I could learn during my residency in Tenerife was that the *Pongo* dance also transmits the attitude in life (ethos) of keeping oneself open to alterity. If we look at the geographical location of the Canary Islands, it is somewhere that has historically been exposed to all types of visitors and influences since it was used as a mission base

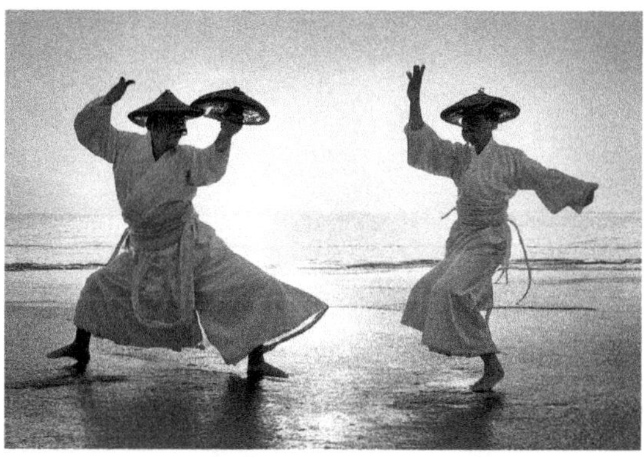

Fig. 13 — *Pongo* Dance. The author training with his teacher Lucio Rubio at Punta de Teno beach in Tenerife.

between Europe, the Americas, and Africa. Pirates and overseas traders would use the islands as a temporary stop when crossing the Atlantic Ocean. The *Pongo* dance responds to the cultural need to develop a practice to relate to the unexpected visits of foreigners and their potential threat. This folk dance has played the role of training the population to be physically and ethically ready to encounter otherness without being closed or forcefully resisting. The *Pongo* dance has functioned in the social body like a membrane or an organ that permeates foreign influences, external affections, and new knowledge. It is like a shield with holes that allows exchange while providing protection. From a political perspective, what I could learn from this is that shielding does not necessarily imply rigid protection; neither unconditional resistance nor inflexible closure. Shielding, understood as a membrane, can be a tactic of permeability and flexibility in order to relate to unknown differences. In this light, hospitality behaves like a membranous and porous shield, it does not exclude the presence of the stranger or the foreigner but rather it is inclusive and welcomes the external influences establishing a practice of listening that facilitates adaptation while maintaining roots and the ground. This understanding of shielding, rather than insisting on strict control as an immunological defence against an outer enemy, proposes the abolition of borders to allow freedom of mobility and possibilities of association. Taking risks is as important as protecting oneself.

Liz Rosenfeld

Trans-Feels / Trans-Shields: Some Scores for Cruising

"Husband or Wife?"

"Huh", I responded.

"Husband or Wife? I just need to know where to send you."

Feeling the endless line of frustrated travellers behind me, as I clearly became the rock in the wheel, I realised it was a question of language. *"Frau oder Herr?"* I was asked at airport security. Even translated into pragmatic English for efficiency, I froze. It's as though I pushed the hidden button and a weighted blanket of disassociation enveloped my body.

I know this weighted blanket. I'm thankful for it. It feels good. Feels like the utopian promise of the darkroom, a space where bodies *should* disappear, dissolve beyond lines of material flesh, and encounter forever orgasms and infinite pleasure principles. I often think about why dissociation is only referred to in reference to traumatic and stressful moments. Especially in these sorts of moments when I am not passing as either. I think about all of this—in this moment—all of it in a flash. Why can I only articulate disassociation when I feel anxious, because dissociating can also feel so good.

Again, *"Frau oder Herr?* Husband or Wife?"

Of course, I would say neither. None to all of it. I don't want a husband or wife. Nor man or woman. There is nothing remarkable about this moment for most trans and non-binary people. Pretty usual. And in my particular position, not only am I already shielded by the expectations of my middle-class whiteness, I have come to experience that the social stigma of being a 'fat woman'—one that I have lived with for all of my life—has transitioned as well. I realize that my current physical questionability is perhaps even more protected by my corporeal expansion /

the way my body takes up space / my general largeness is now deemed acceptable when visibly read as male. Or perhaps, in my case, *more male leaning.*

I feel a gentle hand on my back. The person behind me, they lean in. A voice filtered by layers of mask whispers, "Do you speak German? Do you understand? Can I help you?"

I turn around to meet knowing queer eyes. Knowing as in so many knowings. An acknowledgment of existence. A kind of hotness. In this glance, we could have already fucked in the toilet to the left of the duty free shop, on the other side of security. A knowing of not being able to know the right words to answer the questions in this particular moment. Because no words are ever the right words. The question of gender is still frustratingly real, while also deeply clique and cringey, because who cares and also, we have to care.

In public spaces like airports, I have come to find relief in the mask. It hides my new confusing salt-and-pepper pubescent facial hair. Confusing as in both I don't know what to do it with it yet and clearly, my moustache reads as an awkward middle space.

Above the rim of my mask, I smile back with my eyes. A nonverbal thank you.

A knowing.

I could be on my knees, right now, covered in cum.

Their eyes respond, they deepen. They know I am okay. I can continue.

Regardless of my clear or unclear gender, I have always been stopped by airport security. I turn to the officer and say in what sounds to me like my most non-binary voice, "it doesn't matter".

Once I walk through the scanning machine, they send me to the female officer for a pat-down.

Because my fat could always be some other material: A hole. A screen. A disgust. An uncomfortable reminder of chaos. An apron. A sex toy. An invitation in. A glimpse into movements of other kinds of time. A flagging of certain and uncertain desire. A power tool for dissociative longing. A coat of non-binary time.

My flesh. My fat. A robe to unravel in the depths of darkrooms. Holes to form. Rolls to fuck. An abundance to navigate and a barrier to get through. Another kind of flagging. Androgynous abstraction.

This fat. This flesh. I've hurled it around in unruly ways. Flogging. Dancing. Fucking. Rubbing. Resisting. Un-defining. Tracking time. Creating prints, and making scores.

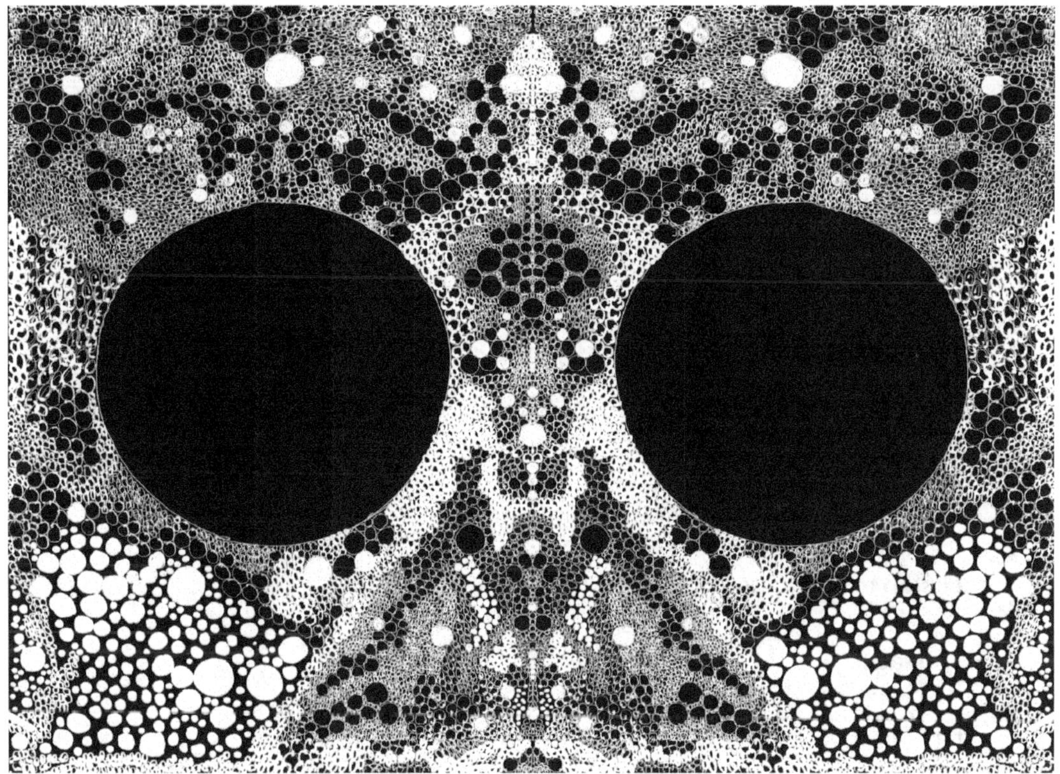

Fig. 1 — Liz Rosenfeld, Scores for Cruising, #1, 2022. Courtesy of the Artist.

Trans-Feels / Trans-Shields:
Some Scores for Cruising

To Sonically Resonate / To Sonic Resonance

Resonance and resonate are often confused. The resonance of something refers to what is produced. The resonant frequency of a system or sound that can change when something speeds up or slows down. A reverberance. A vibrancy. An oscillation. To resonate is to be filled with a deep penetrating sound. To hold a particular meaning / importance. To be held.

How can I ever really know the technical resonance of my voice?
My voice: it acts as both shield and a dead giveaway. I can feel that it has dropped. I can feel my vocal cords satisfyingly elongating. However, externally, no one has noticed.

I wake up

I clear my throat

I organically rest into smiling position

I inhale the sound "(H)EEEEE".

I hold it for a few seconds

I listen to my voice and notice how it feels

I release

I inhale a yawn, I try to yawn. I try to stretch out my throat

I release

I inhale the sound "(H)AAAAA" and then I speak it

I listen to my voice, while staying in yawning position

Apparently, I sound deeper. I am 'supposed' to sound 'more masculine'.

**and Ground(s) and
Aperture(s) and**

And openings
and optics
and scopes
and mirrors
and hills
and diameters
and terrain
and lenses
and whirlpools
and limits
and creases
and meadows
and light
and passings
and pinholes
and tides
and lawns
and objectives
and gaps
and instruments
and vistas
and inlets
and cavities
and channels
and anatomies
and axils
and expressions
and refractions
and graves
and stones
and entrances
and exits
and sphincters
and ratios
and planes
and inlets
and unifiable orifices.

Cracks can be Fissures that can lead to Holes

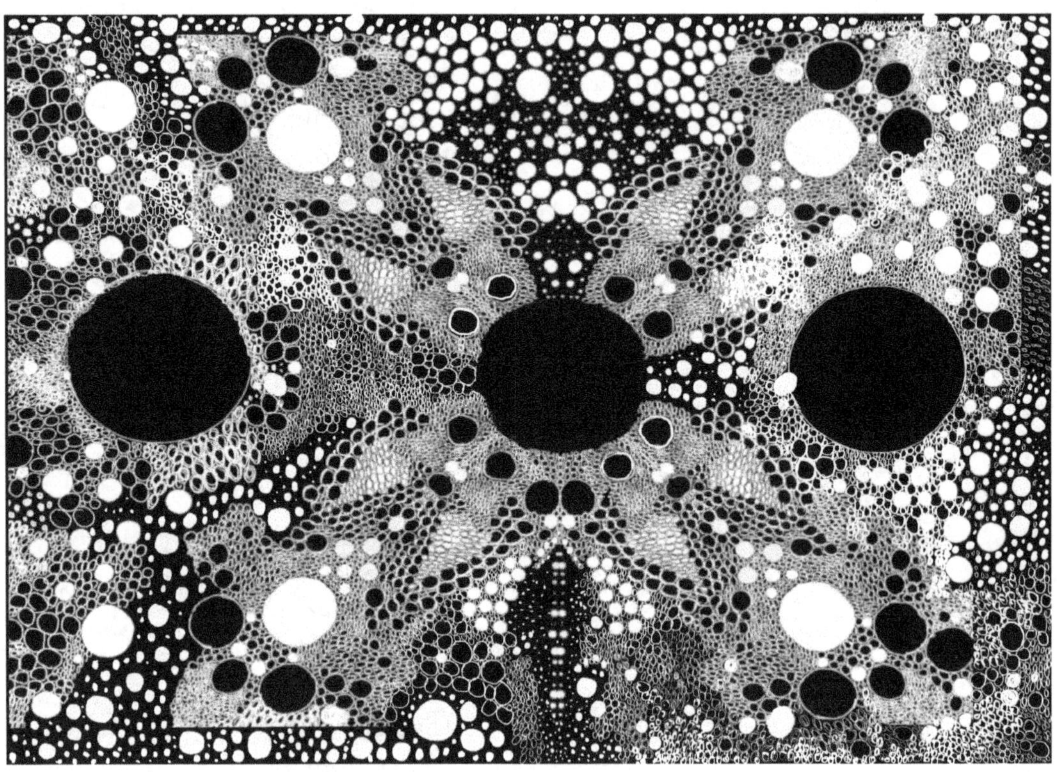

Fig. 2 — Liz Rosenfeld, Scores for Cruising, #2, 2022. Courtesy of the Artist.

Mapping

The human body houses 50000+ holes
Make a list of your holes
          (There is no correct number. There is no correct hole)
Envision a map between your holes
Create a choreography from this map
          (There is no correct way to define choreography)
Enact

Fluids :: Mopping up

Stand over the belly
Feet placed on either side
Ankles holding hips in place
Ass to the back of the room
Face to face
Form a right angle between bodies
Hands on calves
Holes open
Fluid overflows and overflows
A waterfall
A sheet
A buffer
A safeguard
A hot slick shell
On hands and knees
Head grazing the floor
Whatever is leftover
Un-absorbed
Mop it up
Wear it home proudly

Topping from the bottom

I may enter
I may disrobe
I may be looked at
I may stand naked
I may be looked at
I may open up
I may expose
I may be looked at
I may ask
I may stay silent
I may decide not to say no
I may be looked at
I may decide if this feels infinite
I may be looked at

Some Devotional Armour

Thinks of cruising as community service
Describes artistic practice as devotional work
Embodies duration and endurance
Commits to emotion as material
Asks how we can be together while being alone
Investigates why desires are made the way they are made
Watches, sees, and decides when to open
Creates time as it is encountered
Eavesdrops and absorbs quietly
Effortlessly moves light in space
Writes poetic duvets
Nurtures kin with intuitive sharp knives
An indestructible shell of porous metal with soft knowing eyes
A rock, a sensitive force
Observes, sees, and penetrates
Rigger of visions
Navigates collaborations between mind and body/body and mind
Waiting for pleasure in patience

The three digital drawings are part of a larger series.

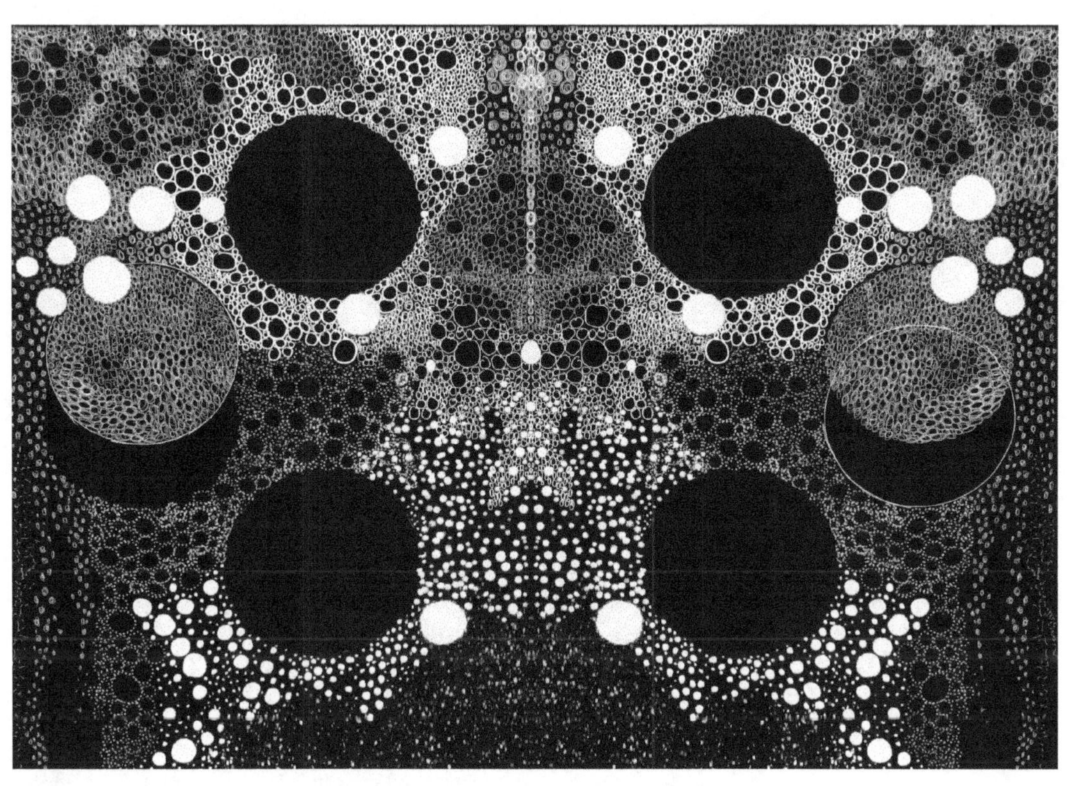

Fig. 3 — Liz Rosenfeld, Scores for Cruising, #3, 2022. Courtesy of the Artist.

Bella Ruhl

Sartorial Shields: Butch Lesbian Gender Styles as Defensive Technology, 1950–1969

I didn't have any [court clothes]. I borrowed them [...] That was the one, great advantage of being gay [...] I beat'em every charge [...] [They were for] assault. One was on a police officer [...] He was in there, his head was all wrapped up, he had a concussion, broken nose, eyes [...] about a six footer. And there I am, looking as pathetic as I could. And the judge, he says, 'You did that? [...] Why you couldn't weigh a hundred pounds soaking wet' [...] I says, '98.' He says, 'I don't believe you did this, no I have to throw this out.' — Sandy, quoted in *Boots of Leather, Slippers of Gold* by Madeline D. Davis and Elizabeth Lapovsky Kennedy

Sandy, a working-class butch lesbian who came out in the 1950s, refused to wear women's clothing in daily life, and, indeed, owned none.[1] She instead wore clothing manufactured for men and performed an aggressive and boisterous queer masculinity modeled on rebellious male pop culture figures of the time. Her specifically lesbian gender nonconformity made her a target of homophobic violence; however, as the epigraph shows, she was a fierce street fighter, and masculine garments enabled physical and symbolic resistance. When the need arose, however, she was also able to perform normative femininity in order to protect herself. Sandy's humorous account speaks to the many overlapping forms of strategic protection and exposure which butches leveraged to make room for themselves in the face of cultural conservatism in mid-century New York State. *Warning: this chapter includes references to homophobia, sexism, and sexual violence. It also includes references to historical trans and lesbian sexual and gender identities, using the historical terms with which the described historical actors self-identified.*

Introduction

Following the Second World War, lesbian communities coalesced and grew in major industrial centers. Gathering primarily in bars, dance clubs, and house parties, working-class queer women constructed a distinctive subculture with its own internal logics, styles, and forms of expression. A key organizing factor of this social world—which centered on the

[1] The epigraph is from Madeline D. Davis and Elizabeth Lapovsky Kennedy, *Boots of Leather, Slippers of Gold: The History of a Lesbian Community*, 1st edition, New York: Routledge, 1993, 233. Davis and Kennedy refer to their interviewees by first name only, while other sources refer to actors with first and last name. I will follow the original texts with regard to naming historical actors in order to minimize confusion between individuals with similar names and to offer as complete of information as possible.

formation of social and sexual relationships—were the dyadic and specifically lesbian gender configurations known as butch and femme (or fem).[2] These binary gendered and sexual styles consisted of a matrix of characteristics, including clothing, gesture, sexual role, and emotional expression which quoted from, while simultaneously subverting, heterosexual gender performance.

Modeling themselves on James Dean and Marlon Brando, white butch lesbians projected an image of bravado, swagger, and rough-and-tumble mid-century working class masculinity.[3] They wore starched button-down shirts or white T-shirts and Levi's 501 jeans or chinos and greased their hair back into a pompadour. Many rode motorcycles, worked in factories, and were quick to fight strangers and each other. Black butches, also known as studs, wore similar styles but also exhibited a more elevated aesthetic based on fashionable menswear, including "elegant [...] three-piece suits"[4] in their extensive wardrobes. Butch gender presentation, consisting of both style and repertoire, was as much an embodied performance as a fashion aesthetic. According to Piri, a Black butch from the Buffalo community, butches could be identified by "[m]annerisms [...] the way they dressed [...] the way they talk, the way they acted"[5]. Those who performed assertive masculine behaviors were admired within the community, and femmes valued a butch who could pick up on their signals of interest and take initiative during courtship, creating pressures and (sexual and social) incentives which rewarded and reinforced butch performance.

Paradoxically, just as their masculinity rendered them visible as gender deviants to the broader society, triggering what gender theorist Judith Butler describes as "a set of punishments both obvious and indirect" which follow from "[p]erforming one's gender wrong"[6], it also functioned to protect them physically and psychologically. This functioned on multiple levels: "passing" as men in the streets could offer a temporary reprieve from sexist and homophobic harassment, the materiality of T-shirts and pants offered both physical coverage and mobility generally denied to women, and in an embodied sense, many butches

[2] See Davis and Kennedy, *Boots of Leather*, 287; Audre Lorde, *Zami: A New Spelling of My Name: A Biomythography*, Berkeley, CA: Crossing Press, 1982, 178, 224.
[3] See Davis and Kennedy, 116.
[4] Davis and Kennedy, *Boots of Leather*, 209.
[5] Davis and Kennedy, *Boots of Leather*, 210.
[6] See Judith Butler, "Performative Acts and Gender Constitution: An Essay in Phenomenology and Feminist Theory", in *Theatre Journal* 40, no. 4 (1988), 528.

describe feeling safer in menswear. While masculinity could offer butches some kinds of protection, navigating the state and its mechanisms was safer as a gender-conforming woman; butches used both strategies to shield themselves from violence, while seeing both as essentially performative.

Cold War Context

The conventional historiographical representation of the postwar period in the United States is defined by conformity and social control, a façade which would fracture in the 1960s with the emergence of anti-colonial resistance movements and the counterculture. In the fraught context of the global Cold War, the heterosexual white suburban nuclear family was valorized as a symbol of the US-American nation state and norms perpetuated through mass media functioned to establish a standard of heterosexuality, gender duality, and conformity.[7] At the same time, when one looks beyond media discourses and centers an analysis of documented behaviors, it becomes clear that the 1950s were also a period of intense experimentation and a rapidly changing social fabric.[8] Women were entering the workforce in increasing numbers, resistance to racism and segregation was growing, and sexual and gender 'deviants' were organizing themselves into communities and networks. The backlash against these changes was swift and fierce. Political and social dissidents, including homosexuals, were surveilled, pathologized and subjected to state violence, as politicians and civilians, swept up what Black lesbian poet Audre Lorde described as the "protective paranoia of the McCarthy years"[9], jostled to root out those deemed disloyal to the American project.

Physical violence, harassment and abuse, incarceration, and sexual assault were among the many ways in which the dominant heteropatriarchal regime, consisting of both institutional (police officers) and vigilante actors (civilians, particularly men, alone and in groups), responded to

[7] Joanne Meyerowitz, "The Liberal 1950s? Reinterpreting Postwar U.S. Sexual Culture", in *Gender and the Long Postwar: Reconsiderations of the United States and the Two Germanys, 1945–1989*, ed. by Karen Hagemann and Sonya Michel, Baltimore, MD: Johns Hopkins University Press and Woodrow Wilson Center Press, 2014, 295.

[8] Meyerowitz, "The Liberal 1950s?", 296.

[9] Lorde, Zami, 187. Alongside the anti-communist "Red Scare" came the "Lavender Scare", a more extensive purge of suspected homosexuals from government positions. See Elaine Tyler May, Homeward Bound: American Families in the Cold War Era, New York, NY: Basic Books, 1988, 13.

lesbian visibility in Buffalo and New York City in this period. Though female homosexuality was not illegal, queer women, butch and femme, could be imprisoned for "vagrancy, lewdness, disorderly conduct, and obscenity"[10], and cross-dressing was widely understood to be illegal at the time. During bar raids the police used a rule of thumb that required three pieces of clothing which matched the presumed sex of the wearer. At the time, garments which were worn by both men and women were designed to be gender specific: once women began wearing pants in the 1940s, women's slacks were cut with a zipper in the back or on the side rather than in the front, and while men's shirts had buttons on the right side, women's had buttons on the left.[11] As a result, transgression was visible and could be systematically policed, both through legal and social means.

Public space was highly contested, and butches and femmes had to learn how to fight off straight men who came into their pubs looking to cause trouble. A white butch named Toni from Buffalo New York explains the resistance which gender nonconformists faced in public spaces during the 1950s and '60s:

> [Y]ou walk down the street and they knew you were gay and you'd be minding your business and there'd be two or three guys standing on a street corner, and they'd come up to you and say, 'You want to be a man, let's see if you can fight like a man.' Now being a man was the last thing on my mind, but man, they'd take a poke at you and you had to learn to fight. [...] And it got to be really bad, I actually had walked down the street with some friends not doing anything and had people spit at me, or spit at us, it was really bad.[12]

Another white butch from Buffalo, Leslie, adds "you would run into flack from men. Women too would cause trouble, they might feel that you would follow them into the bathroom and attack them"[13]. Toni emphasizes that for visible butches, "[o]ut on the street you were fair game"[14] for gangs of men looking to pick a fight. As the most visible representatives

---

[10] Meyerowitz, "The Liberal 1950s?", 299. The 'three pieces' rule of thumb is referenced almost unanimously in the primary source material.

[11] See Alix Genter, "Appearances Can Be Deceiving: Butch-Femme Fashion and Queer Legibility in New York City, 1945-1969", in *Feminist Studies* 42, no. 3 (2016), 608–609.

[12] Davis and Kennedy, *Boots of Leather*, 231.

[13] Davis and Kennedy, *Boots of Leather*, 82.

[14] Davis and Kennedy, *Boots of Leather*, 118.

of lesbian culture, butch gender non-conformity served as a lightning rod for homophobia.

It was specifically the incongruence of visible queerness that made them targets for male violence. This is exemplified by the experience of Sandy Kern, a Jewish butch from New York City, who describes being attacked by a gang of young men when she met up with her femme girlfriend in a Brooklyn park one night.[15] Explaining of her lover that "[s]he wasn't obvious by a long shot, but the two of us together—they knew right away that we were lesbians", Kern points to her own masculine aesthetic, consisting of "sneakers [...] dungarees [...] and a sweatshirt tucked into [her] pants" as the indicator which triggered the attack.[16] In other words, masculine styles made butches a visible target for harassment and social censure.

Shielding the Community

Despite the risks, however, butches often chose visibility over the option to shield themselves by passing as men or conforming to feminine styles. Tough bar dykes of the 1950s and '60s valued projecting a masculine image as much of the time as possible and were unwilling to give in to social pressure.[17] This generation, coming of age in the 1950s and early '60s, was, according to Kennedy and Davis, "always prepared to fight to protect themselves and their community if necessary"[18], a stance which reflected their role as the first line of defense against hostile outsiders and the vanguard of lesbian territorial expansion. By projecting tough masculinity through clothing and gesture, butch lesbians thus formed a symbolic shield for their community.

As Sandy describes in the epigraph, butches saw themselves as defenders of lesbian public space and if a man either propositioned or insulted a butch's girlfriend, she "would naturally get up and fight the guy [...] we all did at that time, *those that were out in their pants and T-shirts* [...] we'd knock them on their ass, and if one couldn't do it we'd all help"[19]. Sandy's associative description reveals the synecdochical relationship between butch clothing styles and the protective role that they took in relation to

[15] Joan Nestle (ed.), *The Persistent Desire: A Femme-Butch Reader*, Boston, MA: Alyson Publications, 1992, 58.
[16] Nestle, *The Persistent Desire*, 58
[17] Davis and Kennedy, *Boots of Leather*, 225.
[18] Davis and Kennedy, *Boots of Leather*, 231.
[19] Davis and Kennedy, *Boots of Leather*, 232 (my emphasis).

the rest of the community, with whom they would close ranks when the need arose. In a time when women's clothes were intentionally restrictive, menswear allowed butches greater capabilities in defending themselves physically. As Toni explains, butches had to "wear clothes that [they] could really scramble in if [they] had to"[20], in other words, pants and shirts, low-heeled shoes, and short hair, which allowed the physical mobility necessary to fight and run when needed. Paradoxically, though it also marked them as other and made them vulnerable to attack, the materiality of menswear—on the level of structure and fit—and masculine personal styles proved conducive to the role that butches played as the first line of defense for lesbian public space.

Embodied Security

Despite the danger in which it put them, masculine clothing and gendered repertoires served a crucial function for New York butches on an emotional level, offering a protective psychic layer against the psychological effects of marginalization. The shared feelings of strength and power that butches describe when wearing masculine clothing, associations appropriated from the dominant heterosexist culture, made their rebellion possible. Leslie Feinberg, author of *Stone Butch Blues*, a fictionalized and melodramatic semi-autobiographical account of mid-century butch life in Buffalo, explains the pride that butches felt in never compromising their style, even when they knew that a police raid was underway. "We knew [...] what was coming. We needed our sleeves rolled up, our hair slicked back, to live through it"[21], Jess, the book's protagonist, explains. The dignity and self-respect butches felt in their clothing, along with the sense of solidarity that it cultivated, allowed them to weather extreme experiences of degradation, marginalization, and attack.

For many, a cultivated image of toughness concealed butch emotional vulnerability and served as a defense mechanism produced in response to the trauma of marginalization and violence.[22] Masculine clothing and aggressive behaviors were key to projecting this image, as, according

[20] Davis and Kennedy, *Boots of Leather*, 231.

[21] Leslie Feinberg, *Stone Butch Blues*, Ithaca, NY: Firebrand Books, 1993, 8. Though Feinberg, and by extension the fictional Jess, was transgender, both lived parts of their lives as self-identified butches, making these early insights relevant to the current study.

[22] Ann Cvetkovich discusses the concept of 'stone' butch sexuality as a hardening in response to trauma in her seminal work *An Archive of Feelings: Trauma, Sexuality, and Lesbian Public Cultures*, Durham, NC: Duke University Press, 2003. Her insights offer a conceptual foundation for the present reflections.

to Stormy, "[l]ots of us had to look real tough, because underneath we weren't really secure about ourselves. We were scared"[23]. Reflecting on the Black studs who frequented a 1960s gay bar in New York City, Lorde, herself agnostic towards the butch-femme gender system, describes them as "tough in a way I felt I could never be. Even if they were not, their self-protective instincts warned them to appear that way"[24]. The contrast between the hard exterior shell that butches formed to protect themselves and their internal emotional world is exemplified by a story shared by Piri, who recalls that she "had a reputation that's so bad, [she] used to go home and cry about it. It was like, 'Hey, that's Piri, don't fool around with her [...] she'll cut you up' [...] I wasn't like that [but] I used to hear it all the time. And I used to get really upset and cry about it a lot"[25]. For many narrators, aggressive masculinity made them *feel* safer, even as their visible nonconformity marked them as other and opened them up to attack.

Masculinity also functioned for some butches as a defense, both emotionally and materially, against sexualized violence. The cultural link between feminine clothing and violability, vulnerability to sexual violence, meant that in a symbolic and embodied sense masculine clothing offered a refuge for butches who had suffered sexualized violence. Feinberg, through the character of Jess, connects the permeability of the skirt to sexual violence when, after being subjected to rape, Jess vows to "never wear a dress again"[26]. This total disavowal is not only a reflection of Jess' gendered self-image, but also a practical response to the violence and culturally enforced vulnerability imposed on female bodies—an attempt to protect hirself physically and emotionally from assault.[27]

Connections between feminine clothing and sexual violence—as well as masculine dress and resistance—that are interwoven throughout the novel also appear in historical accounts. Mabel, an older Black butch from New York City describes in an interview with archivist Joan Nestle the risk of sexual assault she faced while working as a domestic laborer in white homes in sartorial terms. "In every house", she recounts, "the men would try to touch me on my buttons"[28]. The metonymic association

---

[23] Davis and Kennedy, *Boots of Leather*, 211.
[24] Lorde, *Zami*, 224.
[25] Davis and Kennedy, *Boots of Leather*, 232.
[26] Feinberg, *Stone Butch Blues*, 50.
[27] Feinberg preferred the neopronouns zie/hir, which I apply here to Jess out of respect for the semi-autobiographical nature of the text.
[28] Nestle (ed.), *The Persistent Desire*, 44.

of clothing closures with physical violation and harassment rested on the physicality of 1930s women's styles, which were fastened with buttons. Men's clothing, in contrast, was closed around the legs, and fastened with belt buckles, covering more of the body, protecting it, and rendering it less easily accessible. Mabel's association of working-class feminine dress to the particular status of violability with which her Black female body was culturally marked reveals the interplay of the material environment and the embodied experiences of violation. Her permanent adoption of masculine styles in the 1940s is linked to a preference for the physical boundary that male clothing represented, despite the social costs.

Passing Protection

Moving through public space alone at night was dangerous for butches. Bars and house parties offered the relative safety of collectivity but could only be reached by traversing the city through darkened streets. Particularly while traveling or when running away from home, butches appear to have used passing as men to protect themselves from unwanted attention. This strategy also protected them from the misogyny and sexual harassment experienced by femmes and gender-conforming women. By donning men's clothing and using binders and other stylistic means to construct a socially legible masculinity, butches were able to move with greater freedom through the public sphere.[29] Stormy, a white butch from Buffalo, explains that "you [felt] safer if you went out dressed more like a guy so people wouldn't hassle you late at night"[30]. Another white butch from New York City, Judy, concurs, claiming that masculine clothing offered her "instant freedom to walk the streets literally unmolested"[31] and made it possible for her to seek out queer nightlife. These narratives reveal butches' deftness in adopting gendered styles to blend in to normative society in a selective and performative way.

However, unlike their transmasculine contemporaries, butches did not share the objective of continuous cultural legibility as men.[32] While there

[29] See Davis and Kennedy, *Boots of Leather*, 214–215. For butches, passing as men was a temporary act of self-preservation and defense.
[30] Davis and Kennedy, *Boots of Leather*, 228.
[31] Nestle (ed.), *The Persistent Desire*, 96.
[32] Assuming there was a hard boundary between transmasculinity and butch identity in this period is ahistorical, however there are key differences which allow an analytical distinction to be drawn between the two subjectivities for the purposes of this research.

were (and remain) many overlaps between butch and transmasculine identity, and many individuals lived both realities or moved between categories during their lives, butches consciously resisted the cultural legibility which trans* men sought within the dominant binary sex-gender system. Instead, and particularly within the relative safety of the bar, they cultivated an image of explicit nonconformity, which was essential to the creation and defense of a growing, visible, and increasingly rebellious pre-Stonewall lesbian community in New York state. As Davis and Kennedy point out, "to recognize [butch lesbians'] masculinity and not their queerness distorts their culture and consciousness and negates their role in building lesbian community"[33]. In other words, passing as a man was a temporary strategy for safety from harassment in public spaces, and was generally understood as a protective strategy, rather than a projection or representation of the self.

Performing Femininity

Despite the subcultural ideal of continuous presentation as butch, some individuals were able and willing to leverage the social language of femininity when necessary, particularly in confrontations with the law and in order to retain employment. As Sandy's story, with which I opened this analysis, reflects, most butches would at least occasionally use feminine gender presentation as a tool to survive and navigate the demands of a fiercely heteronormative public culture. Sandy saw her appearance in court as a form of performance and took advantage of the opportunity to benefit from the stereotypes surrounding femininity—weakness, timidity, and fragility. Her charade of delicate womanhood, complete with a dress as a costume, functioned to protect her from the disciplinary mechanisms of the state.

Kennedy and Davis underscore the performative nature of these interactions, explaining that "when known butches t[ook] on a feminine appearance [...] [o]ther gay and lesbian [bar] patrons treated them as if they were in drag"[34]. While appearing publicly in feminine clothing was understood as dishonorable for butches, personal agency determined the line between shameful and entertaining. Sandy, for instance, was a respected leader in the Buffalo community, and was adamant about the importance

[33] Davis and Kennedy, *Boots of Leather*, 234.
[34] Davis and Kennedy, *Boots of Leather*, 228.

of wearing men's clothing and performing a tough masculinity, enforcing this perspective among the younger butches who looked up to her. Though her choice to refuse a professional position with a dress code and instead work at one of the bars represented "[q]uite a drop in pay, [...] [she] could dress there the way [she] wanted to"[35]. She was only willing to compromise on this point in contexts in which she was able to employ agency in her approach, asserting to herself and to her community the superficiality of this performance. Thus, even more explicitly than masculinity, femininity functioned as a protective façade.

Unlike Sandy, some butches were willing to temper their aesthetic to maintain stable employment. Kern "never had trouble wearing a skirt and lipstick [to work]" and describes feminine clothing as "a sort of shield"[36] in professional contexts. By integrating into her surroundings, she was able to avoid challenges at work and retain a steady income, while dressing and acting as she wanted to in her free time. Likewise, Buffalo army veteran Bert explains that for a job she particularly liked, she chose to make certain compromises for the sake of maintaining her position. She explains: "when I worked for the child-care center I used to wear men's shirts but I wore skirts [...] had a D. A. haircut, but you know if you put lipstick on that was alright"[37]. As Bert's example suggests, even in these circumstances butches found strategies to signal their queerness and project a degree of socially legible masculinity. Gesture could also supplant dress as a dominant means of signaling, even within queer spaces. As historian Alix Genter points out, in some contexts "it was gendered visual cues around mannerisms and behaviors, not dress, that lesbians emphasized in self-fashioning and butch-femme identification"[38], particularly among older butches. Their ability also to gauge the parameters of social acceptability reveals a fluency in the construction and deployment of gendered styles in various settings to achieve diverse goals—a skill set learned and honed, no doubt, in in contexts of social censure.

While Kennedy and Davis ascribe subtlety to the upwardly mobile and lower middle class, Genter suggests that individuals of all classes who were subjected to mandatory dress requirements were able to find

[35] Davis and Kennedy, *Boots of Leather*, 111.
[36] Nestle (ed.), *The Persistent Desire*, 58.
[37] Davis and Kennedy, *Boots of Leather*, 107. The hairstyle favored by butch lesbians in the 1950s was the 'Duck's Ass' or 'D.A.' style, for which the hair was greased and combed backwards from the face to a point at the back of the neck.
[38] Genter, "Appearances Can Be Deceiving", 627.

strategies to navigate these rules without losing their sense of self and community. In particular, she argues that New York City butches "found ways to use women's clothing and styling to be inconspicuous while expressing their identities to those in the know"[39]. Carmen Vascones, for example, a working-class Puerto Rican-American butch from the Bronx who Genter interviewed for her article, describes asking her mother to sew her a set of narrow-fitted and long wraparound skirts, which allowed her to bypass the school dress code while maintaining a recognizably masculine silhouette.[40] Paired with men's shirts and vests, narrow, straight-cut skirts allowed Vascones to conform selectively and avoid outright censure while asserting autonomy and signaling queerness. In contexts such as high schools, where clothing was heavily regulated, such compromises were unavoidable and shielded butch-identified teenagers from disciplinary action.

But punishment for gender nonconformity was not only reserved for dress-code regulated settings, and it was not only social stigmatization which butches faced for their choice of clothing. Legal restrictions on transvestitism, or "masquerading as the opposite sex" were inconsistently enforced, and "[t]he police used such regulations to harass Black lesbians more than whites"[41]. Piri, who, unlike other narrators, remembers the law as requiring only two pieces of women's clothing, was stopped by the police while driving but was not arrested because she was wearing women's shoes. "At that time", she explains, "when they pick you up, if you didn't have two garments that belong to a woman you could go to jail [...] It would give them the opportunity to whack the shit out of you."[42] Audre Lorde recounts the paranoia which dogged queer spaces during this period as a result of the three-piece law:

> There were always rumors of plainclothes women circulating among us, looking for gay-girls with fewer than three pieces of female attire. That was enough to get you arrested for transvestism, which was illegal. Or so the rumors went. Most of the women we knew were always careful to have on a bra, underpants, and some other feminine article. No sense playing with fire.[43]

[39] Genter, "Appearances Can Be Deceiving", 609.
[40] See Genter, "Appearances Can Be Deceiving", 610.
[41] Davis and Kennedy, *Boots of Leather*, 231.
[42] Davis and Kennedy, *Boots of Leather*, 231.
[43] Lorde, *Zami*, 187.

Even a scrap of lace, hastily stitched to a pair of men's crew socks, could serve as a shield against arrest and exposure to police brutality.[44] While these laws were selectively interpreted and applied, the only defense against arrest and potential assault was selective and discreet conformity.

Faced on one hand with sexist social norms and on the other with homophobic abuse and police violence, sartorial choices determined a process of shielding and vulnerability for butch lesbians in New York State during the postwar period. Using clothing and gendered performance, butches protected themselves while resisting pressures to conform. By sending an aesthetic message of strength and power to the dominant culture, subverting its symbolism for their own ends, they created, through dress and behavior, a form of shield protecting themselves and their community.

[44] See Genter, "Appearances Can Be Deceiving", 617.

References

Judith Butler, "Performative Acts and Gender Constitution: An Essay in Phenomenology and Feminist Theory", in *Theatre Journal* 40, no. 4 (1988), 519–31.

Ann Cvetkovich, *An Archive of Feelings: Trauma, Sexuality, and Lesbian Public Cultures*, Durham, NC: Duke University Press, 2003.

Madeline D. Davis and Elizabeth Lapovsky Kennedy, *Boots of Leather, Slippers of Gold: The History of a Lesbian Community,* New York, NY: Routledge, 1993.

Leslie Feinberg, *Stone Butch Blues*, Ithaca, NY: Firebrand Books, 1993.

Alix Genter, "Appearances Can Be Deceiving: Butch-Femme Fashion and Queer Legibility in New York City, 1945–1969", in *Feminist Studies* 42, no. 3 (2016), 604–631.

Audre Lorde, *Zami: A New Spelling of My Name: A Biomythography*, Berkeley, CA: Crossing Press, 1982.

Joanne Meyerowitz, "The Liberal 1950s? Reinterpreting Postwar U.S. Sexual Culture", in *Gender and the Long Postwar: Reconsiderations of the United States and the Two Germanys, 1945–1989,* ed. by Karen Hagemann and Sonya Michel, Baltimore, MD: Johns Hopkins University Press and Woodrow Wilson Center Press, 2014, 297–319.

Joan Nestle (ed.), *The Persistent Desire: A Femme-Butch Reader,* Boston, MA: Alyson Publications, 1992.

Elaine Tyler May, *Homeward Bound: American Families in the Cold War Era*, New York, NY: Basic Books, 1988.

deufert&plischke
A Worn World Book

Could I knit better I'd knit
myself my own biographical
clothes!

I wear clothes and I know
they are there to get me started.
When they are worn out I have
to go on living naked or
I have to get myself new
clothes. When they are too big
I have to think of growing
up or to try to get smaller
ones or stay naked, needless
to say. When they become too
small, I have to get bigger ones
or get used to the size I am
wearing. When I am old I wear
clothes and I know they will
survive me.

In my grave they stay on
my skin, probably survive
my skin so I won't
be naked after death.

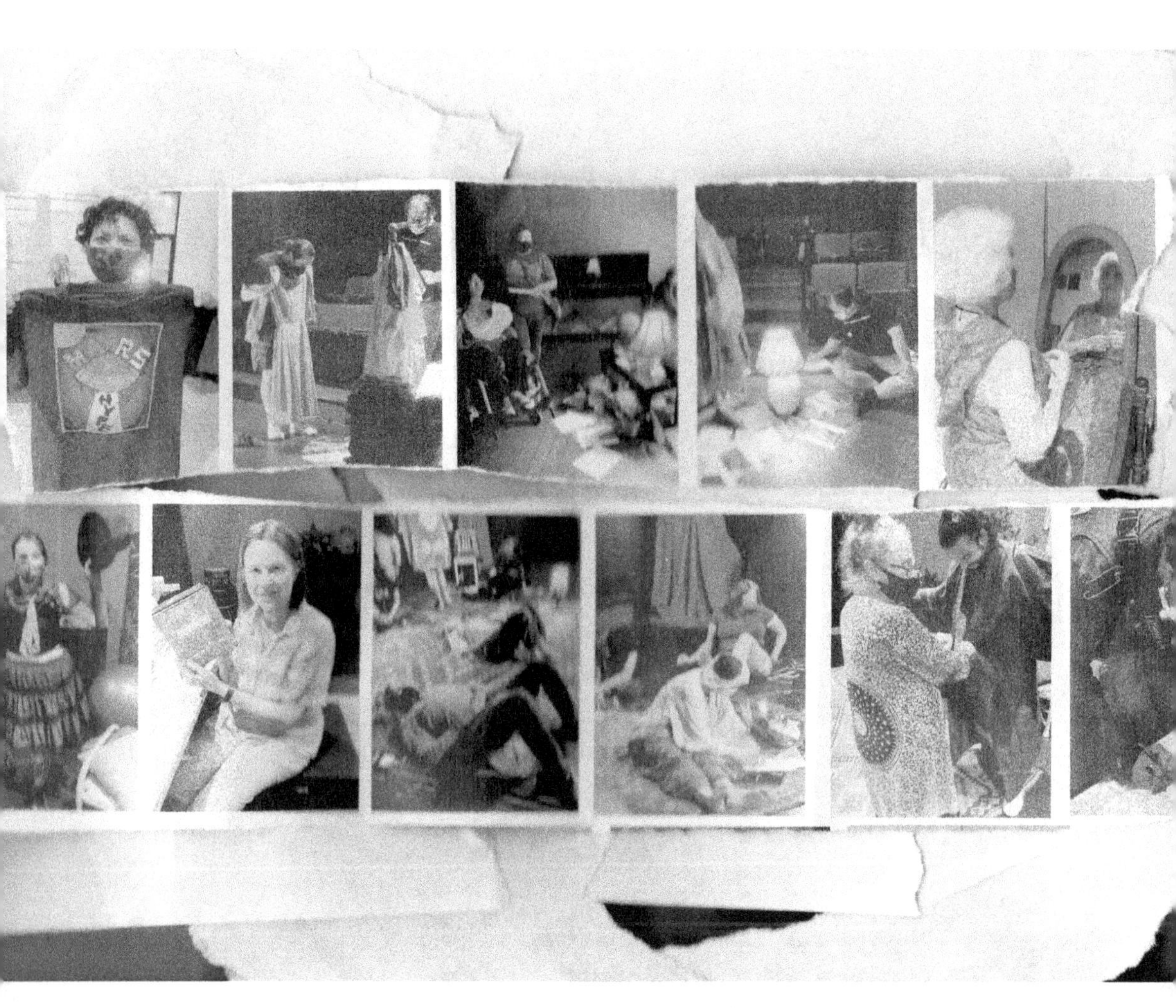

fear
thing.
The state of
being yet
The tendeny
of
non-exis
not bein
no
nothin
A Worn World addresses
the themes of modesty,
desire, pleasure and fear
expressed through clothing.
22.95

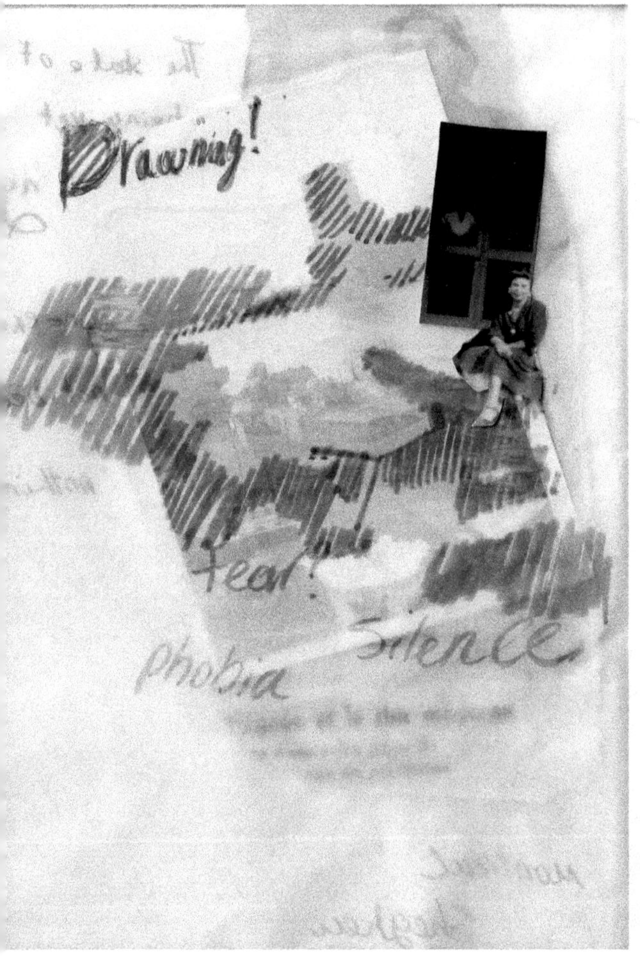

In close contact with the
skin, the sensitive organ
they "touch", they are the dir
expression of a personal
affirmation: they convey ou
stories, ours, memories, eve
our cultures, and specific
places, reflect sociologic
and economic biases, eva
our feelings of belonging a
our resistance.

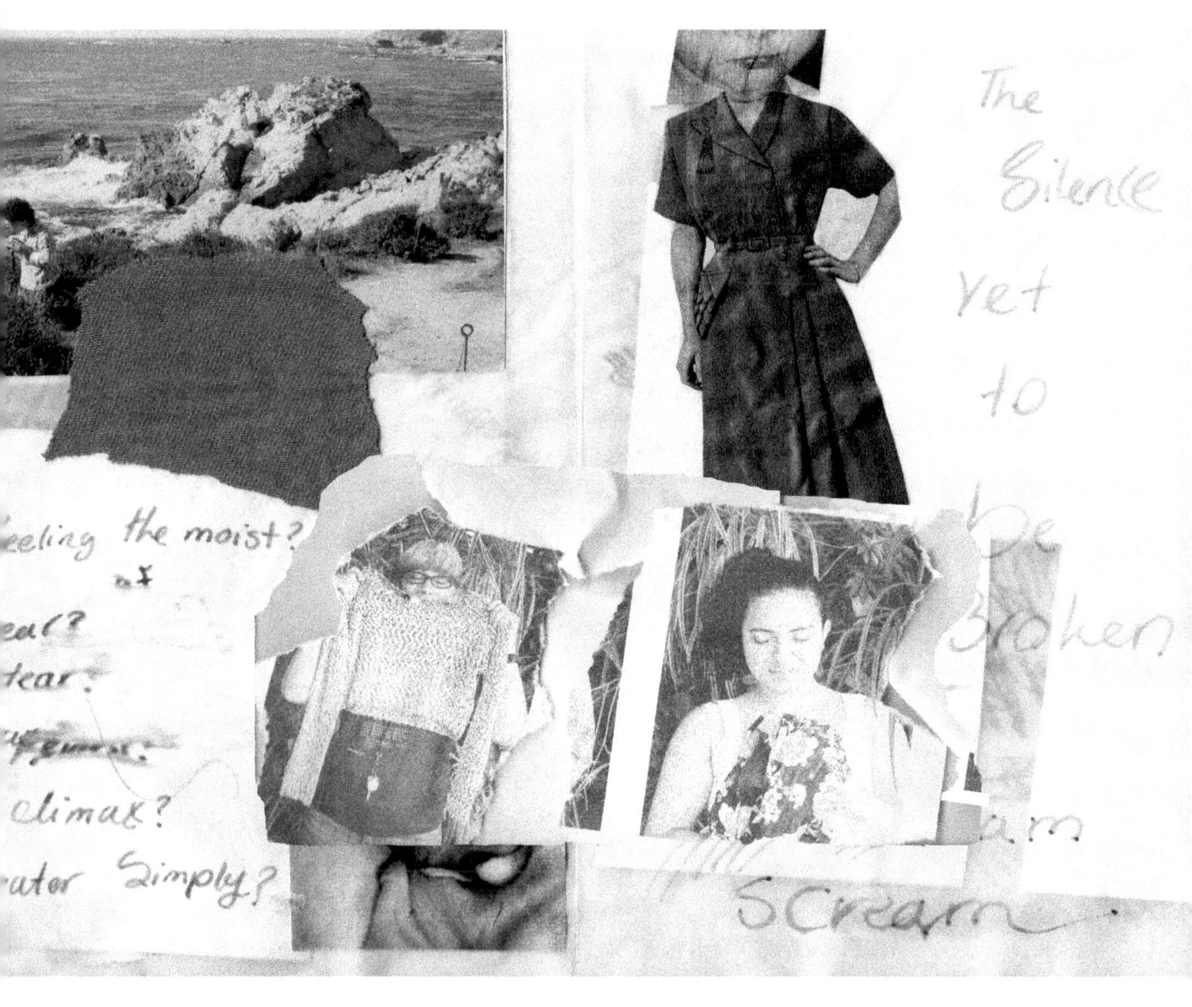
eeling the moist?
ea(?
tear?
climax?
ater Simply?
The
Silence
Yet
to
be
Broken
Scream

Clothing has the power to
address important themes such
as self-image, gender Identity,
coming of age, family.

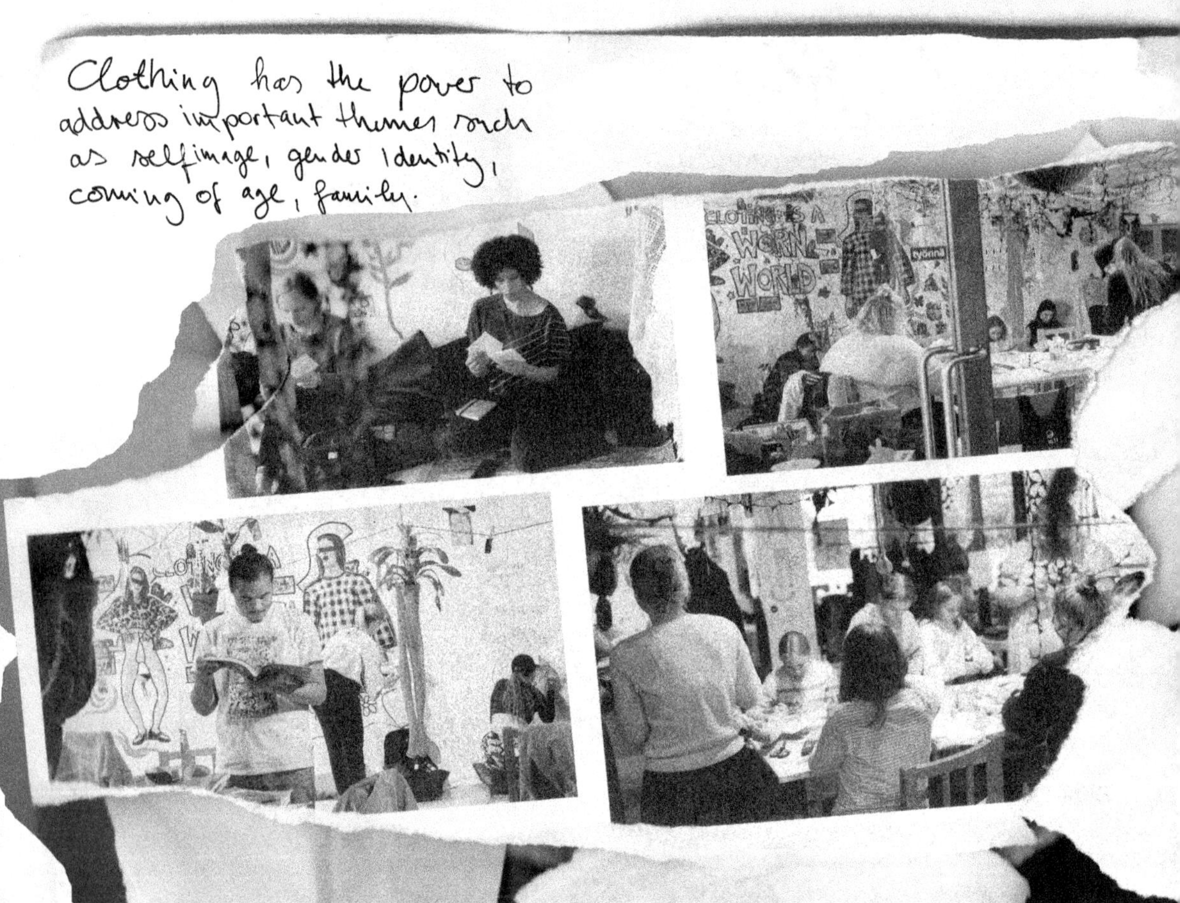

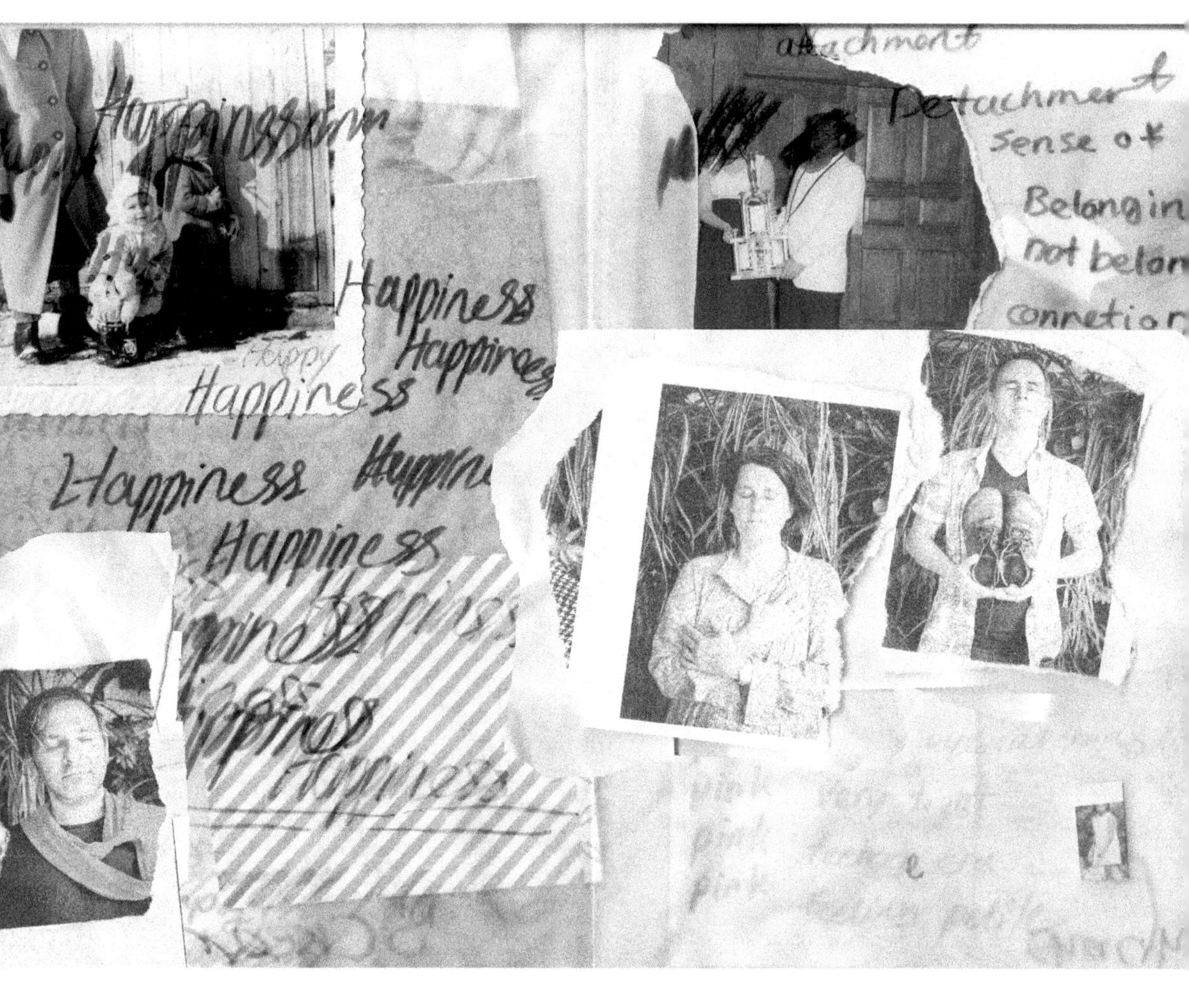

Happiness
Happiness
Happiness
Happiness
Happiness
attachment
Detachment
sense of
Belong in
not belon
connection

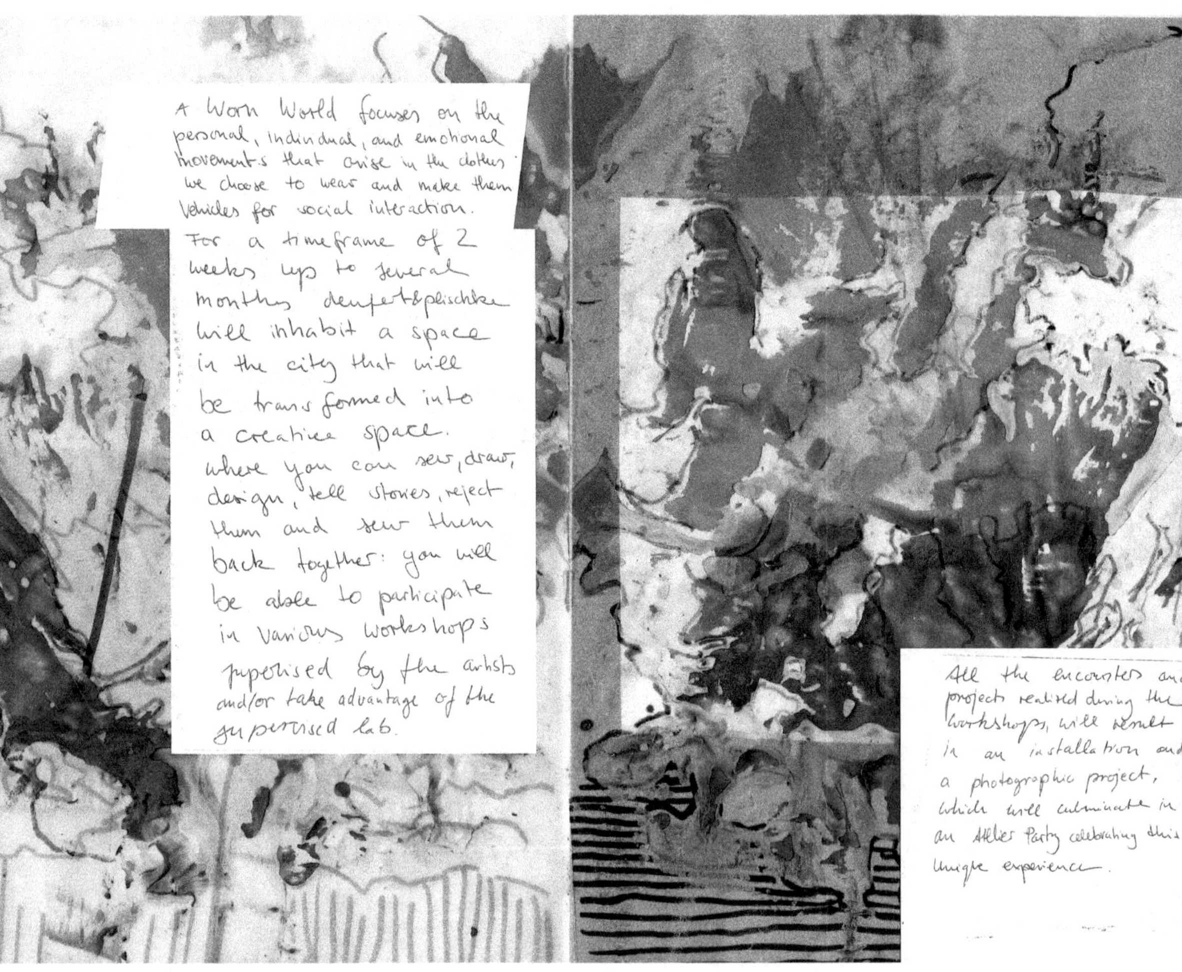

A Worn World focuses on the personal, individual, and emotional movements that arise in the clothes we choose to wear and make them vehicles for social interaction.
For a timeframe of 2 weeks up to several months denfert&plischke will inhabit a space in the city that will be transformed into a creative space. where you can sew, draw, design, tell stories, reject them and sew them back together: you will be able to participate in various workshops supervised by the artists and/or take advantage of the supervised lab.
All the encounters and projects realized during the workshops, will result in an installation and a photographic project, which will culminate in an Atelier Party celebrating this unique experience.

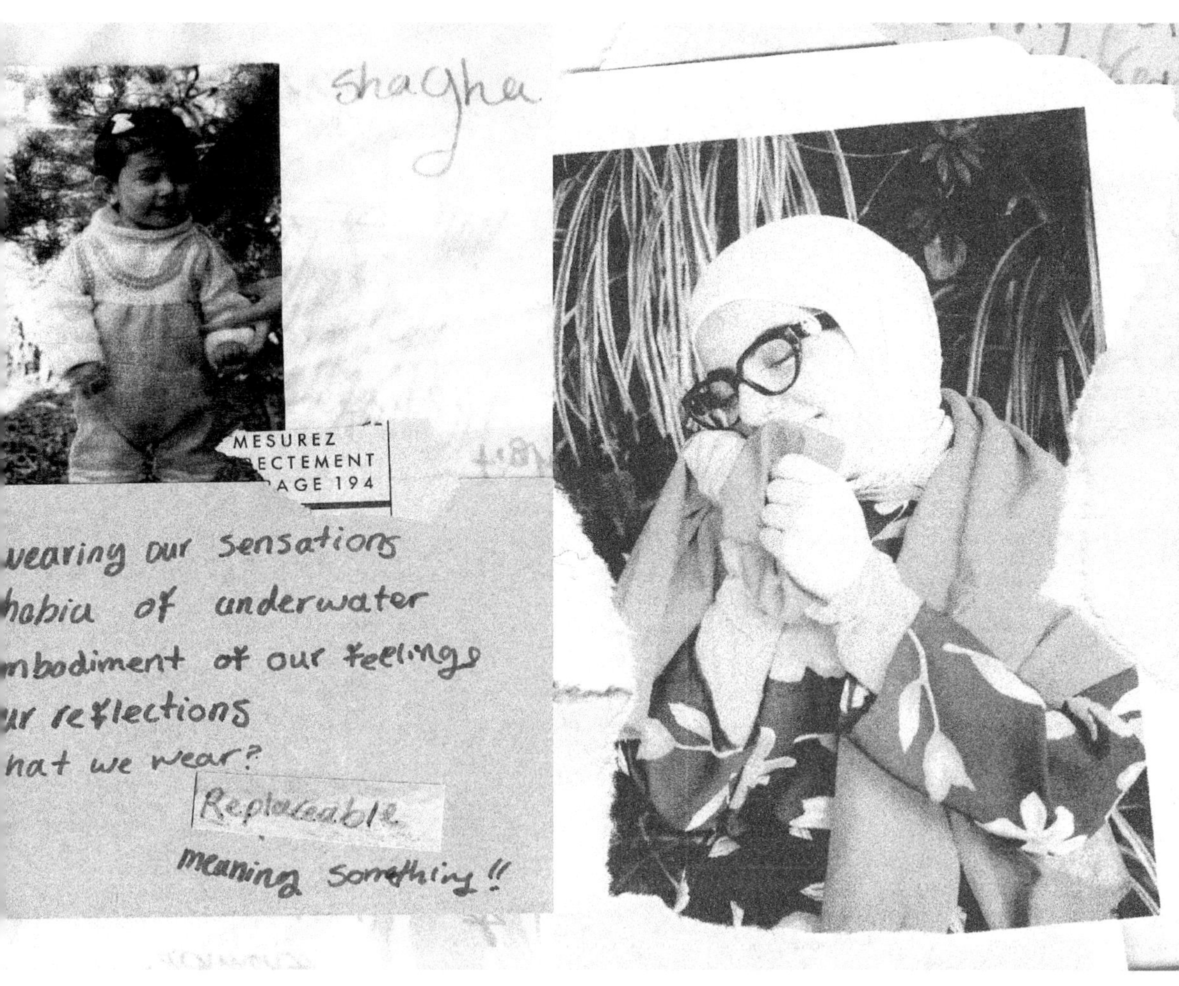
shaghe

MESUREZ
RECTEMENT
PAGE 194

wearing our sensations
habia of underwater
mbodiment of our feelings
ur reflections
hat we wear?
Replaceable

meaning something!!

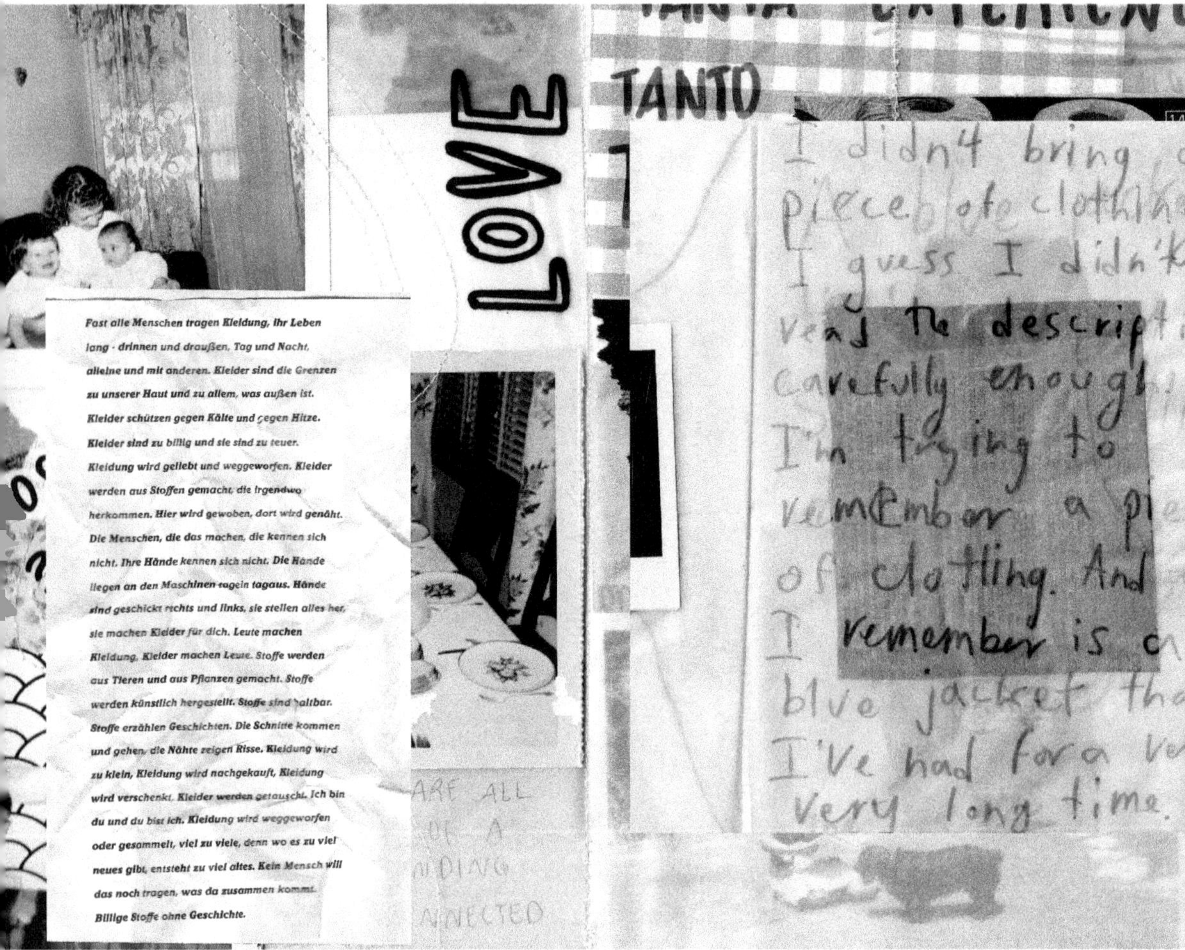

Fast alle Menschen tragen Kleidung, ihr Leben lang · drinnen und draußen, Tag und Nacht, alleine und mit anderen. Kleider sind die Grenzen zu unserer Haut und zu allem, was außen ist. Kleider schützen gegen Kälte und gegen Hitze. Kleider sind zu billig und sie sind zu teuer. Kleidung wird geliebt und weggeworfen. Kleider werden aus Stoffen gemacht, die irgendwo herkommen. Hier wird gewoben, dort wird genäht. Die Menschen, die das machen, die kennen sich nicht. Ihre Hände kennen sich nicht. Die Hände liegen an den Maschinen tagein tagaus. Hände sind geschickt rechts und links, sie stellen alles her, sie machen Kleider für dich. Leute machen Kleidung, Kleider machen Leute. Stoffe werden aus Tieren und aus Pflanzen gemacht. Stoffe werden künstlich hergestellt. Stoffe sind haltbar. Stoffe erzählen Geschichten. Die Schnitte kommen und gehen, die Nähte zeigen Risse. Kleidung wird zu klein, Kleidung wird nachgekauft, Kleidung wird verschenkt. Kleider werden getauscht. Ich bin du und du bist ich. Kleidung wird weggeworfen oder gesammelt, viel zu viele, denn wo es zu viel neues gibt, entsteht zu viel altes. Kein Mensch will das noch tragen, was da zusammen kommt. Billige Stoffe ohne Geschichte.

Contributors

Diego Agulló

is an independent researcher and a dilettante artist working in the intersection between art and philosophy, mainly in the field of contemporary dance and performance. Diego investigates the affinity between body and event, between dance and problems, focusing on the unexpected encounter between the body and the forces of chaos and when the unpredictable irruption of an event demands to be articulated through an artistic practice. Diego studied philosophy and has lived in Berlin since 2005. His work covers different media such as dance, performance, books, video art, laboratories for research, the organization of participatory events and daily Qigong / Tai Chi training. www.diegoagullo.com

Bojana Cvejić

is the author of several books, including *Choreographing Problems* (Palgrave, 2015) and *Toward a Transindividual Self: A Study in Social Dramaturgy* (co-written with Ana Vujanović, Oslo National Academy of the Arts, Sarma (Brussels) and Multimedijalni Institut (Zagreb), 2022) and numerous essays in journals and art catalogues. As a dramaturge, she has contributed to performances in dance and theatre and has co-authored several videos and installations exploring dance and social choreography: *...in a non-wimpy way* (with Steve Paxton), *Yvonne Rainer's WAR* and *Spatial Confessions*. Bojana co-initiated and is active in collective self-organized platforms for experimental production and critical theory in France (Performing Arts Forum (PAF), since 2005) and former Yugoslavia (Walking Theory (TkH), 2001–2015) that have shaped her work contextually. Her current research includes the politics of transindividuality, figures of belonging collectively and social choreographies of dis-order. Since 2017 she has divided her time between Oslo, where she is Professor at the National Academy of the Arts, and Brussels, where she teaches at P.A.R.T.S. and works in the independent art and cultural scene.

deufert&plischke

have been working as an artist duo at the interface of dance, society and media since 2001. Kattrin Deufert and Thomas Plischke have collaborated with each other and with others from the very beginning. Their performances and transdisciplinary works are always created in dialogue, questioning the hierarchy between artists and audience and opening new spaces in which there is room for the imagination of those involved. The spectrum ranges from long durational performance in a gallery space to theatrical installation for participation in a museum, to the collective invention in a small town or even together with an entire village. deufert&plischke curate festivals; their formats and series tour the world. For several years, deufert&plischke have been living and working as a family of artists with their two children Moritz and Simon. In 2020, they founded spinnereischwelm, a venue for contemporary art in the small town of Schwelm in North Rhine-Westphalia, Germany.

Žiga Divjak

was born in 1992 in Slovenia and is a theatre director. In his pieces, he uses stripped-down documentary theatre and a strong focus on text to address social and political reality. His works are clear-eyed, recognizably engaged artistic statements with robust ethics that tend to emotionally challenge and yet strongly intellectually affect their viewers. For his performances, he has received several awards, including two Borštnik Awards for Best Directing and two Grand Prix for Best Performances at the Slovenian National Theatre Festival, Borštnikovo srečanje. He lives in Ljubljana.

Rana Issa

is a writer, translator and curator. She is co-founder and artistic director of Masahat for Arab Arts and Culture in Exile, an institution that programs and produces cultural expression by Arab and global South artists and writers in Norway. Her book *The Modern Arabic Bible* (Edinburgh University Press, 2023) and her academic contributions in the cultural and literary history of the Arab *nahda*, particularly her interest in Arabic historical linguistics and lexicography, were the key to going back to Arabic as her preferred writing language. She is currently finalizing a queer memoir in Arabic and Norwegian about broken characters in her Palestinian and Lebanese family. Rana is a recipient of fellowships from the Houghton Library, The Center of Advanced Studies in Oslo, the Norwegian Research Council, the Norwegian Nonfiction Union for Writers and Translators, the Free Word Foundation, AFAC, among others. Her text *Khatim Izdihar* (Al-Jumhuriya, 2021) is part of *Hartaqāt* (2023), a performance by

Rabih Mroue and Lina Majdalanie. A graduate of the American University of Beirut and the University of Oslo where she taught until she left academia in 2022. Rana dreams of a liberated Palestine.

Janez Janša
See team of the publication series, page 254.

Janez Janša
is a visual artist, working in the cross section of traditional visual art practices, conceptual art and new media. In 2003 he represented Slovenia at the 50th Venice Biennial. His work has been shown in the São Paulo Biennial, Prague Biennial, Limerick Biennial and numerous other venues. He has been teaching at the Academy of Fine Arts and Design of the University of Ljubljana since 2009.

Janez Janša
is a conceptual artist, performer and producer living in Ljubljana, Slovenia. He is the author of numerous videos, performances, installations and new media works which have been presented in several exhibitions and festivals around the world. He is the director of the film *My Name Is Janez Janša*, co-founder and co-director of Aksioma – Institute for Contemporary Art, Ljubljana (together with Marcela Okretič) and artistic director of the Aksioma | Project Space. He has been teaching at the Academy of Fine Arts and Design of the University of Ljubljana since 2016.

Mazen Kerbaj
is a Lebanese author of comics, visual artist and musician, born in Beirut in 1975. He is the author of more than 15 books and his short stories and drawings have been published in anthologies, newspapers, and magazines. His work has been translated into more than ten languages in various local and international publications. His paintings, drawings, videos, live performances and installations have been shown as part of numerous solo and collective exhibitions, in galleries, museums and art fairs around the world. In 2015, Mazen was the recipient of a DAAD one-year artist in residency in Berlin, he has lived and worked in the German capital ever since.

Cikacé Lestine
is a professional wannabe. Depending on the contexts and occasions, they might appear as an emerging performer, a soon-to-be writer, an aspiring DJ, a dedicated teacher, a burnt out activist, or a drag king boyband superstar.

Isabell Lorey

is a political theorist and professor of queer studies in the arts and sciences at the Academy of Media Arts Cologne. She is co-editor of transversal.at, the publication platform of the European Institute for Progressive Cultural Policies (eipcp). In 2009 she completed her habilitation in political science at the University of Vienna. She has taught at various international universities. Her book publications include: *Figuren des Immunen. Elemente einer politischen Theorie* (diaphanes, 2011); *Immer Ärger mit dem Subjekt* (transversal texts, 2017); *Die Regierung der Prekären* (Turia + Kant, 2012; new edition, 2020) / *State of Insecurity. Government of the Precarious* (Verso, 2015); *Demokratie im Präsens. Eine Theorie der politischen Gegenwart* (Suhrkamp, 2020) / *Democracy in the Political Present: A Queer-Feminist Theory* (Verso, 2022). Almost all books have also been translated into Spanish.

Sophia New

is an artist and pedagogue based in Berlin. In her performances and video works she is specifically interested in issues of the everyday, distance, intimacy and scale within art making. In 2002 she co-founded *plan b* with Daniel Belasco Rogers and together they have made over 28 projects in different cities, festivals, and galleries. They also have a long term practice of gathering personal data (GPS & SMS) through which they have an on-going body of work which takes many material forms both analogue and digital, and has caused them to become more politicised about how daily data is being used. Sophia was a member of teaching staff on MA Solo Dance Authorship (SODA) at the HZT-Inter-University Centre for Dance Berlin between 2012 and 2022 and was the course leader for MA Performance: Politics and Social Justice at the University of the Arts London. Together with Daniel they were Guest Professors for the Interdisciplinary Practice and Theory for Studium Generale at the University of the Arts Berlin 2020–2022.

Sandra Noeth

See team of the publication series, page 255.

Nicola Perugini

is a political anthropologist who teaches politics and international relations. His research focuses mainly on the politics of international law, human rights, and violence. He is the co-author of *The Human Right to Dominate* (Oxford University Press, 2015), *Morbid Symptoms* (Sharjah Biennial 13, 2017), and *Human Shields. A History of People in the Line of*

Fire (University of California Press, 2020). Nicola has published articles on war and the ethics of violence; the politics of human rights, humanitarianism, and international law; humanitarianism's visual cultures; war and embedded anthropology; refugees and asylum seekers; law, space and colonialism; settler-colonialism. Nicola is currently working on the project *Decolonising the Civilian*, which examines decolonisation and national liberation wars, international law, and the status of civilians in armed conflicts.

Hanna Poddig

born in 1985 in Hamburg, is an activist and author. She is involved in the anti-nuclear movement as well as in climate struggles, trying to find creative ways to block industry and to provoke debates. She also supports activists facing trials which means spending a lot of time in court. Furthermore she was part of a group translating texts from the anarchist crimethInc collective into German. She shares her knowledge in books, workshops, talks and trainings.

Frédéric Pouillaude

is professor of Aesthetics in the department of Arts in the Aix-Marseille University in France. His works include *Le désœuvrement chorégraphique. Étude sur la notion d'Œuvre en danse* (Vrin, 2009) / *Unworking Choreography: The Notion of the Work in Dance* (Oxford University Press, 2017) and *Représentations factuelles. Art et pratiques documentaires* (Cerf, 2020).

Liz Rosenfeld

is a Berlin based interdisciplinary artist who works with performance, moving images, drawing and experimental writing practices. Liz addresses the sustainability of emotional and political ecologies, cruising methodologies, past and future histories in regard to the ways in which memory is queered. Liz's work deals with flesh as a non-binary collaborative material, specifically focussing on the potentiality of physical abundance and excess, edging questions regarding the responsibility and privilege of taking up space. Embracing an auto-theoretical style, Liz's writing is rooted in questions that contend with how queer ontologies are grounded in variant hypocritical desire(s).

Bella Ruhl

is a media historian working at the intersections of material cultures studies, queer and feminist history, and archival theory. Having completed a bachelor's degree in History at the University of Arizona with highest honors,

Bella moved to Berlin to undertake a master's degree in Global History at the Freie Universität and Humboldt Universität. While writing her MA thesis, she then spent a year in Vienna as a Fulbright research grantee. Bella is currently pursuing a doctorate in Media, Culture, and Communication at New York University and is working on a number of grassroots archiving and digital humanities projects alongside her academic research.

Tenzing Sonam

was born in Darjeeling, India, to Tibetan refugee parents. He is a filmmaker, writer and artist, and is currently based in Dharamshala, India. A recurring subject in his work is Tibet, forming an intimate engagement at different levels: personally, politically and artistically. Through his films and artistic and archival work, he has attempted to document, question and reflect on the issues of exile, identity, culture and nationalism that confront the Tibetan people. His work includes award-winning documentaries, two narrative features and a number of video installations. His most recent feature film, *The Sweet Requiem*, premiered at the 2018 Toronto International Film Festival. His latest art exhibition, *Shadow Circus*, was shown at Savvy Contemporary in Berlin as part of the 2019 Berlinale Forum Expanded and at the 2022 Kochi Biennale. He is co-founder and co-director of the Dharamshala International Film Festival, one of India's leading independent film festivals.

Sandra Umathum
See team of the publication series, page 255.

The team of the publication series *Corporeal Matters*

Daniel Belasco Rogers
was born and grew up in London. Having studied Theatre Design, he spent
the 1990s touring experimental theatre with the group Reckless Sleepers
and working for the Contemporary Art Society. When he moved to Berlin
in 2001 with his partner Sophia New, they started to work together as the
duo *plan b*. They work in the fields of performance, installation, new media
and visual art, regularly contributing to conferences and symposiums as
well as teaching in colleges and universities throughout Germany. Between 2020 and 2023, he was Guest Professor for Interdisciplinary Artistic Practice and Theory on Studium Generale at the Universität der Künste,
Berlin. He has translated for contemporary artists as well as museums and
has been the copy editor for the *Corporeal Matters* series since the first
publication in 2023.

Janez Janša
is a professor at the HZT-Inter-University Centre for Dance Berlin and a
contemporary artist who focuses on the relationship between art and the
social and political context in his performance, conceptual and interdisciplinary art works. His particular areas of research are the performativity of
name, the relationship between art and war, as well as time and tempo-
ralities in art and life. He was the director of *Maska* (1998–2021), an institute for publishing, artistic production and education based in Ljubljana,
Slovenia, and founder and editor of two book series and several readers
on contemporary dance and theatre. He was editor-in-chief of *Maska –
Performing Arts Journal* (1999–2006). He is the author of a book on Jan
Fabre's early work, *La discipline du chaos, le chaos de la discipline* (1994).
Janez is a co-founder and the first president of the association of freelance
artists *Asociacija* in Slovenia and a member of the editorial boards of the
journals *Performance Research* and *Maska*. In 2007, together with two
other artists, he changed his previous name into the name of the conservative three-time prime minister of Slovenia. Together with Janez Janša and
Janez Janša, he is the owner of the Janez Janša registered trademark.

Ana Lessing Menjibar
is a German-Spanish performer, choreographer, multidisciplinary artist and
art director, born and based in Berlin. In her interdisciplinary practice, she
interweaves body, sound worlds and language in multimedia installations
in which she experiments with the transformative potential of flamenco
in the context of contemporary dance and performance. She graduated

from the performance art Master's program, Solo/Dance/Authorship at HZT-Inter-University Centre for Dance Berlin. Previously she studied Visual Communication at the University of the Arts Berlin and has worked as an art director and publisher in the field of culture and art for many years. Amongst many other places, Ana has performed, directed or exhibited at Uferstudios Berlin, sophiensaele, Komische Oper Berlin, tanzhaus nrw, and the Kammermusiksaal der Berliner Philharmonie, at Villa Romana (Italy), PHotoEspaña or at the Centre Pompidou Málaga (Spain).

Sandra Noeth
is a professor at the HZT-Inter-University Centre for Dance Berlin and an international curator. She specializes in ethical and political perspectives toward body-practice and theory and in dramaturgy in body-based performing arts. Recent artistic-theoretical research and publication projects focus the role, status and agency of bodies in bordering processes; the relation between arts, bodies and unequal politics of protection; the embodiment of violence; the performativity of class dynamics in arts as well as the ambivalent status of the body in international humanitarian law. Sandra was Head of Dramaturgy and Research at Tanzquartier Wien (2009–2014) and worked as an educator with SKH-Stockholm University of the Arts and Ashkal Alwan Beirut, among others. She is the author of *Resilient Bodies, Residual Effects. Borders and Collectivity from Lebanon and Palestine* (transcript, 2019) as well as a co-editor of *Breathe. Critical Investigations into the Inequalities of Life* (with J. Janša, transcript, 2023) and of the publication series *Corporeal Matters* (with J. Janša and S. Umathum, transcript, since 2023).

Sandra Umathum
is a performance scholar, writer and dramaturge. From 2019 to 2022, she was a professor for (Applied) Theory Dance, Choreography, Performance at HZT-Inter-University Centre for Dance Berlin. Before that, she held a professorship for Theater Studies and Dramaturgy at the Ernst Busch Academy of Dramatic Arts in Berlin (2013–2018) and a guest professor for Dramaturgy at the University of Music and Theater "Felix Mendelssohn Bartholdy" in Leipzig (2010–2012). She has co-edited, among other publications, *Disabled Theater* (diaphanes, 2015), *Postdramaturgien* (Neofelis, 2020) as well as the publication series *Corporeal Matters* (with S. Noeth and J. Janša, transcript, since 2023). Sandra's research focuses on the theory and practice of contemporary performance; on illness, disability and non-normative bodies in performance and dance and on shooting (with cameras and with guns). She currently lives in Vienna.

Contributors

Imprint

Corporeal Matters

Series Editors
Janez Janša, Sandra Noeth and Sandra Umathum

Book no. 3
SHIELDING
Body-based Studies on Integrity and Protection

Editors
Sandra Noeth, Sandra Umathum and Janez Janša

Authors

Diego Agulló
Bojana Cvejić
deufert&plischke
Žiga Divjak
Rana Issa
Janez Janša, Janez Janša and Janez Janša
Cikacé Lestine and Sandra Umathum

Isabell Lorey
Sandra Noeth
Nicola Perugini
Hanna Poddig and Sophia New
Frédéric Pouillaude
Liz Rosenfeld
Bella Ruhl
Tenzing Sonam

Design Ana Lessing Menjibar
Design Support Peter Löffelholz
Copy Editing Daniel Belasco Rogers
Printed by Majuskel Medienproduktion GmbH, Wetzlar
Print-ISBN 978-3-8376-7280-0
PDF-ISBN 978-3-8394-7280-4

Shielding. Body-based Studies on Integrity and Protection is based on a Research Week curated by Sandra Noeth and Janez Janša at HZT Berlin in January 2022.
The publication is financially supported by the Berlin University of the Arts (UdK) and the HZT-Inter-University Centre for Dance Berlin.

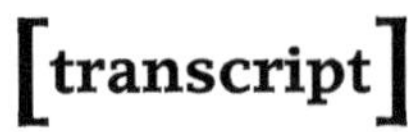

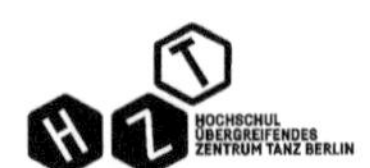

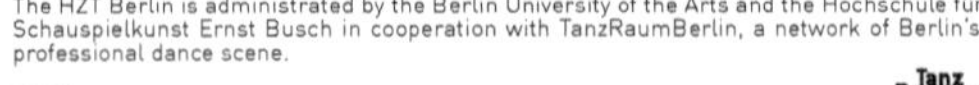

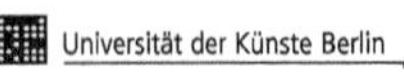

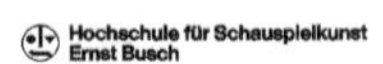

GPSR Authorized Representative: Easy Access System Europe, Mustamäe tee
50, 10621 Tallinn, Estonia, gpsr.requests@easproject.com